BLESSED ARE THE PEACEMAKERS

A Psychological Thriller Where Faith Confronts Violence

STEPHEN McCUTCHAN

Primix Publishing
11620 Wilshire Blvd
Suite 900, West Wilshire Center, Los Angeles, CA, 90025
www.primixpublishing.com
Phone: 1-800-538-5788

© 2024 Stephen McCutchan. All rights reserved.

No part of this book may be reproduced, stored in a retrieval system, or transmitted by any means without the written permission of the author.

Published by Primix Publishing: 09/18/2024

ISBN: 979-8-89194-100-7(sc)
ISBN: 979-8-89194-098-7(e)

Library of Congress Control Number: 2024901997

Any people depicted in stock imagery provided by iStock are models, and such images are being used for illustrative purposes only.

Certain stock imagery © iStock.

Because of the dynamic nature of the Internet, any web addresses or links contained in this book may have changed since publication and may no longer be valid. The views expressed in this work are solely those of the author and do not necessarily reflect the views of the publisher, and the publisher hereby disclaims any responsibility for them.

CONTENTS

Chapter 1. I'm Nobody Now 1
Chapter 2. Making a Name for Self 6
Chapter 3. Running For Your Life 11
Chapter 4. Hospital Visit 18
Chapter 5. Release from Hospital and Visit from police 28
Chapter 6. Never Trust A Man 38
Chapter 7. An Internet for Revenge 44
Chapter 8. Revenge Can Be Fun 50
Chapter 9. Recruiting First Soldiers 54
Chapter 10. Rookie Assignment 59
Chapter 11. Where Is Natalie 63
Chapter 12. It's Bigger 75
Chapter 13. A Little Panic Goes a Long Way 80
Chapter 14. Worship at Voz de Dios 84
Chapter 15. Eric Ivory 88
Chapter 16. Natalie Completes Her Mission 92
Chapter 17. It Hits the Fan 100
Chapter 18. Panic Spreads 105
Chapter 19. A Dark Night 112

Chapter 20.	A Soldier's Journey	117
Chapter 21.	Barbara's Plans	121
Chapter 22.	Battle Strategy	127
Chapter 23.	Building a Counter Plan	142
Chapter 24.	Preparations for the weekend	151
Chapter 25.	Texas, Wisconsin	160
Chapter 26.	No Victory Is Complete	168
Chapter 27.	The Media Reacts	182
Chapter 28.	Barbara Regroups	192
Chapter 29.	Gathering the Tribe	203
Chapter 30.	National Campaign	214
Chapter 31.	Brian Has an Idea	223
Chapter 32.	What to Tell a Nation	230
Chapter 33.	A Call to a Nation	241
Chapter 34.	It Happened on Easter	248
Chapter 35.	Mom Is Acting Strange	255
Chapter 36.	The President's Address	263
Chapter 37.	A Woman's Leadership	275
Chapter 38.	The First Clue	283
Chapter 39.	A Weekend From Hell	293
Chapter 40.	Barbara Disappears	303
Chapter 41.	I Will Be Heard	310
Chapter 42.	Code Broken	315
Chapter 43.	Relationships Are Important	321
Chapter 44.	Explosive Love	329
Chapter 45.	Resurrection	334

I'M NOBODY NOW

CHAPTER 1

First Sunday in Lent

I'm nobody now, but soon the whole city will know who I am—all of North Carolina, maybe the nation.

Jeremy straightened his tie and walked down the sidewalk towards the church. He saw on the sign that it was a Presbyterian Church, whatever that was. He adjusted his backpack so that it did not pull on his newly purchased suit. The Leader always said if you cut your hair and wear clothes that fit in this phony society, no one will see you coming—until it is too late.

He hated to lose his flowing blond hair. A scrawny nineteen-year-old with oversized ears, his hair distracted people from his skinny frame.]

His blond tresses falling over his shoulders caught the attention of the girls. At least Natalie liked to run her fingers through it. Natalie was the first girl to give him serious attention. It was sad last night when he said goodbye to her. He wanted to have sex right then, but she said he needed to preserve his strength. He knew it was so, but his whole body tingled when she stood next to him, trying to be brave herself. The Leader told them they were both part of a larger cause. Soldiers have to make sacrifices so the world can be better.

He continued walking toward the church, smiling.

Join me, he thought, *you unsuspecting morons.* A group of church ladies nodded to him—they looked like Easter cupcakes in spring floral dresses—and walked next to him on their way to worship.

"Good morning," he said to a couple exiting their green sedan. An elderly man smiled at him and opened the door for a woman wearing a Tartan plaid skirt. They held hands as they began to walk towards the church.

"Hey, how are you?" the woman said. "It's so nice seeing a well-dressed young person attending our church. Please stay for the coffee hour after the service."

"Thank you, mam. Maybe I will."

The Leader drilled them over and over again about this hypocritical society and how to talk hypoc language. "Say it the way they think it should sound. They will think they are still in control," the Leader said. "You know how they like to think they control their world. Give them that illusion and you will set them up for the big fall."

He hated being a nobody. Soon no one would think of him that way. His smarmy brothers may have gotten good grades and are now making big bucks, but they will get lost in the crowd.

Not him. Someday they will build a monument to him and his friends. They will carve his name on a plaque celebrating the sacrifice he made for a better world. They did that for other soldiers who died in a war, why not him?

He pulled out a comb and ran it through his hair. He thought about the priceless look on his no-account mother's face when he walked into the house last week with his new suit and haircut. He hadn't worn what she considered proper clothes since he told her to fuck off three years ago.. His mother had hugged him and began to slobber all over him. "Oh Jeremy, you look so nice. I'm glad you decided to change. Your brothers will be so proud of you." Fat chance, he thought, listening to her mention his brothers.

As he slowly walked toward the church's massive wooden doors, he remembered when chaos walked into his family's home. His skirt-chasing, corporate bigwig dad came home drunk. Jeremy made a crack about lowering the sperm count in the world, and his father became livid. His dad was too wasted to land a good punch. Jeremy laughed as *dear daddy*, swearing up a blue storm, tripped over a chair in the kitchen and fell flat on his face.

He wished he had taken the opportunity to kick him in the face while he was down. Instead, he ran out the door and bunked with a friend for a few days until things cooled down.

When he came home, Mom announced Dad had split. She got a restraining order preventing him from coming onto the property. *It was her one act of courage during their whole sordid marriage,*.

Not long after that, they officially divorced. His two older brothers chose to live with their father. Just as well. They never liked him, and the feeling was mutual. They just ignored him. They would not be able to ignore him much longer. He was going to make them famous.

It was a brisk spring day with a Carolina blue sky as he started up the steps of John Knox Presbyterian Church. "Welcome to John Knox," a grinning older man greeted him at the door.

"Thank you, sir." Jeremy displayed his warmest smile. He'd had to practice that a number of times so he wouldn't barf in the process. "Can you please tell me where the restroom is?"

Following the man's directions, he entered the church's bathroom, noticed the wood trim, blue walls, and clean floors. It was nicer than anything room in his own home. He thought he would relieve himself before the service started. He was a little nervous, but he was also excited. After all the planning, it was going to happen. He didn't want to do anything stupid like wetting his pants to interfere with his shining sacrifice. At a standstill, he glared at his image in the mirror. A washed-out face stared back, one with short hair, and it startled him. Hard, nervous eyes. But his mirror image showed excitement and his familiar smirk. After all the planning, it was going to happen. Glory. Recognition. His name would be spoken.

As he moved away from the mirror, he peeked under each stall, checking for feet. *Now*, he thought, *focus. Focus on the cause, on the Leader's words.* He chose the handicapped stall so he would have more room to make a few adjustments to the equipment in his backpack, to be easy to grab his shiny new Glock 19 when the moment arrived.

As he stood in the stall, he thought about the past months of preparation. The good part about Dad and his brothers leaving was that now he had a large room in the house all to himself. His mom, such a weakling, agreed when he forbade her from ever entering his room. His father was so guilty he tried to buy Jeremy off by getting him some state-of-the-art electronic equipment. He had plenty of room to hide everything else he needed for this mission. After this is over, the police will have a field day going through his room, he thought.

When he hooked up with the Leader, things began to fall into place for him. He wanted to be part of making this a better world, and the leader had a plan.

He knew he would not leave the church alive, but that was all right. *I'm going to make a real difference. Most people live their whole lives, die, and are soon forgotten. The world will always remember me, he thought,* as he gripped his bony knees. It made him feel important. It made the anticipation of the action like foreplay in what he imagined sex must be like. Not knowing what it was like, especially with Natalie, was his one regret. She would think of him, though, and be proud of him.

The bell chimes announced the beginning of the worship service. It was time to find his place in the big room. An usher smiled and gave him a piece of paper that he assumed was the program. As he walked down the center aisle, he glanced at the tall pillars along the sides. He noticed that the windows either had colored glass or pictures of what he supposed were Jesus and people around him. The ceiling was high, almost like they wanted to make you think you were looking at heaven. He found a seat on the outside of a pew about halfway down. That will be the best location, he thought. About halfway down, he thought. That will be the best location.

The Leader was right. A church is a perfect place to begin the action. No one used all those screening contraptions at a church like they did in other public spaces. When people saw his backpack, they just assumed he was some hard-working college student who always carried his books around with him.

MAKING A NAME FOR SELF

CHAPTER 2

Frank Sessions walked down the aisle behind the choir as the worship began at John Knox. With the support of the choir, the people sang with full voice *What Wondrous Love Is This*. He was grateful to be the pastor of this 700-member church. It was wonderful to no longer feel the depressive grief that plagued his life after his wife's violent death in the drug store robbery a few years back. Deep within his soul, he sensed a renewed commitment to give back to this congregation who supported him during his dark journey. What better time to begin than the season of Lent.

Many clergy will tell you that some Sundays you are dull. You walk through the liturgy without any joy. Not today, Frank thought. Today was different. The music, the Scriptures, the prayers are filled with the message that life is not just a series of chance events without meaning. God is alive, God cares, and life is going somewhere.

He had gained almost forty pounds during his time of depression, but now he had trimmed his six-foot two frame down to almost two hundred pounds and he felt renewed energy. He almost felt giddy as he walked up the steps to the chancel singing the last verse of the hymn and turned to invite the people to join him in a prayer of praise.

There was a bounce in his step as he entered the pulpit, ready to read the Scriptures in preparation for his sermon. There was so much violence and dysfunction in the world, and people exhibited increased anxiety. He wanted his congregation to know there is reason for hope. The season of Lent followed Jesus through the final days of his ministry. It was a time of violence but not a time without hope.

"This morning I choose to begin at the beginning. Please turn in your pew Bible to the very first page, Genesis 1. These verses remind us that once everything was in chaos, and there was no order. scene of total chaos. Feel the black space churning with energy but lacking any form or order. Now listen to God speak words and life begins to take on order and meaning."

As he read from the Scriptures, he mentally urged the people to listen for God speaking to them again and to understand a reason for courage and hope regardless of the chaos of their world.

When the Scripture reading was finished, Frank began to preach his sermon. He spoke of the recent chaotic events in various parts of the world. He acknowledged the sense of anxiety rising when people thought those in charge were incompetent or in over their heads. He referenced the Scripture and emphasized the contrast between the chaos that causes people such fear and the almost effortless way God provided patterns, structure, and meaning by speaking a word.

He was feeling good about the sermon and was about at midpoint when he saw a well-dressed young man rise from the pew and step into the aisle. His first thought was to be amused and sympathetic. *The poor guy has to go to the bathroom and can't hold it any longer.*

At first, only those sitting behind the man notice him rise. A slight rustle from those behind caused some in front to turn their heads as Frank hesitated. *What's that in his hand?* His eyes saw the gun, but his brain was slow to process what was happening.

The young man raises his arm in a lazy, jerky fashion as a smile forms on his lips. "Times up, Frank," he shouts. "Time to stop the lies."

The first shot from the gun shattered the round stain-glass window above Frank's head.

Part of Frank wanted to duck or run. Then he sensed a calmness descend upon him. He leaned toward the mike and spoke in his deepest, most authoritative voice. "Young man, put the gun down before someone gets hurt."

"Gets hurt?" Jeremy said in a cold voice devoid of any emotion. "You mean like this?" He turned and fired at George Ford who was sitting with his wife four pews in front of where Jeremy stands. George falls back, blood streaming from his head. His wife screamed as she reached for him.

The whole congregation was frozen in terror. They had heard about such events in the news, but it was always somewhere else. Now, here in their church, where they always felt secure, a lunatic was shooting at them.

Frank wraps his arms around his Bible and steps down from the chancel. The words coming from his mouth surprised even him. "Young man, in the name of God, I command you to put the gun down!"

Jeremy turned back towards Frank and fired into the floor of the aisle in front of him. The tile shattered and flying chips hit Frank and some others near the aisle.

"You are not in charge, preacher. You tell these people all this silly stuff about looove (he stretched the word out) and forgiveeenessss, but they go right on fucking their neighbors, sending their kids off to fight their wars, and cheating decent people out of their savings."

At least he's talking rather than shooting, thinks Frank. How do I keep distracting him? "You are right that the world is messed up," said Frank. "That's why we are here. To ask God to help us make the world better."

"Some of us are willing to die to change the world, preacher. The Leader showed us that violence is necessary before the world wakes up to the truth."

A man in the outer aisle at the rear ducked down and slipped out to call the police. Soon the sound of sirens interrupted the deathly silence of the sanctuary. No one dared move. It was as if each hoped by sitting like a statue they wouldn't draw attention to themselves.

"Who are you, son? Tell us what you want."

"You don't know me," Jeremy answered. "Until today, I was nobody. But that ends today. I am Jeremiah the prophet. The Leader knows you and says this church is a house of lies."

He twirls around, swinging his gun in a full circle, shooting into the congregation. People ducked almost reflexively.

"Before that happens, some of you must die, or no one will listen. Those of you I let live need to tell everyone else it is no longer safe to gather in churches full of lies."

Eighty-year-old Maude Naggle rose to her feet. "I know you, Jeremy Bellinger. Your mother and father would be ashamed of you. Stop this right now."

Her face is stern, and there is no quiver to her voice. She speaks with such force and lack of fear that Jeremy hesitates and stares at her. "I'm sorry you are here, Mrs. Naggle, but it is too late to stop now. The Leader told us even our friends will have to die to bring in the new world."

Then he shot her, and she fell across the pew as shouts erupted around the sanctuary. He turned and shot a man trying to protect a small girl in the pew near Jeremy.

"NO," Frank screamed. He lowered his head and charged, legs pumping. He held the Bible like a shield.

Before Frank could close the distance, Jeremy fired as he shouted, "The lies stop now."

Frank falls to the floor.

There is a large bang as the doors at the rear of the sanctuary burst open. A SWAT squad enters with their guns at ready. They see Frank go down. They shout their commands.

Jeremy laughed at them as he raised his gun in their direction. Two of the police fire simultaneously and Jeremy's head explodes, spilling his blood and brains on those who are near him.

Several people fainted as the echo of guns bounced off the walls of the sanctuary.

An EMT crew follows the police and immediately begins attending to those who fainted or were wounded in the sanctuary.

Wiley McClaren, the clerk of session of the church, leaped from his pew and ran towards the prone body of Frank Sessions. Bill Atkins, a doctor who is with his family in the rear of the sanctuary, jumped up and joined Wiley. The doctor and an attendant turn Frank's body over.

The doctor pounds on Frank's chest and then listens for a heartbeat.

"Is he all right?" asked Wiley.

Atkins looked up at Wiley. "We'll know for sure when we check him out at the hospital, but I think the bullet hit that Bible he was carrying and both the Bible and his knuckles slammed back into him. It caused a myocardial contusion so that the conduction system ceased sending out an electrical stimulus."

Wiley stared at him.

"Sorry, in layman's terms the heart is bruised. My blow to the chest got it going again."

Despite the macabre scene, the doctor began to chuckle.

"I guess the word is more powerful than the sword," he says, "or, in this case, a revolver."

Wiley looked at his beloved pastor, released his breath, and started to sob with relief. While Frank was unconscious, Wiley believed that the Bible absorbed the bullet and kept injury to Frank at a minimum.

"He'll have a very sore chest," said the doctor, "but I think he will recover just fine."

Then the doctor looked around. "What in the world happened here?" That is the question the whole community would be asking for weeks and months to come.

RUNNING FOR YOUR LIFE

CHAPTER 3

Blood and brains spilled out on those who sat nearby. Several people fainted, and there was a brief moment of haunting silence followed by an explosion of screams and shouts from all directions. The scene was total chaos.

Wiley saw one man, like a fullback spotting an opening, burst through a side door with his 6-year-old daughter under one arm shoving his wife ahead of him as he used his phone to unlock and start his dark blue Infiniti QX. "Stop screaming, and get your ass in the car," he shouted as he opened the back door and shoved their daughter inside. He thinks he can protect his family by running from the scene of violence.

A slightly built, balding man piled his family into a red Mercedes-Benz parked on the street. As he tried to exit, he hit a gray Hyundai in front of him. He immediately backed up and rammed forward again forcing the Hyundai up over the curb and providing space for his Mercedes to drive away. Wiley guessed he had disabled the airbag because it didn't deploy.

Several cars tried to leave a small grassy church parking area but found the single exit from the lot blocked by a blue Prius. One large man leaped out of his car shouting at the woman sitting in front of the exit. "Get the hell out of the way, you idiot." The driver of the Prius had her hands on the wheel but she was frozen in place. A police car came barreling down the street with siren blaring.

Still yelling, the man grabbed the car door handle and began to yank at the door. The woman's eyes expanded, and her lips formed a scream as she recognized someone trying to enter her car.

"Get back in your car, turn the motor off, and sit there until we get this straightened out," said an officer who walked up to the scene.

"I got to get my family to safety, lady." He raged at the officer, but she was not intimidated.

"I understand this is a frightening time, sir," the officer said, "but there are plenty of police officers around, and your family is no longer in danger. Now I'd suggest you calm down."

Seeing they are surrounded by patrol cars and media trucks beginning to arrive, the man's shoulders fell as he walked towards his car. He spoke to others who had climbed out of their cars. "What the hell is happening? This is a church, not the 'OK Corral.'"

The police began to rope off the area.

Wiley caught a glimpse of a green Subaru quietly leaving its parking spot a block away. He didn't know why but it seemed the one image of calmness in the midst of chaos.

He continued to observe all of this as he stumbled around the parking areas and lawn. He had witnessed a near massacre inside the church and held the unconscious body of his beloved pastor in his arms. He had reason to hope, but was not certain, that Frank would survive. Whether John Knox Presbyterian, where he had served as clerk of session for several years, would survive this horrific event, he was not sure.

A slight chill filled the air. Under normal circumstances, the bright sun and the Carolina blue sky would have lifted people's spirits as they exited the church on a spring morning. A cloud briefly passed overhead causing a quick shadow to envelop the lawn where people ambled in an incoherent fashion. Some walked in circles and most moved as if in a daze. Unlike watching a thriller movie, this time they could not exit the theater and resume their lives.

A police captain used a megaphone to address both the people in cars and the larger crowd huddled on the lawn.

"May I have your attention? Once the wounded are attended to, it will be important that we talk to all of you who were inside the church at the time of the shooting. We will work as quickly as possible, but in the meantime, if any of you need assistance, please contact one of the officers."

The lawn was freshly cut. Sidewalks crossed in various directions. A couple of brick laid patios prepared for small gatherings with concrete benches allowed people to rest and reflect.

The chill of the air caused many people to huddle together seeking the warmth and the reassurance of friends. Many sobbed while others tried to comfort them. A large magnolia tree that children loved to climb after church stood empty of laughter. Groups began to form trying to understand what they had just experienced.

Wiley catches snatches of conversation as he walked by different collections of people. Two couples and a single man talked together.

"Who was that maniac?"

"I saw him come in," said another.

"He looked like any clean-cut college kid," said his wife.

Wiley moved on.

"Why did he want to shoot up our church?"

"It just doesn't make sense."

Wiley listened as two other men joined the conversation.

"Did you hear him call Frank by name?"

"Do you suppose he's from one of those crazy prison projects the preacher is always involved in?"

It's already begun, thought Wiley. Whenever people are frightened, one of their first responses is to find someone to blame. They hope if someone is at fault, we can escape the turmoil by banishing the guilty party.

"Someone needs to put a stop to those crazy projects."

A woman, who had been sniffling, glared at the speaker.

"The preacher was shot, maybe dead, and you want to start criticizing his efforts to make us act like Christians."

The man who had spoken winced at the criticism.

"We have to protect our church. We can't have crazy lunatics killing our families."

Wiley saw a husband take off his suit coat and drape it over his wife's shoulders. Tears streamed down her face. She said, "Do you suppose Frank is dead?"

A man who had been quiet spoke up. "I'm not sure. From what I saw, he was running right at him when the boy fired his gun."

Wiley joined the group and said, "I was with the doctor who first examined him. He was unconscious, but it appears the bullet first hit the Bible he carried. So he is bruised but, God willing, he will be all right."

"Thank God," a man said. "I've had my share of differences with Frank in the past, but I have to say he was willing to risk his life to save the rest of us."

"He may harp on loving our enemies, but when they threaten us, he knows how to act," said another.

A teenager joined the adults. "How many people were shot?"

"It's not clear yet," said Wiley, "but at least four were killed and several others wounded."

A woman dressed in a business suit walked by. "Oh, God, this can't be happening in our church. We're nice respectable people."

Wiley moved on towards another group huddled nearby.

As a police officer walked by, a woman stopped the officer. She turned to her teenage son, who was cowering in the background. "Go ahead, tell the officer." She turned to the man. "My son says that he thinks he recognized the boy who did the shooting."

"Hold on, young man," the officer said. He keyed the phone on his shoulder. "Find Detective Wilson for me. I have a witness who knows the shooter."

Wiley paused to see what would happen next.

In a moment, Detective Wilson approached. "Tell this Detective what you said to me."

"I ma...may kn...know who that kid was," he said. With hunched shoulders and a flick of his brown unruly hair, he shifted his gaze from his tan loafers to Detective Wilson's shoulder holster. "Not sure. Looked different." His words were muffled like he wanted to eat them before anyone heard him.

"What makes you think you know him?" Wilson asked.

"Name, I guess. Lady called him Jeremy Bellinger."

"What lady?" the officer asked.

The boy grimaced as if suddenly recalling the bloody scene he'd witnessed. "Old lady who was shot."

"You know a Jeremy Bellinger?" the detective said.

"Naw, just saw him around at the Stone," said Floyd,

"The Stone?" the officer said.

"He means Brookstone High School," his father said, lifting his hand to place it on his son's shoulder. But, apparently thinking better of it—too many people around—he placed his hand on his wife's back, supporting her when she turned numb at the thought of her church friend.

"Was he part of a group you hang around with?" Detective Wilson asked.

"No way," Floyd said. "He was a dweeb."

"Jeremy!" his mother responded.

"Well, he was, mom." Floyd scuffed at the grass with a shoe. "Maybe I got the wrong guy. He sure looked different in there." He glanced at his dad for support.

"How did he look different?" the detective pressed.

"The guy I knew . . . didn't really know, just saw around, was, you know, different."

Detective Wilson reached out a hand and placed it on Floyd's shoulder. He looked him in the eye and spoke calmly. "Son, I know this is a real confusing time, and people are very frightened. You won't be doing anything wrong if you describe what you know. I'll check it out, and if it is a different guy, then we will move on–no harm done. Now tell me what the guy you recognize from your high school looked like."

Floyd's head dropped, he turned his back from his mother and faced the officer. He spoke softly.

"He was a shit-head. Always dressed in rags. Best thing about him was his hair. Blond, reached almost to his waist, curly. That part of him he kept clean, but the rest was garbage."

"I understand," said the detective. "You say he didn't belong in your group."

"No way. Mostly a loner, though sometimes he tried to flirt with the girls."

"Any special girls?" Wilson asked.

"Don't know," Floyd turns his face away from his mother's sight. "Just some of the ho's."

"What!" his mother said. "Floyd Simpson, you don't talk about other people that way!"

"Mom, I'm just trying to tell the detective what I know. If he's going to track down people who know Jeremy, he might as well start with those girls. Though I don't think Jeremy had the ball . . .the gumption to stick em . . . I mean to have a serious relationship with any of them. He was really lame."

"Thank you, Floyd," said Wilson. "I may need to talk with you some more, so, with your parent's permission, I need your cell phone number."

Wiley turned away from the conversation as he noticed a hush fall over the crowd as the doors opened and several attendants began to wheel bodies out of the church. Several of them were in white body bags. Six people were brought out on stretchers. Some did not appear to be injured, but were being treated for shock, fainting, or from falls. Some friends rushed to their sides to speak words of comfort.

It was the body bags that drew most people's attention. Broadcasters and local print journalists had arrived, and a couple of camera operators were trying to get shots of the bodies as others were setting up for broadcasts. Reporters began circulating among the people looking for significant people to interview.

Several began to focus in on one vocal man who spoke loudly to anyone who would listen to him. When he saw the reporters, he seemed eager to be interviewed.

The reporter approached him, "People are pretty shaken, but tell our listeners what happened here."

"That crazy kid shot up our church." He didn't wait for another question but continued to share his opinion. "I'll tell you what we should do," he said. "I'm from Wyoming, and we had the common sense to pass a law that allows people to carry weapons for our own personal protection even into churches. If someone had their own gun in there, that snot-nosed twerp wouldn't have gotten his second shot off, and at least four more people, five if the pastor is bad off, would still be alive.

HOSPITAL VISIT

CHAPTER 4

Frank was sedated when he arrived at the hospital to enable the doctors to examine him thoroughly. He began to regain consciousness.

His sense of pain was the first form of awareness. He knew his chest hurt but, at first, he could not remember where he was or why he was in pain. The next to awaken was the sense of smell. He had been in enough hospitals during his ministry to recognize the antiseptic smells around him. Then came the sounds–people talking in hushed tones, the clang of instruments, occasional chuckles, and the general bustle of several people moving around him.

Finally, it occurred to him he could open his eyes and see what was happening. Before he did, his memory began to restore itself.

First he recalled the sounds of guns, shouts, and sirens. *I was at the church. Something horrible happened there. People were screaming. I was trying to run towards the shooter. So why am I now in a hospital?*

It wasn't a personal sense of fear but almost a dread of what he would hear that made him hesitate to open his eyes. Slowly he raised his eyelids, at first with a slit, and then he blinked.

"Doctor, I believe he is coming out of the anesthetic," a nurse said as Frank became aware of his surroundings.

The doctor lowered his face mask "Welcome back, reverend. You experienced some broken ribs and went into some shock, but we've checked you out, and you are going to be just fine," said the doctor. "We were concerned that your heart might have a cardiac contusion or, in lay terms, been bruised by the trauma of the bullet, but I haven't spotted any significant damage."

Frank watched the doctor. He noticed he was working hard not to grin. "What is it?"

"Oh, nothing," the doctor said.

Even in his groggy state, Frank could tell the doctor wanted to laugh but held back because he didn't think it would be appropriate.

"OK," said Frank, "what you want to say is that I dodged the bullet this time, isn't it?"

The doctor, who Frank had known casually from his work in the hospital, let loose with a loud guffaw. "If I needed any proof, it is clear you haven't lost your sense of humor, Frank." The staff around him began to giggle.

They immediately sobered when Frank asked, "Can you tell me more about what happened and how long I've been out?"

"I'm afraid there were some serious injuries.

They brought you to Methodist Hospital directly from the church. You were unconscious for a couple of hours. We put you under because we wanted to check all of your vitals, but it all checks out," the doctor said.

"That was only part of my question," Frank said.

The doctor reached out a hand and touched Frank's shoulder. His voice caught as he continued. "It's not pretty, Frank. We'll take you back to your room, and your family can fill you in on the details."

The memory of the events began flooding in on Frank. His pain was much deeper than what had happened to his body. The nurse called the doctor's attention to the spike in Frank's blood pressure.

The doctor placed his other hand on his shoulder and leaned in as he spoke. "Frank, I'm Jew and not a very good one at that. I know you more by reputation and occasional interaction here at the hospital. I know you are a good pastor, and your first impulse is to rush back to your people."

"Yes," said Frank. His face communicated his gratitude that the doctor understood. "If I'm all right, I need to get out of here."

"Frank, listen to me. Your people have experienced a terrible trauma, and they will need your counsel. However, you won't be helping them if you collapse on your way home, and they are forced to give their attention to you instead.

"We need to take you back to your room, and it may be a couple of days before you can return to work."

"But they need me now. I'm their pastor."

"What they experienced was tragic, and they will need you for the long haul. Others will assist them today as best they can, but you need to recover your strength to help them on the longer journey."

A small smile appeared on Frank's face. "You may not consider yourself a good Jew, doctor, but you do possess a genetic wisdom handed down through the ages. I'll give you a few more hours to heal me."

The doctor turned to the nurses and attendants who had been listening with unusual intensity. "Are you listening to this ladies and gentlemen?" He smiled as he included Frank in his comments. "The good reverend thinks another Jew can perform miracles, and he is giving me an extra few hours to accomplish that."

He turned back to those assisting him. "Get him ready to move back to his room. I'll head over there now and reassure his family."

Frank was conscience of the curative effect of the doctor's gentle humor on the nurses and attendants who wore the strain of the community events on their faces. He was anxious to see his family and find out more what has been taking place at the church. They wheeled him out of the ICU. He verbally thanked all those around him.

His adult children, Jacob, and Rachel, were waiting at the door to the room as they brought him in and transferred him to the hospital bed. Jacob was dressed casually and carried his six-foot-four slim body with confidence. Yet he was clearly worried.

Rachel, dressed in her police uniform, spoke first. "Dad, the doctor says you'll be all right but need some bed rest. I told him I had some fresh handcuffs and might put them to good use."

"Just what I need," said Frank–"a parole officer."

"I was on patrol over on the east side when I heard some of what happened on the police chatter box. I radioed in and was heading to the church when my captain told me they were bringing you to Methodist University, so I came directly here. I called Jacob, who was studying, as usual, and he met me here."

"I was on the brink of solving a profound theological mystery that had puzzled theologians for centuries when my sister interrupted my concentration. Dad, you have to stop challenging people with guns. People are going to begin to doubt you are a disciple of the Prince of Peace."

Frank knew they were trying to ease the tension, but their faces revealed their concern about more than his personal welfare. A nurse stepped in to check his vitals, and he saw she, too, had been crying. His children had weathered some tough times with him in the past. The hospital staff was accustomed to responding to trauma, but all of them were struggling to keep their composure. Frank knew his injuries were part of a much larger event that had shattered the calm of many people's worlds.

As the nurse left the room, Jacob and Rachel came closer on either side of the bed. Both of them grabbed one of his hands.

Frank looked at his hands being held. "I have some memory of a young man standing up with a gun and beginning to shoot." His face contorted in pain. "Oh, God, he shot poor old Maude Nagle, didn't he?"

They both nodded. "And some others," said Jacob.

"There was a lot of panic. We are still waiting for a report on how many were hit."

"I've radioed in," said Rachel, "and they will keep me up to date as the reports come in."

"I talked to Wiley as I was coming over," said Jacob. "He tells me there could have been many more if you hadn't charged the shooter. You distracted him. It allowed the police to get in position and bring him down."

"Did he say anything about why he did it?" asked Frank.

"This wasn't an opportunity to try to capture and question him," Rachel said. "He was getting ready to shoot others. The police had no choice but to shoot. He's dead."

"Right before he shot her, people heard Maude say she knew his parents. The police located them. Some officers have been dispatched to talk to them. Maybe they will get some information that will be helpful," said Rachel.

"Those poor parents," said Frank. "I see the two of you, and I realize how lucky I am."

"Yeah," said Jacob with a smirk on his face. "At least one of us turned out all right."

"Careful, civvie." Rachel shifted her belt that held her gun, handcuffs, mace, etc. "I might have to arrest you for showing disrespect for a police officer."

Frank began to laugh, and then his face contorted in pain. "Oh, it hurts to laugh." Then he saw the concerned look on his children's faces. "But it feels good too."

"It's bad out there, isn't it?" Frank said. "How many would you guess were hurt or killed?"

He turned to Rachel. "What are the police saying?"

Rachel looked at Jacob for support, then back at her father.

"Dad, I won't lie to you. It's horrible. At least four were killed and many injured. Let me step out into another room and get an update. I'll be right back."

Frank thought about Rachel as she left the room. He remembered her saying that she joined the police after her mother was killed when she entered a convenience store while a robbery was in process.

"After her death," Rachel said, "I kept thinking it was all such a waste. Then it occurred to me if I became part of the police and helped stop others from being hurt, at least it wouldn't all be a waste." Even though she was slightly built, he knew she had developed martial skills that had surprised more than one overconfident male as he got back up off the ground. Even in this tragic moment, he was very proud to be her father.

He turned back to his son who was also watching his younger sister walk out of the room. "Who'd of ever thought my bratty sister would turn out to be such a skilled police officer. I'll bet it won't be long before she makes detective. She's good at that sort of puzzle solving thing."

"If I remember correctly, both of you were skillful at the game of Clue and helped Mandy and I figure out that crazy rapist case a couple of years ago," Frank said.

"Have you heard from Amanda lately?" asked Jacob. "I'm surprised you let that one get away."

"I didn't let her get away. We just both have our professional responsibilities, and we live quite a distance from each other."

Frank smiled at the thought of Mandy or Amanda as Jacob called her. Then he reeled in his thoughts and turned back towards Jacob. "Jacob, I know the main focus of your efforts is with the academic, but I was wondering . . ."

"Whatever you need, you got it."

"I think what I will need for the next month or so is some help with the congregation. You have some inherent pastoral skills. I'd like to ask for your help."

"Sure, I can break some time free. What do you have in mind?

A nurse came in to check the monitors and to change some bandages. Frank felt the tenderness of his ribs as she worked. When she left, he continued his conversation with Jacob.

"It's clear I'm going to be slowed down for a week or so," he said. "I can't begin to imagine the trauma the congregation is feeling right now."

"Even those who weren't present during the incident will be traumatized," said Jacob. "Those who saw people getting shot will be in shock."

"That's what I mean, Jacob. Your graduate work has combined both theology and psychology. You also have an innate sensitivity to what people are experiencing. I want to draw upon those skills as I help the congregation work through this."

"Sure, Dad, I'll be glad to help. I have some colleagues and professionals in the field I'm sure we can draw upon as well."

"Thanks, Jacob. I also realize I may need some help with how I handle all of this. It's like being in a war zone. If I start acting crazy, I'm counting on you to point that out to me."

They looked up as Rachel walked back into the room. She was carrying her laptop with her. If you can bear a mixture of deep sadness and an amusing secret on your face at the same time, Frank thought that would describe Rachel's face.

"What did you find out?" Frank asked. He felt a small twinge in his chest as his muscles tightened preparing himself to hear the news.

"The initial report is four people are dead and eight to ten injured either from bullets or pieces of tile that careened off the floor. Some others were hurt when they fainted or tried to get out of the way."

"I guess I should be grateful there weren't more," Frank said. "I can't begin to comprehend the emotional shock they are experiencing."

Rachel pulled herself up to her full five foot eight heights and spoke in an official tone. "As you know, the police are going to want to talk to you as soon as you are able."

"Sure, I'm aware of that. In fact I think I can talk to them anytime."

"Well, since the closer to the incident they talk to you, while your memory is still fresh, is vital, I've arranged for one officer to talk with you through Skype. I've brought in my laptop to assist you. I'll just plug it in and set it up for you."

Both Frank and Jacob had a puzzled look on their faces as Rachel busied herself getting her laptop connected. "Jacob, can you help raise the bed to a sitting position for Dad?"

When it was ready, she placed her laptop on Frank's bed and turned the screen towards him. Even as she did that, she turned and gave a big wink to Jacob and began to smile.

"Didn't anyone ever tell you when someone is firing a gun at you it is a good idea to duck, Frank?"

Frank's mouth fell open in surprise as he stared at Amanda Singletary's face on the screen. Her olive complexion and the slight Asian slant to her eyes evoked good memories for Frank.

"Mandy, how are you? It is so good to see you."

"I'm rather relieved to see you, too, Frank. I didn't know that being in the ministry was such a dangerous business."

"I'm afraid it is a tragic business, Mandy. I'm still partially in shock trying to understand what happened."

"The report Rachel gave painted a grim picture, Frank. As bad as it is, I hope it is just an isolated tragedy."

Frank felt his body tense. "What don't I know that would suggest otherwise?" Frank asked as he glanced at Rachel and then turned back to Amanda.

Rachel spoke up. "I was just telling Amanda the police want to know what the shooter was referring to when he kept speaking about the Leader saying this and the Leader saying that. It's remote, but the police want to be alert to the possibility that this might be part of something bigger."

Frank's face contorted in pain to which Amanda responded with concern. "Frank, are you all right?"

"I'm all right. I have some bruised, maybe broken ribs when the Bible hit me." He smiled. "I guess he threw the book at me." Then he grew serious. "When you spoke of the possibility that this might be larger than just my church, it startled me. Before we get too far into that, I want to hear how you are doing?"

"I'm fine," said Amanda. "In fact, before I heard about this, I was in a mood to celebrate. I got an opportunity to join the Justice Department, and I've moved to Washington."

"That's great, Mandy," said Frank. "A new position, huh. So what shall we call you now?"

"Call me, Frank. I didn't know calling someone was in your repertoire." She raised her right eyebrow but continued to smile.

"I'm sorry, Mandy; I've meant to call you for some time now. Things have been busy lately."

Just then Frank heard the doorbell ring in whatever room Mandy was in. She looked up away from the screen, and a large smile appeared on her face. "Come on in Mark. I'm on Skype with an old friend. I'll be through in a minute. Fix yourself a drink, and make yourself comfortable."

Frank's eyes widened and he did his best not to change the expression on his face. "You have company?" Frank said with a slight edge to his voice. "We shouldn't keep you."

Rachel and Jacob tried not to show any response as their dad struggled to hide his reaction to the arrival of a man in Amanda's apartment.

"Oh, that's Mark. We're going out to dinner. Our reservations aren't for another hour. We have plenty of time."

"I see," said Frank. "Well, I hope you have a lovely evening."

Amanda lowered her voice and moved closer to the screen. "Why Frank, I do believe I see a slight flash of jealousy. Isn't that lovely. I didn't know you cared."

"I do care, Mandy. I was just surprised, that's all. I sincerely want you to have a nice evening."

"If you were feeling better, I might bust your chops for ignoring me for the past couple of months and then being jealous that I have a social life. Now, however, I'll just enjoy that small revenge.

Is Rachel in earshot? I want to say something to her about this case."

Rachel moved into the view of the laptop. "I'm here, Mandy. What's up?"

"Hopefully nothing if your earlier speculations are wrong," said Amanda. "However, I would like you to keep me informed as to what develops. If this does turn out to be bigger, my new department may be able to be a resource for you."

"I'll count on that, Mandy. I'll keep you up to date."

"Good. Frank, give yourself some time to heal. Rachel and Jacob put him in handcuffs if necessary. I'll call later to hear about developments. In my case, I do know how to use the telephone." She gave a big smile and reached for the button to turn off the computer. As her image faded, Frank saw a hand reach across the screen and hand her a drink.

"When was the last time you and Amanda talked?" Rachel asked.

Frank's face twisted in a half scowl. "I sent her a Christmas card."

"Well, let the trumpets blast. Frank Sessions, the great communicator, actually signed a Christmas card, addressed the envelope, and spent money on a stamp. Woohoo."

"Rachel, it's complicated, OK. I am glad to talk with her, though. I assume that you set that up?"

"It seemed like a good idea," said Rachel with a grin. "I didn't know that it was going to unleash the green-eyed monster of jealousy, though."

Frank's face colored. "I'm not jealous. It is good Amanda is dating. She is a wonderful woman and deserves to enjoy life to its fullest."

"But?" said Rachel as she stared at her father.

"But nothing," said her father with a slight irritation in his voice. "I was just caught off guard is all."

Jacob chuckled. "I think she caught you, Dad."

Rachel turned on Jacob with a glint in her eye. "Speaking of communication, how is Brandy doing these days?"

Jacob shifted and looked away. "She's doing fine, I think. We've both been busy lately."

"What is it with the men in my family? You both seem to have real problems with long-term commitments. You get close, and then you run?"

"Spoken by the expert in playing the field."

"Believe me; if I ever found a man of half the quality of either of those two women, I would never let him go. Of course, it just may be there are no males with the DNA to have that type of quality. Oh, the burden of being part of the superior gender."

"OK, OK, let's lower the sabers. Your old man needs to get out of here and get home. How about checking with the nurse's station to see what my status is?

RELEASE FROM HOSPITAL AND VISIT FROM POLICE

CHAPTER 5

Jacob came back into Frank's hospital room. "All right, Dad, I've signed all the papers. We can get you dressed, and the doctor will be in to give you final instruction,"

Frank looked around his bare room. He noticed a wardrobe door partially open. "Do we have any clothes for me to wear, or am I supposed to leave here in the gown designed to humiliate all patients who dare to enter here?"

"As an expert in police work," said Rachel as she entered the room, "I confiscated the clothes you wore in here. As a compassionate daughter, I also stopped by the house and brought you a sweat suit and some underwear. I figured that loose clothing might be best for now."

"Jacob, help me into the bathroom so I can get into these clothes without embarrassing your ever observant sister."

Once inside the bathroom, Frank removed the gown and replaced it with the sweat suit Rachel had brought him. His skin was sensitive to the touch of the rough material, but it felt good to get out of the gown.

Then, as he opened the door and emerged into his room, the doctor was arriving. He was still dressed in his surgical scrubs and was rubbing some disinfectant from a dispenser on the wall onto his hands. "Good, you're ready to go," said the doctor.

"As much as I enjoy your hospitality," Frank said, "frankly I can't wait to get out of here."

"If you didn't feel that way, I'd consider having you committed," said the doctor. "Now, Frank, from what I've observed and your reputation, the biggest threat to your full recovery is your unwillingness to give your body time to heal. I've prescribed some pain pills that your son can pick up at the drugstore."

"Thank you."

"Let me advise you of something else. Your heart did take quite a hit. It will recover fine, but you would be wise not to stress it for another week at least. No exercise, no driving, low stress, and get plenty of rest."

"The first two I can manage," Frank said. "I'm afraid removing stress from my life is a little impossible under the circumstances."

"I know, and you are going to be important to helping this community as well as your church put things back together. However, if you have a stroke or heart attack, you are going to be an additional burden rather than a help to all of us. We need you, Frank, so be wise."

"We will do our best to support him in getting recovery time," Jacob said.

"I don't know whether you recall it, but when you were coming out of the anesthetic, we had a little conversation about my being a sort of lapsed Jew."

"I remember part of that conversation."

"Well, I wasn't raised that way. I prepared for my bar mitzvah under a very wise rabbi. One of the lessons that he drummed into me that has helped me more than once as a surgeon was the meaning of the Sabbath."

Jacob's ears perked up. "The Sabbath?"

"Yes, the Sabbath," the doctor continued. "He kept emphasizing that the practice of the Sabbath is a regular reminder you are not God. Whenever you get stressed out by all the burdens and pressures on you," the rabbi told me, "you need to stop and say 'I'm not so important that God can't get this done without me,' and I honor God by giving a little space for God to work while I restore myself."

"As my Baptist friends say, 'That will preach,'" said Jacob.

Frank watched the pleasant look on the doctor's face change as his forehead creased and the lines around his mouth tightened.

"You are very important to what is going to happen in this community over the next several months," the doctor said. "Give God a chance to use you in one piece."

"Thank you, doctor," said Frank. "That is sound advice and even better faith. When I get to feeling better, I'm going to talk to my friend, Rabbi Siegel, about nurturing you back into synagogue life. They could benefit from your presence."

The doctor stroked his chin. "I'm a hard nut to crack, but my guess is that the three of you are also.

"I want to see you back in a week for a checkup, but you are free to go—well, except for stopping by the registration desk and committing your life's savings to paying the astronomical bill awaiting you."

Then he turned to Rachel. "Young lady, in addition to taking care of your father, let me thank you for serving this city. I hope your people will put a stop to this craziness soon." Then he left the room.

The nurse came with the wheelchair, and Rachel and Jacob accompanied their father to Jacob's car. When he was settled in, Rachel stuck her head into the window. "Dad, I need to return to the station and see what I can contribute. Jacob will take care of you, but if you need anything, give me a call." Then she kissed him on the cheek and departed.

As they were leaving the parking lot, Frank said, "Jacob, I promise I won't get out of the car, but could you please drive by the church on our way home."

"Sure, Dad. It still has all the yellow tape around it, but I know you will want to see it at least from the outside."

As they drove, Jacob said, "I know that you are concerned about what is going to happen on this next Sunday. I talked to Marcia, your General Presbyter. I told her that I would work with you to select some Scriptures, and I would lead the liturgy, but I would like her to speak a few words. She agreed completely."

"Boy, that was thinking ahead. Thank you. It's hard to figure whether people will want to come or stay away."

"Marcia and I talked about that as well. We decided that there will be some of both, but that those who do come will need a service. You can decide closer to the time if you want to be visibly present or not, but you will have no responsibilities for leadership."

As they drove by the church, there were still some uniformed officers both enforcing the isolation of the crime scene and continuing their investigation. Jacob slowed to allow Frank to look at the church. An officer approached them. Jacob rolled down the window and explained who they were.

The officer leaned into the window and addressed Frank. "I'm sorry for your loss, sir. I just can't imagine why anyone would do this to God's house."

"I think it will be best if we can use this same sanctuary for the funerals. Will you check with your superiors and inform me the earliest that the building will be available." He handed him a card with his home phone number on it.

"Yes, sir," the officer saluted and backed away.

Jacob turned the car around and drove Frank home.

When they turned down his street, Jacob pulled over to the curb. "Uh, Dad, unless you want me to turn around and find you a comfortable motel, you are going to have to decide what you want to say to the media. There are at least a dozen cars parked outside your house."

"Oh, for the love of Mike. I guess they have their job to do. Let's treat them with respect, but let's be brief," Frank said.

As Jacob drove into the driveway, a couple of police officers approached. "Sir, we've been assigned to guard the house until we can get this sorted out. You tell us what you want us to do with regards to the reporters, and we will do it."

"If you could clear a path to the door, I will speak to them for a few minutes before I go in."

"You got it," said the officer and two officers began clearing a path to the door while telling the reporters, "The reverend will speak to you briefly before he goes inside."

Jacob helped Frank out of the car and assisted him in gingerly walking towards his front door. Even though the reporters were anxious to get a story, they also were respectful of his fragile state.

Jacob opened the door. Frank turned to address them.

"As you know, what happened at John Knox Church was a tragedy. I solicit the prayers of your readers and audience for the families of those who died or were injured but also for all the members of the church who have experienced this horrendous event."

"Do you know who he was, pastor? The shooter seemed to know you."

"I'm sure that this will be sorted out during the investigation. I do not presently know who the young man was or why he acted as he did."

"It's been reported that the shooter kept saying, 'It's a lie.' Do you know what he was talking about?" another reporter shouted.

"No, I don't. He was obviously very upset and disturbed. We may find out that he had been wounded by the church or Christianity somehow. We'll just have to wait and see."

"Do you think you were the specific target?" a reporter asked.

"I don't know why I would be, but again we will have to wait until the police conclude their investigation. Friends, I know there is a lot more that you want to know, but I am still recovering both physically and emotionally. Perhaps later we can have a more extended conversation."

"Will there be church there this Sunday?" shouted another reporter as Frank turned to enter the house.

Frank smiled as he said, "It's called worship. The church is a building. Both will be there on Sunday."

There was soft laughter as Frank entered the house and closed the door.

"I always admire how you handle the press," said Jacob. "Where do you want me to help you get settled?"

"I think my favorite easy chair would be a good beginning," said Frank. "Then I would like a nice tall glass of ice tea and maybe some relaxing, soft music."

For the next hour, Frank sipped the iced tea as he listened to a piano medley of some classic hymns of faith. As the music played, Frank tried not to think about the specifics of the events that had taken place. He sought to allow God to bring thoughts to his mind, gently nurturing himself for the challenges ahead. Jacob had left the room providing him a sanctuary of silence.

His reverie was interrupted by the ringing of the phone. He allowed Jacob to answer. In a few minutes, Jacob entered the room with the phone in his hand. "It's the police. They want to know if they can stop by with some initial questions. They promise that it will be less than an hour because they recognize that you are still in recovery."

"It is important that they get right on this. Tell them to come by."

Jacob proceeded to confirm the appointment.

"I want you to stay during the interview, and if it is going too long or getting too stressful, step in and help me close it down." Frank paused and then said, "Jacob?"

"Yes, Dad."

"I noticed that Brenda, the reporter, or as you speak of her as Brandy, the friend, was not among the reporters at the door. Is there anything wrong between you two?"

"Oh, it's just that we have sort of stepped back from each other recently. It was becoming intense, and I wasn't sure that I could meet up to her expectations."

"Expectations?"

"You know. First I didn't call enough. Then, when I did call, I wasn't sharing my feelings. You know I take my studies seriously. I think she may be a little jealous of my devotion to my work."

"She is devoted to her work as well, Jacob. I'm sure there were times that interfered with your dates."

"Yeah, and I tried to tell her that. She kept saying that it wasn't the work but the feelings she cared about."

"How do you feel, Jacob?"

"I don't know. I think she is terrific, and all, but love is so complicated. Books are a lot easier."

"Well, I just missed seeing her among the reporters, and I wondered."

Jacob smiled. "Knowing Brenda, the ace reporter, I'm sure she is scheming another way to get an exclusive interview with you—maybe when I'm not around.

"It's OK to say this is none of my business, but, in addition to Brenda, the ace reporter, Brandy, the friend, is a terrific woman and seemed to be pretty good for you. If you want to talk about it, I'd like to help."

"Maybe later, Dad. Let's get through these next few days first."

The doorbell rang.

"That must be the police," Frank said. He straightened up in his lounger and adjusted the blanket he had been using to keep him warm while he listened to the music. "I think I will keep this on to remind them that I am not up to full strength," he said.

Jacob gave him a knowing smile and went to answer the door. Two detectives were standing there.

"Hello, officers," he said. "I'm Jacob Sessions, Frank's son. My father is expecting you."

The detectives followed Jacob into the living room where they greeted Frank. "I'm Detective Wilson, and this is Detective Burlingame."

Wilson was a firmly built large man and was clearly in charge.

Burlingame was a lanky, thin man who Frank guessed must have been six-foot-four but probably did not tip the scales at more than two hundred pounds.

"We are sorry for the events at your church."

"Thank you, officers. Please sit down. Have you found out anything new about why this took place?"

Both officers sat in chairs Jacob had set up so that Frank could look at them from his comfortable chair. "We've located the shooter's parents," said Detective Wilson, "and someone is interviewing them to see if we can identify the motive of the young man. We understand from some of the witnesses that he spoke your name as if he knew you. Had you had previous contact with the young man?"

"No, I didn't recognize him as someone I'd ever seen before."

"As a pastor you must work with a lot of groups," said Detective Burlingame." It might have been someone you talked to. Even if you don't remember his face, do you recall a recent interaction where someone got upset at something you said?"

"I'm sorry, I can't think of any event like that either."

"What about during the shooting itself," said Wilson. "Was there anything you saw that might help us in our investigation?"

Frank looked away as he thought. "Things happened fast," said Frank, "but there did seem to be an almost mechanical tone to his speech."

"Mechanical?" asked Burlingame.

"Almost like he was in a daze," said Frank. "In fact as I recall it, his most human moment came when poor Mrs. Nagle spoke up. He almost seemed to regret shooting her, while the other shootings were without any sign of feelings."

While Burlingame took notes, Wilson continued to ask questions. "What else did he say?"

Looking off towards the ceiling, Frank thought a moment. "You know," he said, "I'd forgotten about it 'till this moment, but we record these services. I can have the clerk get a copy of the service to your office, and you can have someone transcribe the whole thing."

"That would be helpful," said Wilson. "I know that you have

worked with the police in a previous case. I'll be interested in your impressions as things unfold."

Frank closed his eyes, and the muscles of his face tightened as he remembered the events of the past Sunday. "The horror of it all," said Frank. "We speak of that room as a sanctuary. It is supposed to be a place where people can withdraw from the stress of the rest of the world and focus on the spiritual meaning of life."

Burlingame looked genuinely uncomfortable. "It must have been horrible as a pastor to see some of your people being gunned down."

Frank gave him an appreciative smile. "We have to find out why this happened," said Frank. "The shooter said, 'it's a lie' a couple of times."

Jacob spoke up. "There is a lot of nihilism and despair among some of the students at the seminary. That is the type of statement some of them might make when they think about the bleak outlook for some of the churches they are serving."

"But it wasn't just philosophical," said Frank. "There seemed to be some deep personal pain and despair."

"Maybe he was raped by some preacher and decided to get revenge," said Wilson. "You hear a lot of that going on these days."

"That would be the ultimate horror, wouldn't it? The sins of a preacher costing the lives of some parishioners who had come to hear Good News."

They were all silent for a minute as each thought about what had been said.

Frank broke the silence. "I know that you have to probe the possibility, but I know of nothing that I or any member of my staff has done that could evoke such a horrible action."

"We will keep your assurance in mind," said Burlingame, "but, as you said, we will need to explore the possibility. It might not be someone in your church."

"Yeah," said Wilson, "you were rather prominent in solving that rape case a couple of years ago. Maybe, in his mind, you were just someone well known on whom he could take revenge."

"I hope you are wrong, officers, but we have to find an explanation for this tragedy. The church and especially the sanctuary is a place of hope and healing. If people become afraid to attend worship, we will have a real problem in this country."

"Hopefully, working together, we can prevent that from happening," said Wilson. "By the way, one of the teens that was present when this all came down said that he recognized this Jeremy fellow. He thought he hung out with a girl called Natalie. Do you know anyone by that name?"

"Sorry," said Frank.

"Well we have an Officer Sessions checking . . . hey, wait a moment, is she related to you?"

Frank felt a rush of pride rise as he responded, "She's my daughter."

"Great officer," said Burlingame, "and I mean this respectfully, but she's a real looker too, wouldn't you say, Detective Wilson?"

Jacob was the first to notice that Detective Wilson's face took on a redder cast, and he stumbled a little as he tried to recover.

"She is a good officer. You should be proud of her. Wouldn't surprise me if she made detective soon." Having said that, he turned and gave Burlingame a sour look.

Frank kept his face neutral, even though he smiled inside.

"Thank you, detectives. We are very proud of her."

"Well, we should be going," said Wilson. "We will keep you informed. If you think of anything else, please call us immediately. Here is our card. We work together so either number will work."

Jacob showed them out and returned with a big grin on his face. "I'd say Officer Sessions is having a big impact on her fellow officers."

"I think you may be on to something, but let's not press the issue," said Frank.

NEVER TRUST A MAN

CHAPTER 6

Eight months before the first shooting

As Barbara Delong Godwin walked down the street, she paused at every store window that held merchandise. She paid particular attention to the store displaying high priced lines. She didn't care what the product was—clothes, jewelry, cars, works of art—as long as it cost a lot of money. She was shopping and wanted to identify two or three expensive gifts. Her husband didn't know it yet, but the Holy Reverend Mr. Bastard was going to buy them for her.

As she walked down the street glancing in the windows, she was aware of the many men who followed her with their eyes. She was stunning even at 50 years of age, and she knew it. For practical reasons she had never had an affair since she married The Reverend Bob Godwin, but she knew if she indicated a willingness, there would be plenty of offers—even from her husband's religious colleagues.

Her father had been very pious, and she was raised in the church, so she learned all about religion. It didn't do him any good, though.

He said all the prayers, gave lots of money to the church, attended worship on an almost obsessive regularity, but God didn't protect him from the drunken truck driver when she was eight.

Even though her mother kept up the practice of religious involvement for four more years, when she was twelve, her beautiful and brilliant mother sat her down and explained the facts of life. Religion and sex are two of the most powerful forces in life and the biggest lies that exist. Barbara was shocked when her mother first made that pronouncement, but, under her mother's tutelage, as she grew older, she began to recognize her wisdom. Both religion and sex can benefit you if you play them right but never believe their promises.

As she crossed 34th Street, some college students drove by and unleashed some whistles and catcalls. She smiled and waved at them. She was pleased that, at 50, she could still attract the attention of such young studs. She took her mother's advice seriously that men were useful for physical pleasure—a lot more fun than masturbation her mother had counseled.

If you hook a good one, they can provide you with material benefits and help you politically achieve what you want. Always remember it is your goals that are important.

A good one, she thought. It was what she thought she was doing when she hooked up with Bob Godwin. He seemed the perfect catch. He was physically gorgeous, very smart, charismatic, and religious. When she spotted him her first year on campus, he seemed the ideal candidate to pursue. He was clearly going to be a rising star in the church, and she knew how to play the religion game well. She understood clergy were never going to receive the exorbitant salaries of some of the corporate execs, but she wasn't greedy. She retained enough of the ethics of her father's faith to consider the economic structure producing billionaires as beneath contempt.

She paused in front of a jewelry store where she spotted an exquisite ruby pendant. She was sure the pendant would match an expensive blouse she had identified earlier in the day. On the other hand, she thought, you don't have to be greedy to appreciate beauty.

Being the spouse of the pastor of one of the larger megachurches in the city did provide some benefits. Especially if she had him by the short hairs, which she was soon going to achieve.

After all, she had been faithful and supported every step of his career. Bob was the one who had betrayed her. She shouldn't have been surprised. She knew from the beginning that men were to be used for pleasure but were never to be depended upon. Now was the time to exact a price.

She turned away from the store windows, amused at the number of men who averted their eyes as if they hadn't been ogling her. She walked to the curb and raised her hand. Two cabs roared to the curb. She chose the one driven by what appeared to be an Indian driver. He was short, paunchy, and easily above 60 years of age. That ought to be safe, she thought.

She gave him her home address and settled back in the seat to think about the conversation she was going to have with her husband. I think I will wait until he has had a drink and a good dinner, she thought. Men crawl better on a full stomach.

Barbara knew Bob would be tired and looking forward to a quiet night at home. Tonight was one of those rare evenings without a scheduled meeting. She chose to surprise him by having a strong drink for him as he entered the house. The table was set with attractive china and she had some soft music playing. As he ate his supper, he seemed to relax and enjoy each bite.

"What a day," he said. "Few people recognize how demanding being a pastor of a large church can be."

She smiled, showing her beautiful teeth, as she offered him another serving of a blueberry parfait she knew he favored. She was wearing a bright red scoop-necked blouse that revealed some cleavage. She saw his eyes sweep her body as she extended the dish towards him.

"Well, Barbie-doll, what have you been up to today?"

She hated that name. People had been calling her Barbie since she was a child. When she was young and playing with Barbie dolls, she identified with the curvy doll that was so popular among her friends. As she grew older, she realized people also used the term to refer to someone who was all beauty and no brains. As her husband had learned over the years, it was a mistake to think Barbara DeLong Godwin was not smart.

"I did some shopping." She paused and looked at him.

"Uh-oh, I'd better hold on to my wallet." He smiled at his own cleverness.

"Maybe, but it gave me time to think about the church and your position as pastor."

Bob was so involved in eating the blueberry parfait that he was only half-listening. "Yeah, we have had a pretty good run at this church. I expect they will offer me a significant raise when the budget is approved. Maybe I can afford an extra gift for you."

"Bob, do you think the people of the congregation love you?"

He looked up as he wiped his mouth with a napkin. "Not sure what you mean. I think most of them are pleased with my ministry, although there will always be a few complainers." He gave her a knowing wink.

"But do they love you?" She paused, folding her napkin, creasing it, and laying it beside her plate. She picked up her wine glass, but before taking a sip, she said, "For example do you think that cute little widow, Felicity Marshall, loves you?" She tried to keep her face neutral as she saw the color drain from his face.

"I'm, uh . . ."he hesitated searching for the right words," . . . a pretty good counselor." He paused. "Most people seem to appreciate my effort to reach out to people—especially those in grief."

Got your attention now, don't I, she mused. She watched his eyes search her face for any sign of what was behind her question.

She deliberately allowed silence to linger, looking down for a good fifteen seconds, tracing her fingers around her plate. She looked up straight into his eyes as she said, "I guess what made me wonder, Bobbie, was whether it was love or disappointment that caused her to send me a recording of some of your moments of passion. Or maybe you told her I wasn't very good at lovemaking, and she sent it to me to educate me. What do you think, Bobbie?"

She sat back and crossed her arms in front of her. She was pleased with herself for coming up with the diminutive for his name. As many years as she had to suffer being called Barbie, it was only just that she could return the favor. His face was now as white as the tablecloth.

"She sent you a recording . . .?" He started and then changed course," Eh, Barbie, I mean Barbara, I can explain. Sometimes my gestures of support are misinterpreted."

"Words can be misinterpreted, Bobbie, but when you unzip your pants, it's pretty clear, don't you think, Bobbie?"

He started to take a drink from his glass of wine, but his hand was shaking and he sat the glass back on the table. "Your right, Barbara, I was wrong, I confess, but it was a moment when I was weak . . ."

"The first time or the second?" she interrupted. "I think the note accompanying the recording said the second time was even better than the first. What was the special wine she mentioned? I'll have to get a bottle the next time I'm at Total Wine."

His mouth opened. He shoved his chair back from the table, stood, and came around towards her, dropping to his knees, laid his head on her arm, and began to weep. "Just twice, Barb. That's all, I swear. I have sinned . . ."

Before he continued, she gripped his hair with her left hand and jerked his head up, so he was staring into her face. "Don't give me that pious shit about having sinned and begging for forgiveness." Without thinking, she grabbed a knife with her free hand and brought it close to his neck. "You are perilously close to seeing if the resurrection is true or just some malarkey the early Christians dreamed up to continue their movement after Jesus was eliminated." His eyes were staring at the knife. If terror can be seen in the pupils, she was looking at it.

She set the knife down, placed her right hand on his face as she released his hair with her left and shoved. Bob was starting to rise as she shoved, and he fell away and landed flat on his back, hitting his head on the floor.

She rose and stood over him, looking into his dazed eyes. "I am your wife, you supercilious bastard. If you don't want a major scandal to tarnish your holy image, here are the required steps. As I name them, you will continue to lie on the floor, and you will nod your head in agreement. Do you understand me?" She stood over his prone body one foot on either side. She caught his eyes looking up her short skirt, and she knew he recognized she was not wearing panties.

"I said you are to nod your agreement."

His eyes quickly shifted back, and he meekly nodded.

"First, you are to remove that whore from the membership of the church."

"Barb, I can't just remove . . ."

She kicked him in the armpit. "I said nod, damn it."

He nodded.

"Second, you will give me all the pass-codes to your computers and accept the fact that you will be monitored from now on."

Again, he nodded.

"Third, you will buy me a ruby pendant and blouse I spotted today in my shopping."

Buying her off was familiar territory. He had no problem nodding this time.

"That's all for now, but there will be more later," she said, stepping away from him. "Get up. You look stupid lying on the floor. I'm going into the sitting room and put on some soothing music. You can clean up the dishes for once. Then you can bring me a margarita, whether you deliver it on your knees or not, you can decide."

She turned and walked out of the room leaving him dazed on the floor.

She would keep him around as long as it was useful, she thought, but she wouldn't depend on him for her future. She needed to think more about that future.

AN INTERNET FOR REVENGE

CHAPTER 7

The sweet taste of victory didn't last long for Barbara. Bob crawled, bent, and groveled for the next couple of days. He insisted on taking her shopping the next day so he could purchase the ruby pendant and blouse she mentioned in her outburst, plus some diamond earrings.

She relived her tirade in her mind. *I almost lost control. I never planned that bit with the knife. It was just suddenly there. Yet, the look of terror in Bob's eyes made it almost worth it. He looked so vulnerable. It actually turned me on. I can't believe, even in his moment of panic, he couldn't help but get an erection when he looked up my skirt and saw my nakedness.* She laughed. *I was so excited I almost ripped my clothes off and had sex right there on the dining room floor.*

That was then. Now was now. *I've returned to being the little bimbo attached to the charismatic pastor of a prosperous church.* She almost gagged. *Life has to be more than keeping Bob's image* shining and milking him for some expensive gifts. I need to get away and think more deeply about what I want in life.

She was sure Bob would pay for any trip she chose. She remembered a friend mentioning a spa resort in Arizona. One of her secrets she kept from Bob, and everyone else, was her skill with social media. Her son David introduced her to the Internet, and she soon found she had a natural gift for it. She became an expert in finding anything she wanted.

The thought of her son brought a new surge of pain. He was another casualty of his father's religious career. He sat in jail, thanks to that Presbyterian pastor, what was his name—Sessions, Frank Sessions. I don't know how yet, but I will make that bastard pay for what he did to David.

David had failed in his attempt to exact vengeance on his father's obsession with success, but in his failed effort, he showed cleverness. Barbara intended to learn from his failure.

David attempted to terrorize the city by mysteriously committing a series of rapes. While he raped the women, he quoted Scripture verses, thus bringing a lot of embarrassment to the churches of the area—but especially his father's church.

They caught him, but before his arrest, he demonstrated how to use his father's religious symbols and the people's fascination with the power of sex to terrorize the city. Barbara wasn't sure how, but she determined to succeed where her son had failed.

It didn't take her long to Google spas in Arizona and identify Canyon Ranch as the place her friend had mentioned. If she believed in signs like her husband did, which she didn't, she would interpret the fact they had an unexpected opening within a couple of weeks to be an affirmation of her plan. She booked the spa and a plane reservation, using the credit card information she lifted from her husband's computer.

Bob came home that afternoon and announced to her he had located an excellent marriage counselor and made an appointment for the following week. "He's expensive, but he is supposed to be the best in the business." It was clear Bob wanted a sign she saw this as his sincere attempt to make amends.

"Bob, I'm not ready to look at this yet. I need time to settle down before I'd benefit from any counseling. I need to take some time away."

"Of course, honey. Whatever you need to do. I've just been so terribly wrong, and I want to make this right."

"I've decided to fly to Canyon Ranch, outside of Tucson, Arizona. It's a resort spa out in the desert."

"I've heard about it. Wasn't Louise telling you about her experience at that ranch last week? They offered massages, healthy food, relaxation classes, meditation sessions—that sounds like a place to help you relax"

"That's the place. I leave Sunday afternoon."

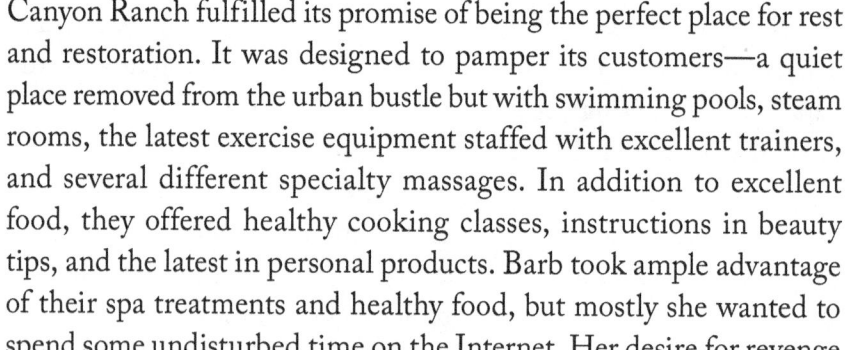

Canyon Ranch fulfilled its promise of being the perfect place for rest and restoration. It was designed to pamper its customers—a quiet place removed from the urban bustle but with swimming pools, steam rooms, the latest exercise equipment staffed with excellent trainers, and several different specialty massages. In addition to excellent food, they offered healthy cooking classes, instructions in beauty tips, and the latest in personal products. Barb took ample advantage of their spa treatments and healthy food, but mostly she wanted to spend some undisturbed time on the Internet. Her desire for revenge extended far beyond Bob and his petty craving for affirmation from the available bombshells in his congregation.

She accepted that a charismatic preacher who stood before an adoring crowd and spouted aphorisms about love, redemption, and power each week was an aphrodisiac for many hungry women who felt unappreciated and neglected in their life. Even the professionally successful were always running uphill in a male dominated, money hungry, cruel society. What could be more thrilling than to sleep with God, and the preacher was the closest you could get to that experience.

She enjoyed the almost sexual thrill of seeing the great Bob Godwin crawling at her feet, panting like a newly trained puppy, eager to please, but it was not enough. What would it feel like to bring all those power maniacs to their knees? What if she saw the same look of terror that was in Bob's eyes in the eyes of the churches all over the city? What if she could get them to admit all that religious pabulum was a lie, and they begged her for a greater vision? Now that would be a climax worth some extended foreplay.

Apart from breaks to get a massage or some other pampering service, Barbara devoted most of her time at the ranch to working the Internet. She didn't have a strategy for how to carry out her plan for revenge yet, but she was convinced the ideas were there somewhere on the Net. Everything from designs for making bombs to how to design a new religion was available.

Her mother taught her both how to use Christianity and recognize its basic lies so as not to be seduced by them. There was power in the Scriptures and the practices of faith, but you also needed to know how they pulled the blinders over people's eyes. It was important to recognize the key symbols of religion because you wanted to know how your enemy thought.

Her mother helped her understand life from a female perspective. God, Jesus, and the Bible are useful concepts, but you need to remember the Bible that explains it all was written by men. You have to read between the lines. That's where the woman's story is.

She recalled how her mother explained the rather titillating account of David and Bathsheba. Her mother told her how Bathsheba had recognized how David was going to need help if the kingdom was going to prosper. So, she seduced him (used her beauty for a purpose) and produced a son that she could train to lead the kingdom. The son, Solomon, was smarter than his brothers and better able to advance the kingdom.

When it came to Jesus, her mother explained, he was a nice man, but people don't always like nice men. Both the religious and political leadership ganged up and crucified him as a lesson to others.

Like Bathsheba, Jesus' lover, Mary Magdalene, recognized the potential of the movement he started, so after they buried him, she went to the grave and made sure the body was removed. She went and told his disciples he was raised from the dead. At first they didn't believe her, since she was a woman, but the idea of what she said began to take hold of his devastated disciples and give them hope. That was the beginning of the church. It's all there in the Bible, her mother explained, if you read the real message.

She particularly remembered her mother reading from 1 Corinthians words that were presumably written by Paul. "If there is no resurrection from of the dead, then Christ has not been raised; and if Christ has not been raised, then our proclamation has been in vain." As her mother had explained it, Paul spoke the truth when he said that if Christ had not been raised from the dead "then we are lying because we told you God had raised Christ."

She searched the Internet, and some ideas began to fall into place. She was rather intrigued with how radical Islamists were able to recruit jihadists all over the world who were willing to die to achieve a greater purpose. What if she could recruit soldiers for her cause? I wouldn't even have to go international. There are several possibilities right here in this country.

On Tuesday afternoon, as a break from staring at the computer screen, she went for a swim at the Canyon's luxurious pool. She put on her skimpy bikini suit and entered the pool. After six laps, she chose to use one of the lounge chairs to absorb some sun. Might as well improve my tan while I'm here, she thought. She added some lotion to her body and positioned herself on the chair. She noticed a teenage girl in the lounger next to hers. The teen was slightly overweight and wore a dour look on her face. She greeted her with a broad smile that she found so effective in connecting with people. "Nice to catch some rays," she said.

The teen inspected her. "You are very beautiful, but don't you just hate it that all these men are trying to undress you with their eyes like you were a piece of meat?"

Barb grimaced in acknowledgment and said, "Men are idiots, but if you know what you are doing, they can be useful idiots. For example, my husband paid for this trip, and I'm going to enjoy the hell out of it."

The teen grinned. "As long as they get what they want," she said. "Life has to offer more than just a few trips and some jewelry. Most of us aren't as beautiful as you are, so what's left for us?"

Barb turned more towards the teenager. "Sex, like religion, is just a tool to be used to get something more important. You have to know what you want out of life; what is worth dying for. Then you use the tools to get there."

"My brother thought he knew what was worth dying for, so he went to war. Now he is dead, and soon people will forget all about him."

"I'm sorry about your brother," Barb said. "War is a terrible thing and usually based on lies our governments tell people. I guess I want to fight the lies in the world."

"Figure that one out," the teen said, "and you can count me in."

The teen went to lunch, and Barb went back to the Internet. She had a germ of an idea. One of the things she noticed as she roamed the Net were how many postings there were from alienated teens. What if she harnessed that energy? What if she recruited them for a cause that gave them a sense of purpose? Young people choose to give their lives in the military for a country feeding them lies and then betraying those who come home. Historically people also died for their faith. In both cases, they believed they were a part of something bigger than themselves. They wanted to believe their lives had an impact—that they had made a difference.

REVENGE CAN BE FUN

CHAPTER 8

When Barb returned from Canyon Ranch, she could tell Bob was anxious about what would happen next. She recognized his lack of information about what she was thinking gave her more power. For once, she thought, he has to wait to see what I will do. She smiled, accepted the awkward embrace, and waited for him to speak first.

"So did you enjoy the ranch?" he asked.

She noted the new lines of strain on his face, and he seemed more hesitant.

"Yes, Bob, the ranch was very nice." She lifted her hands and stretched. "I feel like I'm a new woman."

"That's good," his voice lifted an octave as he searched her face. "It's good, isn't it?"

Not being in charge makes you really uncomfortable, she thought. She almost felt sorry for him.

"Yes, Bob, it's good. How are things at the church?" She turned to hang her scarf in the closet

"Oh, fine. I did do what you asked," he said.

He's wondering what new demand I will make, she thought. "Bob, I think I'd like a private office. I'd also like a personal connection to the Internet. The Internet is like a free university. I can learn so much on the Net. I should have listened more when David tried to tell me how to surf the Net."

"Sure, Barb. Anything you want. I'll get some people to install a connection right away."

Within a week, she had a refurbished office, a brand new MAC with all the Apps she asked for, and a private Internet connection. A couple of men at Canyon Ranch were pleased to show her how to surf the Net and explore unusual sites.

Within a few days, Barb used her natural talent for surfing to find what she wanted. She always kept herself anonymous, not even revealing her gender. At the ranch, a seed of an idea had begun to grow in her mind. She was fascinated to read about how ISIS recruited jihadists in the US via the Internet. Could she do that?

Her husband's betrayal was the proverbial straw that broke the camel's back. However, as she mused about her situation, she realized it was far more than his betrayal. She shouldn't have been surprised. After all, he is a man. Long ago she learned men could be used but never depended on.

The first time he broke faith with their marriage, she was devastated, thinking she had failed to satisfy his sexual appetite. "Am I not sexy enough for you?" she screamed. "Do you really think those tits and ass are better than mine?"

He crawled to her, bought her expensive gifts, and begged for forgiveness. Then, one evening while swimming in a dark pool of self-pity, she experienced an epiphany. It dawned on her she was not the problem.

Bob was a public figure, and like many public figures, he was addicted to admiration. It wasn't the woman as a person who attracted him. What he craved was their near worship of him. Actually, she thought, he did love her in his own demented way. The others were just little strokes to his ego.

While she spent many hours in her private office, she also made efforts to show him all was not lost in their relationship. She tried to balance evidence she felt wounded with actions suggesting progress was being made.

"That was an excellent service tonight, Bob. You were on top of your game. No wonder the deacons voted to give you a nice raise."

"Thanks, Barb. The ushers told me we had at least 50 first-time visitors. By tomorrow afternoon, they will all be called and encouraged to attend again. I'll follow up with the best ten prospects myself."

"You must be exhausted. Let me fix you a drink. Why don't you get out of your suit and relax? I'll bet your shoulders could use a good massage as well." She rose, winked at him, and went to the bar to prepare him a martini.

Bob almost glided into the bedroom to change into some comfortable clothes.

Barb smiled. You still got it, girl.

The larger problem for Barbara was though she knew how to play the religious game, she didn't believe any of it. The world lived a lie because it was comfortable, but the foundation of their faith was a cock-and-bull story. She didn't think Islam, even in its radical form, was any more truthful than the Christian or Jewish lie which mesmerized the world. She couldn't affect the whole world, but she at least could awaken the beast in this country. She giggled at the thought of how to use Christianity against itself.

While at Canyon Ranch, she studied the news reports and commentary about the terrorist activity around the world and those willing to sacrifice their lives for a cause. What struck her was the number of very smart people who felt left out of the society in which they lived. They were idealists offended by those in power but helpless to act in any effective way. Despite above average intelligence, they felt very small and insignificant in the world.

When a militant group like ISIS or Boko Haram was able to disrupt the order and comfort of society, there were two major results.

First, terrorizing the ordinary population made people question their rulers and their ability to maintain security.

Second, it attracted the attention of potential recruits who yearned to have an impact—any impact on their world. To be a part of a movement that made a difference meant they couldn't be ignored. Even if it resulted in their death, history would remember they existed and helped change the world.

What if she harnessed that alienation and brilliance into a coordinated attack on the soft underbelly of religion in this country? Like the Kamikaze pilots from Japan, it will be their lack of fear of death that gives them power.

She connected with a set of young geniuses who taught her hacking skills. These hackers taught her how to surf the Net anonymously and reach into establishment sites and remain undetected. She was determined to know more. She reached out to them and began to test the waters.

Her confidence grew as she gained entrance into this whole underground community of youth who felt left out by society. She forced herself to take breaks for food and sleep.

She began to connect with the alienated teens who were posting on several sites. She positioned herself as the Leader of a clandestine movement who understood they were feeling lost and disrespected. She offered a plan for how to make people sit up and listen. She always signed off as "the Leader."

She needed an event that would both shake up the established order and galvanize the attention of an army of alienated youth. They wouldn't have to feel lost and helpless anymore. The world was about to notice and listen to them.

RECRUITING FIRST SOLDIERS

CHAPTER 9

Barbara continued to explore the Internet. She posted invitations to join a conversation about our failed nation. She quickly discovered mockery and satire critiquing society had a deep resonance among a certain strata of youth.

The Islamic radicals raged at cartoons satirizing Muhammad, but the alienated youth were energized by similar satire that mocked Christianity.

Barbara developed cartoons depicting Mary Magdalene and two other women plotting together to continue the movement that Jesus started. They began by carrying his body off and burying it in a hidden grave.

"One more man who couldn't pull it off," one quipped to the others. "So sad. He was a good man, but he chose some real losers as disciples."

"Let's not let this end here," Mary said. "Remember how he kept telling us he would rise again."

"Sure, but he didn't," said another.

"We are the only ones who know we moved the body," said Mary. "Let's go and tell the disciples we saw him, and he is alive."

"They won't believe us," said Salome. "They'll just say we are telling an idle tale because we are women."

"Don't be too sure," said Mary. "Their life is in chaos. They might believe us as long as we let them think they are in charge. The world is in need of a miracle."

Other cartoons showed churches fooling their members with clever schemes and milking them for their money.

Some depicted clergy standing behind the pulpit with their pants down while preaching on morality.

Most cartoons were simplistic but invited others to submit a more biting commentary. Then the real commentary began to build. Some people even developed games people could play involving teens with X-ray vision hunting down the hypocrisy of the adult world.

At first it seemed all fun and games, but soon the commentary became darker and the critiques of the adult society more pointed.

The contributions came from around the country and from international bloggers as well. Barbara read them with interest and started a few private exchanges with the most interesting bloggers, exploring how far they would go if they could make a difference.

Early on she had developed relationships with a couple of hackers who taught her to communicate while maintaining her anonymity. The hackers liked being on the inside of the plan and promised to help her with some other projects she had in mind.

She quickly spotted several teens from the area around Lincoln. Soon she had private communication with four who were committed to being part of the REAL army. They were eager to be in a movement to change the world. She chose two, Jeremy and Natalie, as the best prospects for the initial action. Her next challenge was how to set up clandestine training sessions in a remote location and begin to test their psychological readiness for dramatic action. Her hope was that as they trained they would be caught up in the intrigue and the possibility to make a real difference

She identified a particular veteran returned from Iraq. He was furious with the government that had sent him there. His name was Jeb Magreer. His Internet skills allowed him to search for others who shared his anger. He saw Barbara's posts and made a few responses. He didn't think teenagers could accomplish anything, but he sympathized with them. He had been barely out of his teens when he was recruited to fight in Iraq, and he knew what it felt like to be lied to.

Barbara read one of his posts with interest. "When it comes time to stop talking and take up a gun, there are others who might join you. I could teach you how to use a gun and cause real damage in just a few minutes. But then you have to be serious."

After several similar posts from Jeb, Barbara decided to make private contact. After a few probing messages back and forth, it was clear both of them were serious. She had the advantage because she had his name and did some background checks. She decided to issue a challenge. "Suppose I knew someone who was ready for real action, are you able to secure guns and provide basic training?"

Trust built slowly between them, but they finally developed a strategy. He was fascinated with the possibility of creating havoc in the churches, and she convinced him her plan could work. He agreed to meet Jeremy and Natalie at a cabin in the mountains and give them training in the use of the guns they would need. He secured some life-like dummies to help them overcome any reluctance to shoot real people.

Barbara and Jeb designed a live camera set up where she watched the teenagers train. She also offered instruction sessions with them via the camera while maintaining anonymity behind a mask and disguised voice box. She established some simple codes allowing them to message each other. She taught them how to dress in a way that made them invisible in the crowd. After several weeks, both teens were comfortable with their weapons and convinced they were the front line of a revolution to change the world.

A week into the training, Barbara and Jeb met in person to develop the rest of the design.

She arrived at his cabin in the woods at a time when the teens had returned to school to prevent suspicion with too many absences.

She got out of her green Subaru and stood in front of the cabin as they had agreed. Jeb stepped out from behind a tree off to the side. He carried a rifle, but as he walked towards her, the rifle pointed towards the ground. She saw a quizzical frown on his face. "Holy shit," he said. "You're a fucking woman."

"I'm a woman," she smiled, "but I'm not interested in fucking so wipe that from your mind. I'm here to see if you have the guts to carry out our strategy."

"Lady, I've been waiting to get revenge on those rich bastards who sent me to war for a long time. I'm locked and loaded as they say."

They went inside the cabin. The room was rustic and the furniture was designed for casual comfort. There were no pictures or other decorations to give it any warmth. She did notice, as she entered, that there were some mirrors that enabled someone standing in the doorway to see around both sides of the cabin.

He grabbed a beer for each of them from his cooler and sat across from her at a table.

"So, Jeb, what do you think will happen when this goes down?" Barbara asked.

"For the first time since I got back from raq, I'm beginning to think we can teach the idiots who run the world a lesson or two."

If this is going to spread beyond Lincoln, we need some plans for the next steps," she said. "I need some good training videos on the use of guns and some trusted contacts who can deliver some training on the go."

"I have some buddies I've talked to across the country."

A look of concern spread across her face.

He held up his hand, "Relax, I didn't give them any information that will trip us up, but if we can pull this off, they are ready to join in. Many of them already have the guns and ammo available.

"OK, once we shoot up a couple of churches, there will be panic but also an intense search within Lincoln for what is behind this. We need to enter phase two within a few weeks to make this a national rather than local issue."

"You name the states and find the teens, and I will get the guns and instructors."

"Let's begin in Texas. They are so gun happy. I figure when the young person starts firing, several others will pull out their guns and start shooting. Lots of people can be caught in the crossfire."

Jeb whistled and then grinned. "You are evil, lady. I'd suggest we place a second teenager in a different spot, and when the great defenders start rising, let him pick off a couple of them. They won't know which teenagers have guns, and the shooting will get wild and crazy."

"I like the way you think," said Barbara. "After Texas we'll hit several states at once and paralyze the whole Christian part of the nation—who knows, we may be inclusive and throw in a synagogue and mosque while we are at it."

"Or maybe hold off on that and get people thinking they are the enemy—especially those mosques—full of those rag heads."

"What about the Mormons," Barbara said in glee. "Aren't their teenage missionaries always dressed like little Republican businessmen?"

They continued to plan for another hour and left with a plan in mind.

ROOKIE ASSIGNMENT

CHAPTER 10

When Rachel entered the police station on Wednesday, the desk sergeant told her she was to go to Supervisor Swenson's office. This made her nervous. The shooting at her father's church remained deeply upsetting. Trying to be there for her father and meet her responsibilities as a new police officer at the same time proved exhausting.

Only on the force for a couple of years, she was intent on performing up to expectations. She had missed a couple of days because of the shooting at her father's church, but, otherwise, she thought she had been doing well. A private meeting with the supervisor made her question her own evaluation.

She took a deep breath, straightened her uniform, and knocked on officer Swenson's office door.

"Enter," she heard a base voice say.

Swenson, a middle aged man with graying hair, was pulling a file as she entered. He laid it on his desk and greeted Rachel with a smile. She appreciated it when he said, "Relax, Officer Sessions. You haven't done anything wrong. In fact, all the reports I hear about you are excellent."

"Thank you, sir," she said.

"The truth is I need some help from you." He pointed to the chair in front of his desk. "Please sit down."

"First of all, how is your father doing? That was a terrible incident at his church."

"He's recovering nicely. They sent him home this past yesterday."

"Good, good. What I want to ask you has to do with our investigation of this shooting."

Rachel nodded but stayed silent.

"When Detective Wilson questioned the witnesses at the church, there was a teenager who said he thought he knew the shooter. In fact, one of the things he mentioned was how different he looked on Sunday."

"Different?"

"Yeah, according to this . . . "his eyes shifted to the folder in front of him,

"this Floyd kid—who would name his child Floyd in this day and age—well according to this Floyd, the shooter . . . " he glanced again at the report . . . "Jeremy, I think is his name, this Jeremy was unwashed, wore long hair, and dressed down, as in what we used to call real funky clothes. Only on this Sunday, his hair is carefully trimmed, and he is in a suit and a tie. Anyone who saw him would think of him as college material. The type who would make any parent proud."

"Sort of disguised to fit in to some congregation's expectations," Rachel commented.

"Scary when the people you have to fear dress like what you want your kid to look like," said Swenson.

"Sounds like this wasn't just some kid who'd gone off his rocker. He'd thought through the details of how to pull this off," said Rachel. "Almost seems like someone had told him how to behave."

Swenson looked up. There was an appreciative glint in his eye. "They told me you are smart. That's very insightful, Officer Sessions."

"Thank you, sir." Rachel was pleased but still tense waiting for the other shoe to fall. She knew he had not called her in just to compliment her.

"When Detective Wilson interviewed Floyd, he said Jeremy went to Brookstone High School. He also said the boy hung around someone named Natalie."

"So if we go to Brookstone High and question this Natalie, we might find out why Jeremy acted as he did and who is behind it," said Rachel.

"Almost right," said Swenson. "We've been thinking that if WE went to Brookstone High with sirens blaring and someone is coaching them, everyone might clam up before we got any real information." However, we thought if YOU went in plain clothes and asked around, it would not scare them off quite so quickly. You could not only seek Natalie out but also talk to others who knew them both."

Rachel gulped. She wanted to be part of the police assigned to this case, but she did not expect this type of involvement.

"I'm not sure I can pass as a high school student, sir."

"No, I'm sure you couldn't get away with that. But, if you posed as a college student on an assignment to survey high school attitudes about violence in society, you might pass as young enough and have a legitimate reason for talking to a variety of students."

Rachel nodded. She was growing excited at the prospect. "I'm assuming you can get clearance from the school administration?"

"Already taken care of," said Swenson. "We can provide you with a basic questionnaire, and then you need to be creative on how to work that into a conversation about Jeremy and, hopefully, Natalie."

"When would you like this to take place?" asked Rachel.

"It's important we get this information as soon as possible. Today is Wednesday. Would you be willing to do this tomorrow, before the weekend?"

"I'm scheduled for patrol duty, but I assume that can be changed."

"I don't think that is a problem, but I will inform the desk clerk to change the schedule."

"Then it's a go," said Rachel.

"One more thing, Officer Sessions."

Rachel's chin rose and she felt her stomach tighten again. "Yes, sir."

"Because your father was a primary target in this, normally I wouldn't assign you, but I think you are the best person for this assignment. Do you think you can stay objective despite your personal involvement?"

"It's clear my family is involved in this, sir, but if I am right, this is much bigger than my father and his church. The reason I joined the force is to make a difference in protecting society. I won't let you down, sir."

WHERE IS NATALIE

CHAPTER 11

Officer Rachel Sessions, dressed in faded blue jeans low on her hips, with a hole in one knee, bleached to meet fashion, and a scruffy, untucked orange shirt, with an auburn wig loose around her shoulders, began to mount the steps at Brookstone High School. Her outfit got plenty of hoots and catcalls at the station, which she took as good-natured kidding by her fellow officers but also signs of their support.

The shooting at John Knox Presbyterian had the whole police force on edge. While most of the city hoped it was a one-time horrific event, many on the force agreed with Rachel there was a possibility of another shooting. The question being debated was whether it would be at another church or would the next violent act be at a school, business, or even an open market. The department placed all patrols on high alert. It wasn't clear who or where the event might take place. They were hoping Rachel could at least get a clue to what would happen next.

As Rachel entered the school building, she was stopped and

questioned. She explained that she was part of a community college research group and had been cleared by the administration. They directed her to the office. She noticed several posters and signs attempting to brighten up walls and inspire the students with encouraging quotes. While the youth seemed very young to her, the surroundings were familiar.

The administration office was a brightly lit room encased in large clear windows that allowed the administrative staff to see what was happening in the hallway and who was approaching. The staff seemed busy, some focused on their computers, others helping teachers or students with their needs, and some going in and out of offices. As she entered, several glanced at her but quickly returned to their business. A large matronly woman rose from her desk near the counter. Her dark hair that had begun to turn gray was styled in a bun. She adjusted her silver frame glasses and greeted her with a mixture of courtesy and weariness.

"May I help you?" she asked. It was clear she couldn't decide whether this was an older teenager or perhaps an applicant for a custodial job that had been advertised recently.

"Yes, my name is Angie Whitley from Lincoln Community College. I'm part of a study group researching the high school students' opinion about the level of violence in our society."

"With that terrible shooting at the church this past Sunday," the woman said, "and by a teenager too, I imagine they will have plenty of opinions. Besides, teens these days like to tell everyone their ideas."

I bet you love listening to each young person that walks through this door, Rachel thought, as she stood there. The woman didn't seem to know what to do next, so Rachel took the lead.

"I think my professor cleared my coming," she said. "The idea is I will begin with passing out a survey at a Mrs. Thompson's civics class, and then I will hang around and talk to some of the students between classes and perhaps at the cafeteria during lunch."

"Let me check with Principal Courtland. Wait over there." She indicated a chair against the wall. She turned and walked into an office and closed the door behind her.

While Rachel waited, she watched as teens and teachers came in and out. Their business was usually handled efficiently. She noticed the better-dressed youth got more attention than what she used to call the hippie types. She felt a momentary embarrassment when she recalled she had made the same distinction as a student.

The principal's door opened as he spoke softly to the woman. The woman returned to Rachel with a renewed look of respect. Rachel guessed that the principal had filled her in on the real reason for Rachel's presence.

"Mrs. Thompson's civics class is up one level and the fourth door on the right," she instructed. "The class will start in fifteen minutes." She turned her head both ways to see if anyone was watching and leaned closer to Rachel. "The principal told me to provide a copy of this picture of Natalie taken from last year's annual." Her hand slid across the counter covering a picture. She lifted her palm, and there was a small picture of a rather emaciated, young girl with stringy dishwater hair and a vacant stare looking up at her.

Rachel felt sad as she examined the girl's picture. She might have been attractive with a little more fullness to her face and some light makeup. Instead, the photo reminded Rachel of some of the pictures she had seen of abandoned children in orphanages in Eastern Europe—wasting away while the world ignored them.

She spoke to the woman standing before her. "Is this girl in class today?"

"Hard to say until the attendance sheets are tallied at the end of the day. Principal Courtland did ask me to give you a copy of her class schedule, so you can check." She handed Rachel another small piece of paper. She again leaned closer and asked in a whisper, "Does she have something to do with the shooting?"

Rachel didn't want to join in conspiracy rumors. "I doubt it, but she may know the shooter. If so, she can tell me who his other friends were. Please don't talk about this with anyone else." She looked the woman straight in the eye, conveying the message that though she was dressed like a loafer, she was an authority worth paying attention to.

"Of course," the woman said. "Good luck with your survey, Miss Whitley."

Rachel almost didn't recognize the name she had presented but quickly recovered. "Thank you. Next level and fourth classroom on the right, you say." She smiled at her and left the office complex and headed for the stairs.

She practiced her best slouch and greeted several of the students with a grunt or mumble as she climbed the steps. She searched carefully, but without success, for any signs of Natalie as she made her way down the hall towards the fourth door on the right. As she entered the room, she spotted a young, clearly energetic woman sitting behind a desk working on some notes for the class.

The woman rose to greet her with a welcoming smile. "Good morning. You must be Miss Whitley from Lincoln Community College. I'm Mrs. Thompson. I understand that you want to conduct a survey in my class, I understand."

Mrs. Thompson was a thin, wiry woman with steel gray hair with tight curls. She was dressed in an attractive burnished orange business suit. Rachel guessed she was in her late forties. She projected confidence in her demeanor.

"Yes, I'm Angie Whitley, and our group project is doing a survey of teen attitudes towards violence in our society. It shouldn't take too long for them to respond, and then, if I can, I'd like to ask some general questions of the students. I appreciate you making time for me in this way."

"Since everyone's talking about what happened last Sunday at that church, I think it will be enlightening to hear what they say. What better civics lesson than to help these soon to be adults process what has just happened in their community."

The classroom began to fill with youth. Mrs. Thompson excused herself and turned to speak to the incoming students. Rachel was impressed with the way the teacher greeted them as they entered. She seemed genuinely interested in them. There was a clear range of students from those who were anxious to learn to those who saw the classroom as one more place to hang out. Mrs. Thompson reached out to each of them. Even those who wanted to hide in a corner, and perhaps catch a little shut-eye, seemed touched by some of Mrs. Thompson's energy, and responded with some energy of their own.

Once they were all settled in class and the bell rang, Mrs. Thompson walked to the front of the classroom. "You all are aware that we had a terrible tragedy this past Sunday in one of our local churches. The shooting was by a young man who attended this school."

"Sometimes," came a voice from the back of the room.

There were several knowing snickers from around the room.

Mrs. Thompson responded. "I agree that he was often absent, but he was one of our classmates, nevertheless. We are having a civics class, which means we study how people behave in our civilization—that includes our city."

An eager hand shot up in the front row. "Mrs. Thompson, I think it shows that we should outlaw guns in our society. My dad says that boy shouldn't have been allowed to have a gun to kill those people."

"That's something we need to discuss, Mary, but before we do that, I want to introduce you to a guest from our community college who is doing some research on what teenagers think about violence. She has a survey that she would like you to fill out, and then she would like to hear about some of your opinions. May I introduce Angie Whitley? I'll let her give you instructions."

Rachel stood up with the surveys in her hand.

"You can have my opinion any day," said one of the athletes near the middle of the class. He smirked and nudged another large student on the shoulder.

"Stop that," said a girl in the next row. "Show some respect!"

Rachel decided she needed to ignore the comments and move ahead if she was going to keep control, but she didn't want to appear too adult if she was going to get some good conversation after class.

Mrs. Thompson asked a couple of students to help pass out the survey as Rachel began to explain.

"This is something my project team put together. Shouldn't take you too long. Just want to know what you think. Point is, most adults don't listen to teenagers, and we want them to know what you think."

There were some knowing nods as they started to work on the survey. Everyone finished in about fifteen minutes. Then Rachel said, "So why do you think he did it?"

Everyone was silent.

"There will be a lot of smart people trying to figure this out, but we students at the college figure you, his classmates, are the real experts. Hey, you know Jeremy and some of his friends better than most people."

"I didn't know him," one student said, "but I saw him around. He was usually alone. Nobody paid much attention to him. Maybe he just wanted to be noticed for once."

"He had some friends, just not the type you'd notice," said a student from the back.

"What do you mean by that?" said another.

"You all sit up front and answer all the dumb questions. You think you are so smart, and everyone should listen to you," said the companion of the classmate who had spoken from the back. "I didn't know Jeremy was going to do that, but I understand why he chose to go out in glory."

"Say some more," Rachel said.

"Hey, I know what he is talking about," said an overweight girl in the other corner. "Jeremy knew he was never going to amount to anything. It's like that old movie Mrs. Thompson showed us, what's it called where the guys are trapped and decide to go out fighting."

"Butch Cassidy and the Sundance Kid," said another. "Yeah, that was a special flick. I watched it on Netflix a dozen times."

"That's the one. So Jeremy goes down fighting. People will remember him around here for a long time."

"There are better ways to be remembered than killing a bunch of people," said a pretty girl near the front on the left side.

"Easy for you to say, Miss America," said a mousy-looking girl behind her. "You got every jock in this school wanting to get into your pants. Your future looks fucking bright."

"Hey, watch your mouth, bitch," the first girl shot back.

Mrs. Thompson decided to step in before things got out of hand. "Wait a minute. I think you both are onto something important."

They all turned back towards her. Rachel was impressed that she didn't focus on their language but responded to what they were saying. It was obvious she carried a lot of authority in the class. "You don't need to insult Marcie to make the point that people who are physically attractive have an advantage in this society. Elsie, you are talented with the computer. That can give you an edge too. Lots of people your age struggle to be noticed and to make a difference. The question we want to explore is what set Jamie off to take such a violent route."

The conversation continued to bounce around the room. All were caught up in this energy as they exchanged their ideas. Occasionally there was conflict, and she admired the skill of Mrs. Thompson to smooth over the rough spots and get them back on target.

After about 30 minutes of exchange, before the class was over, Rachel decided it was time to steer the discussion in a different direction. "You are really great in coming up with these ideas. Some of you mentioned that Jeremy had a few friends. They might be able to help my group see this from another angle. Do any of you know who some of those sidekicks are?"

She waited. They seemed uncomfortable. She wondered if she had overplayed her hand and they sensed she wasn't just some college student trying to complete a class assignment.

"Are you a narc?" one of the students in a back corner asked.

Ok, this is where I see if I've got what it takes to be an undercover agent, Rachel thought. She took a step forward and glared at the questioner. "No, I'm not a narc. That's stupid. But I'll tell you this is more important than just an assignment."

The entire class stared at her, waiting for her next words.

"The survey will fulfill the project assignment, but this is my city, and one of the people who was shot was a friend. I want to know why it happened. If I can bring something new back that no one ever thought about before, I can make a difference. My class will listen to me. Haven't you ever wanted your peers to think you are a genius?"

There were several responses around the room. "Go girl." "Right on." "Kick butt."

"Hey, snake eyes," one of the guys said. "You know where some of Jamie's friends hang out down by maintenance. Why don't you take Miss Whitley down and see what she can find out? If her classmates think she is a genius, she might be really grateful to you." There was an emphasis on the word "grateful" that everyone understood.

Rachel looked over at a large student who sat hunched over in the rear of the class. Rachel guessed he was about two hundred pounds and slightly under six feet. He reacted to their comments as if he would prefer to disappear rather than say anything. Rachel tried to look serious but friendly. "Would you do that for me, Mr. . . . Er . . ."

"Snake eyes," said another with a smirk. "Mr. Snake Eyes. Watch out, girl, don't get within striking distance."

They all began to snicker as the bell announces the end of class. Mrs. Thompson was quick to call Robert, whose classmates called snake eyes, to stay after class.

Rachel did notice that his eyes darted from side to side as he approached the front where she waited. She was excited with this break but did not want to appear over eager.

Mrs. Thompson, who Rachel vowed to get to know better after this was over, spoke to Robert. "Robert, this is only if you want to do it, but it would help Miss Whitley if you can introduce her to some of those who often hang around Jeremy. Are you willing to do that?"

"Guess so. Can I skip math if I do that?"

"You can get to math class late if you take the time to do that," Mrs. Thompson said with a knowing smile. "I'll write a note to your teacher. And thank you, Robert. I appreciate your doing this."

It is clear that Mrs. Thompson had a knack for making people feel valued. Robert even stood a little straighter as he began to show Rachel out the door.

She glanced back and mouthed a "thank you" to Mrs. Thompson as she left.

The class had responded with some enthusiasm. They liked someone to listen to their ideas.

Robert found several students hanging around near a door that was labeled maintenance.

"Hey, Snake, how's it going?" one of the girls said.

"Been better. What's shaking with you?"

A pimple-faced boy spoke up, eager to be recognized by Robert. "We've just been talking about the Jeremy shootout. Awesome, man."

"Did you know he was going to do it?" Robert asked.

"No way, Snake. Jeremy had gotten all secret the last couple of months. We thought he was just getting some snatch from the natch, but we didn't think he had the balls to pull this off."

Rachel decides to pick up on the conversation. "What do you mean he got all secret?"

They all turned and stared at her. It was as if this was the first they realized she was present.

Robert vouched for her. "She's all right. She was in our class doing a survey about violence and wanted to meet some people who knew Jeremy. She's from over at Lincoln Community. It's for a class or something."

With Robert's stamp of approval, the group all seem to relax a little.

The girl who first spoke to Robert, and who was clearly attracted to him, said, "Jeremy wasn't really part of the group, but he hung around. Only he hooked up with Natch . . . uh, Natalie, and they started going their own way. We thought they were getting it on with each other or something."

"It was more than that," said another. "It was like they got religion or something, only it wasn't the normal type of religion."

"What do you mean?" asked Rachel.

"They'd go off to these meetings and come back all glowing. They'd strut around like they were important or something."

"So that was what was going on," said the pimple-faced boy. "I thought they were falling in love or some shit like that."

"Naw, Natalie wouldn't even let Jeremy touch her," said another girl.

"Though he sure wanted to," said the first girl. "Natalie was like a lost waif until she found this religion. Jamie followed her around like a puppy dog. He would do anything she asked."

"Say, do you suppose his religion told him to shoot up that church?" asked the boy.

"What type of religion would do that?" asked one of the girls. "He just went crazy, is all."

"Where is Natalie?" Rachel asked. "I'd like to talk with her."

"I think she left school," said one of the group. "I saw her taking lots of things out of her locker on Tuesday, and I haven't seen her around since."

"Yeah, I heard her mumbling something about lies or something. She seemed like spacey. I tried to speak to her, but she was in another zone. She didn't even say anything back."

"Maybe she was more into Jamie than she let on, and she was being sad about his death. I hear those cops blew his brains out. Just like a cop. It's not safe when they are around."

Rachel felt her anger well up at the attack on the police, but she knew this wasn't the time to get defensive. She thanked them and walked with Robert back towards his math class. When they reached his room, she took one of his arms. "I know they were giving you a hard time back in class. While I'm not available for anything more, I want you to know I am thankful for your help. You've made a difference."

Knowing no one else was around, she leaned in and kissed him on the cheek. "Thanks, Robert. Go to math now. You are a good man."

She smiled and left him trying to get himself together to enter the class. She hoped he would feel good about what he had done.

On her way to the principal's office, Rachel tucks in her shirt and puts her hair in a ponytail. She wanted to look her most adult for this next action.

She thanked Principal Courtland and told him what an amazing teacher Mrs. Thompson was.

Courtland, a short stocky man dressed in a dark blue suit, responded with pride,"I hired her myself."

"I wonder if it is possible for you to let me into Natalie's locker?"

"Normally I like to respect our students privacy, but if this is police business . . . ?"

Rachel looked down at the floor, nodded her head, and then said, "Sir, I respect your concern about a student's privacy. My concern is if what I heard from some of those students is accurate; it scares the bejeebers out of me that the shooting last Sunday may not be the last."

Courtland's face lost some color and his eyes widened. His eyebrows lifted. "You mean there might be another shooting? Oh God!"

"I'll be honest with you, sir. I don't know for sure it will happen, but I don't want to take a chance on it. I'll take full responsibility for this action."

"Why is this so important to you?"

"Well, sir, there is something I haven't told you. You remember the pastor who was shot last Sunday?"

"Yes, a very brave man from what I hear in the news."

"He is very brave," Rachel said. "He is also my father. He risked his life to save more people from being shot. If he can do that, I should be willing to take some risk to help prevent it from happening again."

"OK, I will get the combination, and I will stand by your side while you open the locker." He turned and walked back to his office. Rachel noticed when he was walking out, he reached over and closed the blinds of the window that looked down the hallway.

"OK, Daniel, let's jump into the lion's den together. Let's hope and pray we won't find a lion when we get there."

Rachel smiled as she took the combination and opened the locker. She was beginning to like this high school. She already knew it contained one very skilled teacher and one caring principal. These kids were lucky.

The locker swung open. They both looked in.

"It's empty," said Courtland.

Rachel bent down to snatch a piece of paper on the bottom of the locker. "Not quite, I'm afraid."

She opened the paper. On it was printed a simple statement in bold print: "It's a lie" Underneath it was printed, "Others must pay 127OMN."

"What does it mean?" asked Courtland, leaning in to get a clearer look.

"At my father's church, the shooter kept saying the same thing, 'It's a lie.' I don't know what the rest of it means, but I think it clearly points to the fact this is not over."

"What do we do now?" he asked in a shaky voice.

"I've got to get this back to headquarters ASAP. For now, I ask you to keep what you have seen here in strict confidence. We don't want to panic the city until we have more information."

With that, Rachel turned and ran towards the exit. She found her car parked a block away and turned on the siren as she sped back to headquarters.

IT'S BIGGER

CHAPTER 12

On her way, she rang her father.

"Dad, I think we need to convene the Clue Crew. I think I found out this is bigger than what happened at your church."

"Damn, I was afraid of this," said Frank. "What did you find?"

"I can't talk now. I'm driving towards police headquarters at about 60 miles per hour on a crowded street. I'll call you later, but see if Jacob is available for a meeting tonight—even if it's late. Time for the Clue Crew to get to work."

Frank did not prolong the conversation even though he was desperate to know what she had found. "OK, be careful, and call me as soon as you can."

Frank knew what Rachel was talking about when she mentioned the Clue Crew. He smiled as he recalled how she and her brother, together with Amanda Singletary, helped him solve a serial rapist case a couple of years ago that had stumped the police. At the time, she likened it to the game of Clue he played with them when they were children.

His more recent Skype conversation with Mandy, which he still preferred to calling her Amanda, was uncomfortable. He knew her briefly in college and then reunited when she was brought in by the police to help them solve the rape case. After they had moved past the embarrassing way they parted at college, it was a wonderful reunion. His adult children thought their relationship might develop into something more permanent.

Mandy returned to her professional responsibilities in Richmond, Virginia, and he resumed his work at the church. They let their hectic schedules build a barrier to more frequent contact. At first there were several phone calls, then some email exchanges, and finally an exchange of Christmas greetings. It seemed to Frank both wanted more but were hesitant to pursue a deeper relationship. When Frank was honest with himself, he knew the powerful feelings evoked in being around Mandy during the investigation scared him. He felt like he was being unfaithful to his first wife, even though she had been dead for several years.

I guess the Clue Crew will be one member short, but it will still be good to get together with Jacob and Rachel. I wonder what she found out, and why she thinks it is so important. I didn't even know she was working the case. Since when do they have a rookie patrol officer get involved in something like this?

Rachel entered the station on a dead run. Out of breath but feeling the urgency of the moment, she skidded to a stop at the reception center. "Larry," she said to the officer at the desk, "tell Supervisor Swenson I need to see him immediately, and alert Detective Wilson and Burlingame to come to Supervisor Swenson's office."

Larry looked at her with some amusement. What will Detective Sessions be doing while I'm carrying out her orders?" he asked.

"I'm sorry. I know I have no authority, but this is an emergency. It relates to the church shootings. And, . . ." she looked down while her face reddened. A half smile appeared on her face, "I will be making a short detour to the little girl's room on my way to Supervisor Swenson's office." She rushed towards the ladies room.

When she emerged and approached Swenson's office, she saw Wilson and Burlingame quick stepping on the other side of the room heading in the same direction.

All of them arrived as the supervisor was opening his door. "Let's go to the conference room," Swenson said. "Assuming you have important information, I've called the chief to meet us there. He wants to be in on every decision related to this."

"I think it is, sir," Rachel said as they all moved into the conference room. "It's speculation at this point, but I think we are in for some more trouble."

There was an uncomfortable silence while they awaited the arrival of Chief Bergson. When he arrived, Swenson turned to Rachel and asked her to give her report.

She summarized the discussion in the classroom and being led by a student known as "Snake Eyes" to meet with some classmates who knew Natalie. She then told them of that conversation and discovering Natalie had not appeared at school that day.

"What happened then?" Chief Bergson's asked. He was a large bespectacled man with broad shoulders and a commanding presence.

She was a little uncomfortable relating how she convinced Principal Courtland to open Natalie's locker but felt they needed to know the whole picture.

Swenson responded, "I think you acted appropriately under the circumstances. It's important that we determine whether this is just one crazy incident or part of something bigger."

"That's just it, sir. If I understand what I found, it appears it might be something bigger," Rachel said.

"Lay it out for us," Swenson said. She heard the tension in his voice.

"I found this on the bottom of her empty locker." She held out the small piece of paper.

They all leaned in, almost bumping heads, eager to see what was on the paper.

Swenson read the message aloud. "It's a lie" "Others must pay 127OMN."

"What do you make of it?" Chief Bergson asked.

They all looked at Rachel.

"Well, the first part, 'It's a lie,' is what the shooter kept saying at my father's church, so we know they discussed what was going to happen. What scares me is the next line—'Others must pay.' That sounds to me like this is not over."

"And the 127OMN" bit?" asked Burlingame.

"I'm not sure," said Rachel.

"That scares me even more," said Wilson.

"How so?" asked the chief.

"If it was just between Jeremy and Natalie, they were talking to each other already. They wouldn't need a code. A code would only be used if there was a third party involved."

"Bingo," said Burlingame. "Didn't you say that several people at the church kept hearing the shooter say something about a Leader or something like that?"

"Exactly," said Wilson.

"Officer Sessions, this is good police work. You might make a detective yet," said Burlingame.

Rachel knew her face was hot and probably beet red. "Thank you, sir. I'd like to stay on this case if it is OK with both the Chief and Supervisor Swenson." She looked at them expectantly.

"Detective Burlingame is right," said the chief. "That is good work, and I expect Supervisor Swenson can make the necessary adjustments to keep you on the case. I'm assuming she can team up with the two of you, Detectives?"

They all nodded in agreement.

The Chief rose. "I'll let you all work out the next steps but keep me in the loop." As he left the room, he turned and said, "Put additional people on patrol this Sunday. We don't know that churches will be the continuing target, but we need to cover what we can."

Rachel felt a tingling in her limbs and a bounce to her steps as she headed out of the station. She resisted the temptation to look back, but she knew her supervisor and two detectives were watching her, and soon the story of her success at Brookstone High School would be spreading throughout the force. Not bad for a virtual rookie. She had taken the test for the position of Sergeant, but had not heard how she had scored.

She got into her car and headed towards her father's house. She kept the code 127OMN running through her mind, but nothing emerged as she approached the house. She was in hopes that especially Jacob, who was good at puzzles, would help work it out.

A LITTLE PANIC GOES A LONG WAY

CHAPTER 13

This is really cool, thought Natalie, as she hid in the bushes outside Brookstone Methodist Church in Lincoln. The Leader hooked her up with Jeremy and started things moving. The Leader cautioned her not to get too involved but to keep an eye on him. She didn't consider herself to be pretty and not having much experience with boys made Natalie nervous at first. The Leader gave some hints on how to relate to boys, and Natalie was thrilled to find out the suggestions worked. Besides, he was sort of cute, and though she didn't let him get too far, it was fun to know he wanted to do more than she agreed to. For once in her life, she was in charge of a relationship.

She was sad that Jeremy had to die, but, as the Leader said, soldiers have to accomplish their objectives. Now she had a mission of her own. The Leader was smart to have her clean out her locker and leave the school Tuesday after the shooting. They probably didn't even notice her absence, but in case someone recognized her as someone Jeremy hung around with, she didn't want to risk being questioned. And just like in the movies, the Leader provided her a safe house to hold up in until time for the completion of her assignment.

Saturday night came and the first phase of her mission got under way. She felt a little giddy when she thought of her first assignment. At 1 a. m., seeing no one was around, she creeped out of the bushes, climbed the church's steps, and taped a large sign on the front door. Then she went to two other entrance doors and posted signs on them. Each had the same carefully stenciled message.

IT'S A LIE
THOSE WHO WORSHIP HERE MAY DIE
TODAY OR NEXT SUNDAY
GET REAL
#127OMN

She quickly sped away on the bike the Leader provided her. She continued to the next church. There were ten on her list, all sizes, and all denominations. As the Leader said, it will leave the whole city in panic, and people will abandon the churches in droves.

At around 4:30 a.m., she carefully returned to her safe house. Being cautious that no one saw her, she dumped the bike in the rear of a building three blocks away and, keeping in the shadows, made her way back to her room. She set her alarm for 10 a.m. and sank joyfully into her bed. She was exhausted but pleased with what she had done. The Leader told her the news would begin breaking late in the morning, and the sound of sirens awakened her before her alarm went off. It was fun to think she had caused police cars to rush to the various churches.

About 11 a.m., she walked to an I-Hop. She never had much money, so it was special that the Leader gave her $50 to spend on meals for the next couple of days.

The waitress that approached her table was a tough looking woman with blond hair in a pigtail. She looked tired but friendly. She provided Natalie a menu. "Do you want some coffee, honey?"

Natalie looked at her a moment, unused to being treated as a genuine customer, and then said, "I would like that. Also a glass of water. I want to look at the menu for a second."

"Take your time, honey. With all the excitement this morning, we don't have many customers, so you get the top of the line service."

When the waitress returned, Natalie said, "I would like one of those big waffles with the fruit and lots blueberry syrup. Also, I'd like some bacon and one egg scrambled."

"You got it. I'll be right back."

She tried not to stare at the TV broadcasting the morning news. It was hard not to giggle a little when all the news people focused in on pictures of her signs. It was clear the city was filled with fear, and she had caused it.

"Churches all over the city had signs posted on them during the night," the broadcaster said. "All held the same message: 'It's a lie. Those who worship here may die—Today or Next Sunday.'

"It now appears the terrible shooting that took place at John Knox Presbyterian last Sunday was not an isolated incident. While police searched churches for bombs, many pastors cautioned it might be wise not to conduct services today.

"We've heard reports that one creative pastor invited his congregation to go to a nearby park for the worship experience. Even he advised, however, in light of last week's incident, everyone should make sure they were acquainted with all the young people in their midst."

After a couple more bites from her waffle,, Natalie heard a special newscast. "A police spokesperson said they did not know whether the signs were a distraction to mislead or an actual targeting of specific churches. The officer cautioned that all congregations should be extra careful and immediately report any unusual activity near their churches."

They further noted the posters were made by a stencil App on a computer, so there wasn't much hope of identifying the culprit.

You ain't seen nothing yet, Natalie thought, as she continued to eat her breakfast and listen to the newscast.

"We take you now to Lincoln Episcopal for an interview with the pastor. The interview is already in progress."

The cameras switched to focus on a crowd of reporters speaking to a man dressed in a dark suit and clergy collar. "Reverend Wellington, can you tell us whether this church will conduct services today?"

"The vestry met in emergency session as soon as the news of these signs being posted was known. They decided since this church did not receive any sign, they would proceed with extra care. They also noted worship is conducted in nearby towns if people felt more comfortable attending out of town."

"Do you believe this is an anti-Christian attack from a new type of jihadist?"

"Frankly, no one knows who is behind this. I would caution you against making any premature conclusions. Lincoln is hardly a focus for major terrorist' activities. These shootings may well be the deranged act of a couple of people who have a grudge against Christianity or even religion in general.'."

The reporter interrupted, "But there hasn't been any threats against the local mosque, has there?"

"I received a call from Imam Hasan this morning. He and I have been friends for several years. He assured me he would stand in colleagueship with me in protest of these despicable acts. These are not the actions of any faithful Muslims."

I can't wait to get my instructions next Wednesday, thought Natalie. Then they will have a real reason to be scared.

News vans were sent out to tour the city near a variety of churches and to interview anyone who might have an interesting perspective. The problem they faced was they didn't know where to go. It was not even clear that churches would be the only target. Even if they were, would it always be from one denomination, one size, one theological stance, or one geographical location. Mostly reporters roamed the city, hoping if something happened, they would be nearby.

WORSHIP AT VOZ DE DIOS

CHAPTER 14

John Knox Presbyterian, still wrapped in yellow tape as a crime scene, stood empty on Sunday morning. The session agreed with Frank and Jacob that people would need an opportunity to worship together, but in light of both the need to preserve the crime scene and people's sensibilities, they needed to worship at another location. The choice became easier when Frank's old friend, Oscar Ramirez, called and invited them to meet at his church. Not only were Frank and Oscar old friends, but their congregations increasingly shared in joint activities in recent years.

When the news broke about the posted signs, he grabbed the phone and called Oscar to consult.

"I don't want to put your people at risk. Maybe we should call it off until we know more. Who knows how far this craziness will spread?"

"No, mi amigo, we should continue," said Oscar. "Como dice the good book, if we allow ourselves to be "silent, the stones will cry out."

Frank hesitated and Oscar continued.

"My people conocen mucha violencia in their lives, and they are not inclined permitir some pissant kid to silence the worship of our Lord."

Frank chuckled. "Sometime, when there is more time, I want you to show me where you find "pissant" in the Bible. Is that in the Spanish version?"

"I think they called them Pharisees back then, but that seems unfair to the good Pharisees, so I retranslated it slightly."

So about 10:30 a.m., people from John Knox's church began arriving at La Iglesia del Voz de Dios. It was a smaller building than John Knox, and the congregation sat in folding chairs. There were several banners on the walls and on stands that welcomed the season of Lent in Spanish. At the center of the raised platform at the front of the building was a large figure of Christ clearly wearing a crown of thorns. There was lots of laughter among the people in the sanctuary.

Hearing some of the news broadcasts of the morning, members of John Knox were showing signs of the strain of the last week. Then a strange thing happened. Members of the Hispanic congregation reached out to encourage and comfort the members of John Knox. Every Caucasian who entered the sanctuary was immediately befriended by a Hispanic worshiper and accompanied to a pew. The music leader began to lead them in song, some in Spanish and some in English, with the words flashed on a large screen. Every once in a while, she would stop and explain a Spanish phrase or help with a complicated rhythm.

When Marcia, Jacob, and Frank arrived, the people were already in a joyful mood and burst out into cheers as they walked carefully down the aisle. Frank, still a bit shaky on his feet, waved to the people and sat in a front pew. Jacob stood and addressed the congregation. "My father will say a few words at the end, but our General Presbyter, Marcia Newsome, agreed to speak first."

Marcia, a stocky, short African-American woman, rose. "I have read the story of Pentecost several times in my faith journey, but when I walked into this sanctuary and heard both Spanish and English, and more importantly, the sound of joy and love casting out fear, I think I truly experienced a Pentecostal moment.

"In my studies at the seminary, I focused on church history. One of the things repeated throughout the two thousand years of our church's history, across many cultures and languages, is when the going got rough, the faithful recited a creed that emphasized what they believed. It is not yet clear what the intention was of the shooting last Sunday and the signs posted this morning on many church doors, but there seemed to be a common theme of our faith being a lie. We believe the lie being told is in the mind of the shooters. Lest there are any questions about our faith, I want to invite you to stand, if you are able, and say together in two languages the Apostles Creed that the world may know what we believe."

Jacob came forward to speak in Marcia's ear.

"An excellent idea." She turned to the congregation. "Frank has asked, before we say the Apostles Creed, we recite the names of the four people who were killed last Sunday. They are among the saints who watch over us as we declare what we believe."

Jacob spoke up. "I will help my father stand. When he speaks the name of each of the victims of the shooting, you are asked to respond, 'May they go with God.'"

Frank looked pale as he stood, but he felt the strength of the combined congregation and the support of his friend Oscar who came to stand beside him. He scanned their faces and saw a sense of joy in the midst of their pain. This is what the faith is about, he thought. The people of God reach across their differences and are buoyed by hope even in the turmoil of tragedy because they trust God is ultimately in charge.

With a strong voice, he spoke the name of the first victim, and they responded both in English and Spanish the vigorous "May they go with God."

He continued with each of the other victims.

Next Jacob and Oscar led the congregation in reciting the Apostle's Creed.

The service lasted for over two hours with several Scriptures, many spontaneous prayers, and a variety of songs. As they drew to a close, neighbors, some newly acquainted, turned and hugged each other.

Oscar took the mike and spoke over the many voices. "You are invited to continue our fellowship with some comidas muy sabarosa prepared by our congregation. I invite you to go from here with these words ringing in your ears: "God, not death has the final word."

ERIC IVORY

CHAPTER 15

Eric Ivory, Lincoln's own conservative radio talk show host, was excited. He had made very few comments about the church shooting at John Knox Presbyterian on his "Out of the Ivory Palaces" program. While he was still fuming over the humiliating incident with the pastor, Frank Sessions, a couple of years back, he calculated that the best approach was to express sympathy for the victims and wait to see what developed. This past Sunday, the postings on ten different churches in the city made it clear that there was a larger issue than one deranged teenager shooting up a church. Here was a conspiracy, and Eric fed on conspiracies.

He could feel the atmosphere of fear sweep over the city and even begin to creep into the national news. If something new happened, which he was sure it would, he wanted to position himself to be a chief spokesperson for what was taking place in Lincoln. While he had gone easy on Frank Sessions after the shooting, now was the time to pose a question to his radio audience. Was it just an accident that Frank's church was the first target?

"Good morning, listeners. Eric Ivory here to give you the unvarnished truth about what is happening in the religious world. As you, my dear listeners, know, we are at a critical moment in the life of churches here in Lincoln. A number of churches closed their doors this past Sunday out of fear. What are we to make of this when in Christian America we allow some jihadic-like terrorists to close down our churches?"

He paused and let silence linger for a moment and then continued. "Notice, I did not say this maniac was a jihadist terrorist. I said he was jihad like. We don't know the full story yet. With these signs posted on our beloved churches this past Lord's day, we know some people are behaving like those Islamic jihadists. Whoever they are, where did they learn how to spread terror in our hearts?"

Eric Ivory had planned his broadcast carefully. He would hint at but not name the enemy yet. The signs posted on the church doors were proof that this was a larger operation, but its source was not yet clear. Who had recruited this teenage nut, and what was behind these crazy actions?

"I will tell you this, my friends, this is an attack on all good believing Christian Americans, and we dare not let it paralyze us. The words of our Holy Scripture tell us 'Perfect love casts out fear,' so let us be about casting out fear.

"I understand why some churches, out of an abundance of caution, closed their doors this past Sunday. But now it is time to stand up and be counted. This next Sunday let our churches be full as a defiant voice against fear." He had raised his voice and did his best to sound commanding.

Again he inserted a moment of silence before he spoke." "And just to be clear," Eric chuckled into the microphone, "while I believe that the conservative churches are more in line with the Gospel, it was John Knox, with their liberal pastor Frank Sessions, who experienced the first attack. His name was shouted out by the shooter who accused his liberal rantings to be a lie. Even so, his liberal distortion of the faith is closer to the true Gospel than the jihadist terrorists, so for the faithful, liberal and conservative, it is time to stand together against this blasphemy."

He tried to lower his voice and again sound like a commanding leader. "It is time to stand up and be a man in this hour of crisis. When our churches are no longer safe, then where do we find sanctuary? While North Carolina has yet to wake up enough to pass a concealed weapon law, I can tell you that for the next several weeks, when I go to church, I'm going to be prepared—law or no law. Some freedom loving states have it right. If a home is a man's castle, and he has a right to defend it, surely our churches are also worthy of our defense. I dare anyone to try to arrest me for trying to defend our places of worship in Christian America."

Eric continued his broadcast for the full half hour, attempting to position himself as the spokesperson for the good believing Christians of Lincoln in case anyone wanted to know.

Frank was listening to the broadcast with his friend Oscar and his son Jacob.

"It's a good thing Rachel isn't here with us," joked Oscar. "She might have to head over to the radio station and detain our defender of the universe for incitement to riot."

"Let's hope," said Jacob, "that no one acts on his suggestion. I'd certainly be afraid to visit a church that didn't know me if I knew some screwball was packing and nervous about all young males who entered."

Frank stood up and started pacing in his office. "We have to get ahead of this," said Frank, "before the whole city is paralyzed. One of the questions I keep pondering is why this happened in Lincoln? If it was a terrorist plot, there could be many better places to spread fear."

"Maybe that's the point," said Jacob, as he looked up at his father. "If it happened in New York or even Charlotte, everyone who lives in smaller places would assume that they are safe. Since it happened in Lincoln, no one feels safe."

"But why Lincoln and at John Knox?" asked Frank.

"And even more pointedly, why did the shooter know your name?" asked Jacob.

"Well, it has certainly had the effect of reviving the city council of churches. That group had died out, but I suspect it will be a packed meeting this Thursday," said Oscar. "As the good book says, 'Even egotistic preachers and bombastic radio commentators can't separate lo que Dios a reunido.'"

Jacob turned towards Oscar. "Is that quote from the Septuagint. I don't think I recognize it."

Oscar waved the question on with his hand. "La pregunta es, si Dios puede reunirnos, what do we do then?"

"It surprises me to hear me saying this, but I agree with the first part of Eric's counsel. It is important that the churches not give in to fear. We need to be open and proclaiming the Word."

"De acurerdo," said Oscar, "but we also need to be aware that since we dodged the bullet this past Sunday, if anything is going to happen, it will be this Sunday."

"I think the large churches are most in danger," said Jacob. "Small churches would immediately spot a new stranger among them. If an unknown teen came to worship, he would immediately be spotted."

"It's a sad day when churches want to keep teenagers away from their door," said Frank.

NATALIE COMPLETES HER MISSION

CHAPTER 16

Third Sunday in Lent

Natalie's intercom buzzed early Saturday morning just as she had been told. She answered. The message was brief. "A package is at the bottom of your stairs. Pick it up now." She couldn't tell if the voice was from a male or a female.

She peeked out her door to make sure no one was watching. When satisfied she was alone, she descended the steps and found a box waiting. No one saw her. It dawned on her that she had not seen anyone at all who lived in the other apartments.

She picked the package up. The packing tape felt rough but firm. She tried not to make a lot of noise as she climbed the stairs. She smelled some bacon being cooked somewhere in the building but saw no one. She felt very important with her secret hideaway and packages mysteriously delivered to her. The box was heavy, but she felt strong as she entered her apartment.

With her door safely locked, she slit the tape sealing the box and tore it open. Inside she saw a light blue dress. Not too bright or stylish but a lot prettier than many of the clothes she had worn. Also, she found underwear, a comfortable pair of flats, and some basic make-up items. Nothing too fancy. As the Leader instructed her, she did not want to draw attention to herself. She tried the dress and shoes on immediately, and, to her delight, they fit her perfectly. Her hand touched another box in the package and a slip of paper with a note to go to a designated website for further instructions.

She opened the carton first. Inside was a rapid-fire pistol, a nine millimeter semiautomatic Glock 19, with two ammo clips like the one she had practiced with when in training with Jeremy a month ago. She was a quick study. She proved a better shot then Jeremy and also faster at ejecting the empty clip and shoving in the new one. She lifted the Glock, and held it out with her elbow locked as she was taught. She saw the heads of several adults blowing apart as she imagined tomorrow's scene in the church. One of the targets reminded her of the uncle who had raped her when she was thirteen.

She didn't know which church yet. That would be given to her when she booted up her computer and logged on to the site. In training, she had been concerned that she might freeze or hesitate to fire the gun. It helped to shoot at the realistic dummies her trainers provided. She also repeated the mantra that the Leader gave them. "It's a lie. All must die. I'm a REAL soldier for the true Jerusalemites."

She pictured the fear that would paralyze the congregation. She knew that she would die. The only failure was to be taken alive and questioned. Although, even there, the Leader proved clever. Each link in the revolutionary chain only knew a little bit. But who wants to live in a musty old cell. Better to die on the battlefield. She was a true soldier. Like Jeremy, she would be a hero celebrated in the history books. All those other pretty girls, so popular in school, would be forgotten, but not Natalie.

The package also contained a hairpiece for Natalie to wear. No one looking for mousy old Natalie would recognize her. She tried on the wig. It was a soft, dishwater blond. It wouldn't stand out. She looked in a mirror and thought it made her look pretty—she liked going out as a pretty girl with a nice new dress. She would never pick out another Goodwill hand-me-down. Jeremy would like her in this new dress.

She arrived at the Open Door Community Lutheran Congregation at 10:30 a.m., in time to watch early arrivals and the release of people from their educational hour. It was a big church with a large brick patio out front. They had set up a bar with coffee and snacks both for those who were arriving and those who waited for church after they finished their classes. The Leader had researched the church and their routine. Soon she saw several teenage girls emerge and stand on the brick patio munching on some muffins and talking to each other while looking at the other people around them. As instructed, she edged up to them and insinuated herself into their conversation. The Leader gave her some ideas on how to introduce herself to the group while not appearing aggressive enough to draw their attention in a negative way.

"You new here?" one of the girls asked.

"Yeah, my parents just came here from Ohio. Lot warmer here."

"My cousin's from Ohio. Says it's freezing there still."

"Good church? Lots of good looking guys in the youth group?"

"Winners and losers. You know how it is?"

"Don't I. Couldn't be any worse than the numbskulls in Ohio. When are boys going to grow up? They're so juvenile."

"Got that right. Guess we should go in. We usually sit in the balcony if you want to join us."

The girls began to walk together into the church.

When they were in the narthex, Natalie turned to one of them and said, "I'd better stay down here. My parents are going to meet me here, so I have to save them a seat." She rolled her eyes. "I'll catch you later." She moved off towards the center door to the sanctuary.

Two ushers wearing boutonnieres were greeting people and handing them bulletins as they entered. She took a bulletin from an usher and walked into the large worship space. She noticed how different it looked from the plain Baptist church that she had attended a few times with her parents. The stain glass windows had pictures of saints and biblical figures. There were purple banners and the smell of burning candles, a large cross, and a circle made of dead branches with sharp thorns. The Leader had told her that these were symbols of what they called Lent, a few weeks prior to Easter. She knew what Easter was. A time for pretty dresses, bunnies, and Easter egg hunts like the Girls Club had when she was younger.

OK, I'm in, she thought. Now to find a place near the aisle. She felt the pistol wrapped in the sweater she tied around her waist. The extra ammunition secure in her left dress pocket. She had practiced several times this morning ejecting the first clip and loading the second. There were ten bullets in each magazine. That should be more than enough. If need be, the last one would be for her. About halfway down the aisle she found two elderly ladies seated in the pew, and they shoved over for her to sit with them. They smiled at her, patted her on the arm, and welcomed her.

She smiled back, then folded her hands and bowed her head as if she were preparing for worship with prayer. The Leader had prepared her well.

She admitted to herself that the music was lively, and the pictures on the screens placed around the room were uplifting shots of nature—streams of flowing water, beautiful clouds floating in the sky, people gathered together with their hands raised in the air. She didn't understand that, but at least they looked happy.

The service began with a chorus of singers leading the people in several songs, interspersed with comments about the faith. When she had opened her email on the computer, a picture of the pastor was attached. Now she recognized him as he took his seat behind the Plexiglas stand that she assumed he would use when he spoke.

He wore a black robe but also a big purple scarf around his neck that reached almost to the floor. He also had a large cross hung like a necklace.

Soon the portly pastor, Stanley Hawkins, rose and walked to the front of the steps. He smiled and opened his arms as if to envelop the crowd in front of him. "We are overjoyed that you have chosen to praise God with us in the name of our Savior, Jesus. The band certainly put us in a spiritual mood. Weren't they fantastic? Praise the Lord."

Natalie reached under her sweater laid on her lap and gripped the 38 Special.

"I just know that Jesus is with us this morning," said Hawkins with upraised hands.

"It's a lie," Natalie shouted as she leaped to her feet and entered the aisle. She fired her gun into a chandelier bringing glass showering down on the congregation.

The people froze. They had heard the reports of what happened two weeks ago at John Knox, and now the terror was visiting them.

Natalie had her opening speech rehearsed. "The resurrection is a lie, reverend. Mary Magdalene made up that story after she stole her lover's body from the grave. You are all fools."

"Young lady, I will not have you blaspheme the name of our Holy Savior in this place."

"Oh really, preacher. Do you believe in the resurrection for this person?" She turned slightly and shot one of the women who had been sitting with her. Blood spurted from her head as she collapsed forward, showering the couple in front of her.

One of the teens in the balcony screams. "You're that new girl."

"Shut up," Natalie shouted and fired a shot towards the balcony.

"Oh dear sweet Jesus, don't do this," Hawkins pleaded, falling on his knees with his hands outstretched in her direction.

The Leader coached her that after she began firing someone would call 911, and she had about ten minutes to complete her mission before they arrived. Time seemed to slow for Natalie, but she figured she had at least another eight left. "You are not Frank

Sessions; you bloated tub of lard. He got away this time, but you are not so lucky. You can show your people that you believe in the resurrection right now."

Hawkins began to weep. Natalie placed a bullet between his eyes and whirled to face the rest of the congregation as she climbed the chancel steps. Some in the back tried to run out, others crouched behind the pews, many just sat with a glazed look on their faces. "You are going to meet your God. Doesn't anyone want to volunteer?" She shot at some who tried to leave in the rear. A couple of people fell in the aisle. Probably four more minutes left, she thought. She heard the sirens approaching.

An elderly man rose and entered the aisle. "Daughter, don't do this evil. But if you must kill someone, let it be me. I've had a blessed life."

Natalie hesitated, intrigued by the old man's calm demeanor as he walked towards her. She heard the police enter the building. "You live," she said, as she fired several more shots out into the congregation, killing some around him and wounding others. "Because of you, some of the children will also live. Tell them to get REAL and stop living a lie."

Then the special unit with their shields burst into the sanctuary. "I am Iscariot, one who was rejected," she shouted. She placed the gun to her temple and pulled the trigger.

The congregation sat in stunned silence as officers approached Natalie and made sure she was the only shooter. Howls and moans erupted as the medical teams began to treat the wounded.

Detectives Wilson and Burlingame had picked up the call on their scanner and were close behind the first body of police. They called Rachel, who was with her father at Iglesia de Jesus Cristo, Oscar's church. Her phone vibrated, and she immediately lifted it to her ear.

At first, people around her were irritated that she started talking on her phone during worship, but Oscar, recognizing what this must be, halted the service in mid song and waited.

She turned to her father, who still used a wheelchair. "Find someone to help you get home," she said. "There has been another shooting. I need to go. I'll call you as soon as I can." She rose, ran down the aisle, jumped in her car, flipped on the siren, and rushed to the scene.

When the detectives and Rachel entered the sanctuary, an officer approached them and reported.

They spread out to talk to as many people as possible. Rachel went to the balcony and spotted a group of girls in hysterics over in one corner.

"Those teens said that they entered the church with the girl who did the shooting," said one of the adults who was trying to comfort his children. "God in heaven, how can this be happening?" he said. "Now it is both young girls and boys who have gone crazy."

Rachel approached the huddled teens on a pew in the corner. She introduced herself and waited. Her presence calmed them, and one began to speak.

"We were just standing outside waiting for church, and she came up and joined us," said one.

"She didn't seem dangerous," said another. "She said her parents had just moved here from Ohio."

"We invited her to sit with us in the balcony," said a third. Then she clutched one of the other girls. "Oh God, if she would have come with us, we might all be dead," she moaned.

After Rachel finished with them, she came down to the main floor. Detective Wilson motioned for her to come where he stood over the body of who people told them was Pastor Hawkins.

As she came closer, he stood and took her to the side. "Rachel, this gets weirder and weirder."

"What is it?" she asked.

"One of the witnesses said that before the girl shot the pastor, he heard her say, 'You're not Frank Sessions, he got away, but you aren't so lucky,' right before she fired. How is your father connected with all of this?"

"I wish I knew."

"We can take care of what needs to be done here. Why don't you go and talk to your father? See if he can make sense out of any of this."

She ran to her car and called to make sure her father had returned home. She flipped on her siren and raced towards his home. It is time for the Clue Crew, she thought. What is it about you, Dad, that these types of problems keep following you?

IT HITS THE FAN

CHAPTER 17

By the time Rachel reached her father's house, the media had begun to gather. The word had quickly spread that Frank's name had been spoken at the latest shooting. Jacob stood by his father's side. Frank was still in the wheelchair. The reporters shouted multiple questions trying to be the first to get attention. Rachel decided a little drama might focus their attention, so she hit her siren as she drove up. The reporters turned to see what was happening behind them.

Rachel exited her patrol car, smiled at her father, made her way through the reporters, and climbed the steps. Jacob spoke, "Get your pencils and microphones ready. I will provide the answer you have all been seeking." He proceeded to speak several sentences in Hebrew. There was a look of confusion on the reporters' faces. "Oh, I'm sorry, perhaps saying it another way would help." Then he spoke in Greek for several sentences.

Frank grinned. "It's all Greek to me." The reporters relaxed a little as Frank continued. "You are here because of a second shooting at another church. You're probably more familiar with the details than I am."

"We know that the shooter mentioned your name. What was that all about?"

Frank's face turned white as he turned to Rachel.

She responded. "This is still under investigation, but it is true that his name was spoken during the shooting."

"The shooter was a girl this time," said another reporter. "What do you think these kids have against churches?"

"As you can see, my father is still recovering from the first shooting. We heard about this second one while worshiping at another church. Dad," Jacob turned towards his father, "Do you want to say anything further before we go inside?"

"I think there are some very angry youth who have lost all sense of right and wrong in this mad rampage. The first shooter, Jeremy, kept shouting that everything was a lie. The challenge for the churches going forward is to demonstrate what we believe is the truth."

"What was your son saying, or was it just gibberish?" a reporter asked.

"I was having fun with you, but it is more than gibberish," Jacob said. "The Greek statement is a quote from Paul, 'In everything God works for good with those who love him and are called according to God's purpose.'"

A reporter swore under his breath and mumbled, "So God's using demented teenagers to accomplish some grand design? That's enough to make one barf."

"If your interpretation was correct, I would join you in upchucking," said Frank, "but Paul's statement doesn't mean that at all. These events are clearly evil. Paul is saying God is not defeated by evil, and if we work together as Christians, we can draw some good out of this tragic event. That is not your task. It is the challenge to the churches not to let this evil defeat us."

"So what should the churches do?" asked another reporter.

"I suspect many clergy will be gathering sometime this week to decide on what our next steps will be," Frank said. "If you believe in prayer, I'd suggest you pray we act in ways that reflect our faith and not do something in a panic that contradicts that faith."

Jacob again intervened. "That will have to be all for now. My dad needs to rest."

The reporters began to drift away as Jacob and Rachel helped their father into the house.

"Greek and Hebrew!" Rachel said. "People are dying out there, and all you can do is spout Greek and Hebrew?"

"Actually," said Frank, looking at his son who was moving towards the couch, "I didn't understand at first, but as I think about it, it was brilliant."

Jacob flopped his long, lanky body on the couch and smiled. "They were ready to pounce on Dad with all their inane questions. He wouldn't even have a chance to answer before the next question came. The language confused them, and when Dad used that old hackneyed joke about it being all Greek to them, they relaxed and started listening."

"OK," said Rachel, "I guessed it worked."

"Thank you, Rach, for such effusive praise," said Jacob.

"Rachel, is it true my name was spoken in this second massacre?" Frank said.

"Fraid so, Dad."

"And it was a girl this time?" asked Jacob.

"Yeah, apparently she joined with a crowd of girls coming out of Sunday school and came into the church without anyone noticing," said Rachel. "Right before she shot the preacher, someone near her heard her say something about him not being you, and he would die anyway."

Jacob suddenly sat up. "Do you remember the clue to tracking down the serial rapist a couple of years ago was figuring out why he kept using quotes from your lecture at the seminary?"

"But these kids are too young to have heard Dad at seminary," said Rachel. "Both of them were still in high school and were loners. I'll bet they didn't even go to church. How do they know Dad?"

"I don't have an answer," said Jacob, "but we had better figure out that connection fast before all the churches in Lincoln collapse in fear."

The shooting was the main breaking news on all the television stations. Overnight Lincoln, N.C. became known all over the world as the place of the church massacres. The talk shows shared endless opinions about why this was happening, who was behind it, and what it means for the future of Christianity.

A video purported to be by the Islamic State claimed God was punishing Christians for having shown a lack of respect for Islam. This stimulated several commentators to explore whether this was a new form of macabre terrorism. Several others explored the significance of the shooters always being so well dressed and proper looking. One opinion maker even cast an accusing glance at the Mormon Church, reminding his listeners that their missionaries were almost always dressed in the conservative fashion of the shooters.

Several commentators mused about why Lincoln had been the location of the attacks. They mentioned Frank and his involvement with the Evangelical Rapist that had terrorized the city a few years previously. Some conservative spokespeople wondered if Frank's more liberal theology offended young people. The more mainstream commentators wondered whether a dark shadow in his past was now coming to light.

All the commentators focused on Lincoln until a strange event occurred Monday evening on CNN's The Situation Room with Wolf Blitzer. Blitzer signed on and was commenting on the tragedy taking place in Lincoln, North Carolina. Before he could redirect the cameras to a reporter in Lincoln, an unplanned banner began to run across the bottom of the TV screen. In bold print it said, "What is the truth, Wolfie? When are you going to tell the truth about all religions? Not North Carolina, Texas next time."

Observers noticed the strain appearing on Wolf Blitzer's normally calm face as he was being instructed through his earpiece that something unusual was taking place.

"Ladies and gentlemen, I've just been informed that a banner is running across the screen declaring disturbing news. First of all, I assure you this message has not been placed there by CNN News. Apparently a hacker broke into our news feed. Our engineers are trying to trace its source now. However, the message itself seems to alter the focus of these events. The banner suggests that the church shootings are no longer confined to Lincoln or even North Carolina. The threat is it will happen in Texas next time.

"We are going to take an unplanned commercial breaks while we try to figure this out. I assure you we are not suggesting the commercials are more important than this event, but we do need a few moments to investigate this unusual happening. We will be right back."

Pandemonium erupted on other networks as well. It would have been comical if the unfolding events were not so serious. Some went to commercials while others tried to describe the events for their viewers and assure them both their network and CNN were doing all that they could to explain what was occurring.

Internet bloggers went into overdrive trying to explain the event. The public was in a state of frozen shock.

PANIC SPREADS

CHAPTER 18

Frank was sitting in his office working on a sermon. He flipped on the news in time to experience the banner insertion event and the resulting confusion. What the hell is happening? Now it is not only Lincoln, but the whole nation is involved. He studied enough basic psychology to be aware that panic often resulted in bizarre behavior.

He switched to several sites bookmarked on his computer to see what reaction was developing. The CNN site was awash with reactions both from experienced commentators and the usual knee-jerk reactors.

Over the next few days, he watched the panic spread.

"Has North Korea hacked into our communication system?" one commentator asked.

"We ought to round up any young Muslim who visited outside the U.S. in the last five years," said another.

A news commentator on CNN reported that "The NRA released a bulletin advising all Texas Christians to come to church fully armed."

Within hours, gun stores and the Internet sources for purchasing guns were flooded with orders.

The governor of Texas immediately called out the National Guard and placed all law enforcement personnel on high alert. The problem, as immediately identified by many commentators, was where to place the Guard. There was no identifiable pattern to the attacks. No one could say whether the threatened attack in Texas would be in a megachurch or a small one, in a large city or a village.

In Lubbock, Texas, two Mormon missionaries rode their bicycles towards the neighborhood of Rosewood to which they had been assigned. As they rode by the Rosewood Christian church, a car roared up beside them. Three adults with rifles leapt out. Pointing their rifles at the young men, they shouted, "Stop right there!"

The Mormon youth pulled to the side of the road and stopped. "What's wrong?" one of them asked.

"We are protecting our neighborhood," one of the men said as he advanced on them. "You are strangers around here, and you're dressed all snooty like. Show some identification."

Each of the young men immediately produced their cards identifying themselves as Mormon missionaries.

The men frisked them and said they weren't welcome near a Christian church, and they should go back where they came from.

When they reported the incident to their headquarters, the Mormon Church immediately issued a bulletin canceling all missionary visits by young people until the source of the church attacks had been identified.

Some communities issued curfews for all people between 15 and 25 unless accompanied by an older adult.

The FBI frantically explored the Internet trying to trace the origin for the banner. It came to the United States from a foreign source, but they couldn't determine whether the signal bounced through several sites to disguise its origin.

Lots of attention centered on Lincoln, but why was Lincoln

chosen as the site of the original attacks? The only clear fact was the connection with the pastor, Frank Sessions.

Frank slowly recovered from his injuries but the trauma of friends being killed in his church left a deep, aching wound in his soul. Following therapy instructions, he exercised at home but did not venture out of the house.

On Wednesday, his phone rang.

When he answered, he immediately recognized the voice of George Shultz, a member of his session. George didn't waste time on greetings but delivered his message in tight, explicit sentences as if prepared for a battle.

"Frank, when you got mixed up with the police on that rapist case a couple of years ago, I supported you. Figured it wasn't your fault, and you were helping out."

"I think I hear a 'but' coming, George."

"This latest thing is too much. I don't understand your connection with these crazies, but it's has to stop, Frank. Churches shouldn't be battlefields."

"I agree, George, but what do you want me to do?"

"Beats me, Frank, but you seem to be a focal point. Maybe you should leave, at least until this gets settled."

"You may be right, George. If I am a target, I don't want to put our people at risk."

There was a long pause. George's tone softened, almost to a whine. "Aw, Frank, I'm not sure whether that is right or not. I'm just scared for my family is all. I know you are not personally at fault, but you seem like a magnet that draws trouble."

"Listen, George, let's call a special session meeting Friday evening and see if we can pool our wisdom."

"I have a lot of respect for you, Frank. The truth is, I don't want my family and my friends in the church to get hurt."

"I'm afraid they are already hurt," said Frank. "Even those who weren't present were traumatized, and if it spreads across the nation, all the churches are going to be paralyzed with fear."

"Yeah, my cousin in Texas swears he is never going to go to church again."

We are facing a big problem," said Frank. "It's beyond Lincoln and bigger than me. We are caught in a tsunami of fear sweeping the nation."

"You're right. But we have to do something. Do you think the Devil is behind this, and this is the end of the world, Frank?"

"Evil is certainly at work, but personalizing evil by calling it the devil isn't going to help us confront the real enemy. This is not supernatural. It's human terror, and we need to stop it."

"Like you said, the violence is spreading across the nation. What good are we going to do by calling our session together, Frank?"

"When we are in the midst of chaos, George, the first thing we need to do is start right where we are and do something. We have to bring some order to our little corner of the universe."

"I hope you are right, Frank. My world is coming unglued."

"OK, here is the first thing you can do. First call our clerk, Wiley, and tell him we need to call a special session meeting on Friday night at 7 p.m. Offer to divide up the list; you call half, and let Wiley call half."

Frank could hear more confidence in George's voice when he responded. "OK, I can do that. Where should we meet?"

"Let's meet at the church. We need to reclaim that building for our own work."

"In fact, unless Wiley objects, let the elders start spreading the word we are going to worship at John Knox on Sunday as well. We are Christians, George, and we need to come together and declare to the world we believe God, not death, has the last word."

"You're good, Frank. When I called, I was ready to toss you out with the garbage. Now I feel like we have something we can do." He paused and then added, "I just hope to hell it works, Frank. But thanks for this conversation." He hung up.

Frank put the phone down. He noticed his shirt was soaked clear through. I hope it works, too, George. That's the problem with being the pastor. Sometimes you need to show courage even when you are not sure you feel it. Like he counseled George, however, just doing something did make him feel a little better.

Frank knew how to be a good pastor in the presence of another person in need, but he also tried to stay in touch and be honest about the nonprofessional side of his personality. He, too, was scared, but more than that, he felt enormous guilt. A couple of people, including his adult kids, had kidded him about being a magnet for trouble. The problem was that it seemed to be true.

The first shooter named him as if it were personal and the girl at the second church had spoken his name before she shot Stan Hawkins.

He never had a lot of respect for Stan. Though he had to admit his organizational genius had increased the numbers at Open Door Community. Now he felt guilty about all the cynical comments he had shared with colleagues about lightweight faith in a heavyweight pastor. Whatever Stan's faults, he didn't deserve to die like this. Despite their differences, Stan was a colleague in ministry, and he should have built a better relationship with him. Now he's dead, and many of his members are wounded in body and soul without a spiritual leader to guide them.

It was more than Stan's death that troubled Frank. Had he been the trigger releasing this anger and hatred, he wondered? Somehow he was at the center of this hailstorm of violence that threatened the church, now spreading to churches beyond Lincoln.

A strange sound on his computer startled him out of his musings. He examined his screen for the source of the sound. He saw a signal for a call on Skype. He had encouraged his colleagues to use Skype, Google Hangout, and other programs to reach out in support of each other. He was grateful that one of them was reaching out to him. He certainly needed the support.

He searched for the right buttons and adjusted the screen. He wondered which of his colleagues was calling him. He pushed the accept button and looked at the screen.

Her bright teeth and eyes with a slight Oriental slant were the first things he noticed. Next he felt guilt for not having followed up on her call at the hospital. He was pleased there didn't seem to be a scowl on her face.

"Mandy, great to see you."

"Zeke, if you just wanted to work with me again on another case, all you needed to do was ask."

Zeke was what she had called him in college. It was comforting to hear it again, but he quickly switched to the main subject. "Texas now. How could this be happening, Mandy?"

"I hoped you could tell me, Zeke. I barely settled into my new job here at the Justice Department and now this. My boss, who knows I knew you before, asked me to talk to you and see what you thought."

"Your boss. Is that Mark?" He regretted it as soon as the words left his mouth.

"Oh, how delightful. Is that a flash of that green-eyed demon of jealousy peeking out?"

"I'm sorry, that was uncalled for," he said with chagrin.

"Well, the answer is yes, it was uncalled for, and no, my boss is not named Mark, and yes, I do know someone named Mark, but none of the above relates to why I called."

"Your boss, who will remain unnamed, asked you to make contact with me to try to find out why my name came up at both shootings," Frank said.

"And the answer is?" Mandy said.

"My children and I tried and failed to solve that puzzle over the last several days. Now there is Texas. I've never even been to Texas."

"Let's come at it another way. What causes a young person to go on a suicide mission? From what I've heard, they don't even expect to make it out alive," said Mandy.

"You don't suppose you could find time to come to Lincoln for a couple of days and let Jacob and Rachel share in our thinking about that?"

"You know what? My boss, who shall remain unnamed, came up with the same idea." She broke into a broad smile. "I told him if it were on a professional basis, I could probably wrangle an invitation."

"Mandy, I . . ."

"Wait, now I'm the one who needs to apologize. Some day, when you are both healthy, and this problem is solved, we are going to have a no-holds-barred conversation about us, but right now I need help. You are gifted with an instinct for thinking these things through."

"I think I just received a warning and a request in the same sentence."

"We government people are a sneaky bunch," Mandy said. "So how do next Tuesday and Wednesday sound? Of course, we don't know what may happen in Texas by then, and that may change everything."

"My guess is whoever is behind this enjoys watching the tension build, so this so called Leader will probably will give us a week or so before anything new happens."

"I hope you are right. We can use a little time to get oriented."

She looked at Frank with an intense stare and shook her head slightly.

"What?" Frank said.

"Nothing," she said, "I've never met anyone who can be so brilliant in one moment and such a dumb-ass the next. Bye!" Frank saw her reach over and push the disconnect. Her smile faded from the screen.

A DARK NIGHT

CHAPTER 19

Frank stared at the wall in his office. He saw all the symbols of his faith—the cross, the chalice, his robe, and stoles, pictures of different events in church life. He glanced around at all the books stuffed on the shelves as well as several stacks on the floor around his desk. If you can be both numb and angry at the same time, that's how he was feeling.

For reasons he didn't understand, people had died because they were connected to him. That little nutcase came to this church, into my sanctuary, called me by name, and shot several people—friends of mine, people who came expecting to be uplifted, not riddled with bullets. If they hadn't known me, if I weren't pastor in this church, those people would still be alive.

It was like you did something stupid, and caused people to be hurt. You kept playing the scene over and over again, trying to change something, but it always came out the same. Their blood was is on my hands. They sure as hell didn't teach you how to deal with this in seminary. He again glanced at the books. He had read most of them. They were supposed to contain wisdom—both spiritual and practical—but he couldn't think of anything he had read that gave him a sense of direction in the midst of this chaos.

He continued to stare. He turned again to look at several crosses hanging on the wall. Some were what he would call Protestant crosses, without Jesus' body. They spoke of God's victory over evil, the resurrection, the body gone; death had done its worst, but God had triumphed. In some eternal sense he believed that, but right now death seemed very real.

He looked at what he thought of as the Catholic crosses, where Jesus' body still was present. It spoke to him of God's suffering because of the evil of this world. It was supposed to speak of God's willingness to suffer on behalf of the world. *What's clear to me is people are suffering. I'm not so clear about whether you are suffering or just sitting out in the vast somewhere,* he thought.

In his mind he heard the cry of the human Jesus from the cross described in the Gospels of Matthew and Mark. The agony depicted spoke deeply to Frank. Frank remembered the cry of abandonment came from Psalm 22, and he turned to the psalm for his own prayer.

"My God, my God, why have you forsaken me? Why are you so far from helping me, from the words of my groaning?" The words opened up all of Frank's feelings of desolation. He felt forsaken by God.

He continued reading the psalm. "In you our ancestors trusted; they trusted, and you delivered them. To you they cried, and were saved." *Isn't this what the faith is supposed to be about? Haven't we told and retold the tale of God's saving work among God's people? God protected Abraham even when he was foolish. He stayed with Jacob even though he was a conniving rascal. He took a stuttering Moses and helped him free the Hebrews from slavery. Even David's action of adultery and murder didn't deter God from faithfulness. It never depended on the goodness of humans but only in their trust in the faithfulness of God. So where was God now when Frank needed him? What did these church people do to deserve this?*

"But I am a worm, and not human," continued the psalm, "scorned by others, and despised by the people. All who see me mock at me; they make mouths at me, they shake their heads; 'Commit your cause to the Lord; let him deliver.'" Frank felt like a worm, and he wondered how many people were shaking their heads at this moment. He could hear them saying, he preached a good line, he told us to trust in God, but then God wouldn't even come to his rescue. Who can trust in such a God?

He read further, "I am poured out like water, and all my bones are out of joint; my heart is like wax; it is melted within my breast." Calvin was right; the psalms are an anatomy of the soul, he thought. The psalmist described in better words than I can how I am feeling. He felt weak all over—helpless. He had been here before, but each time he wondered if this time he would not find the proverbial light to lift him up.

Deep in his dark muck, at first he didn't hear his phone ringing. When he heard the sound, he at first wondered if it was an alarm. Then reality began to dawn on him, and he reached for the phone.

The phone screen indicated it was his son Jacob. That little bit of familiarity relaxed his body as he lifted the receiver. "Jacob, how are you?"

"Fine, how are you? I gather that your secretary is not at work yet since it took you six rings before you answered."

"She had a doctor's appointment. Everyone's still a little spooked about the building since the shooting. I told her to take her time. We are going to worship this Sunday, but I expect the turnout may be low."

"After the second shooting, I'm sure no one knows what to think. The churches seem to be the target, but no can explain why?" Jacob said.

"And with my name being associated with both shootings, some fear we might get hit a second time."

"Well, in a weird sort of way, that is why I'm calling you," said Jacob. "I know how hard this hit you."

"It all seems so pointless," said Frank. "Just because I'm me, I've put people in danger, Jacob. I'm supposed to help people, not put their lives in danger."

"You may not be up to this, but there is this friend here at the seminary that is back from Afghanistan about a year. He's struggling with the PTSD. In talking to him it occurred to me that you both might gain from talking to each other."

"You may recall," said Frank, "the last person you asked me to talk to is now serving a twenty year sentence in the pen."

"I know," said Jacob. "I think this is different. In fact, I'm hoping he might be able to give you some insight about how to respond to the church violence."

"That may be a son's wishful thinking, but I'm willing to give it a shot. What's the best way to set it up?"

"I think he will be more comfortable if I came with him for the first session. We've had some long talks, and he trusts me. He's part of a support group who has begun exploring how they might turn their experience around. Instead of calling it Post Traumatic Stress Disorder, they speak of themselves as a Post Traumatic Growth or PTG group."

"Tell me some background, Jacob. You said he's been back about a year. Is there family around, or is he all alone?"

"He is single. Had a relationship, but she couldn't cope with his mood swings. One of the group stumbled on an article about how you can convert trauma into new strength and resilience. It was a new thought, but it seemed to give them some energy. Brian says it doesn't make the black holes disappear, but you develop new confidence as you face them."

"Now you have my attention," said Frank. "In fact, I can see that might be useful for the congregation as well."

Jacob chuckled. "That's my father, always thinking about the other person. I was thinking that he might be of help to you. In this case, however, they might go together."

"I should have known that when you started combining graduate studies in theology and psychology I would be on the receiving end after all these years of giving out advice." Frank paused and then said, "However, I think, Jacob, you may be right. Just thinking about the possibilities has given me some energy."

"Given the likelihood there will be another shooting soon, I think we should set this up right away. How does your schedule look for the rest of the week?"

"How about Saturday some time? Other than some work on my sermon, I'm pretty free."

"Thanks, Dad. By the way, his name is Brian. I'll call him and get back to you."

A SOLDIER'S JOURNEY

CHAPTER 20

They entered Frank's office. Frank noticed Brian carefully checking out the room, the window that opened out onto the church lawn, and the position of the chairs. He had thin, wavy blond hair, and was a compact well built young man in what Frank guessed was his early thirties. He moved with grace and appeared to always be balanced so that he could quickly move in any direction. Frank wondered if he had developed that habit in Afghanistan.

"Brian, why don't you sit there?" He indicated a chair that provided a clear view of both the window and the door. "Jacob, take that chair, and I'll take this one."

Each of them took their seats. There was a pot of coffee on the table. Frank offered to fill their cups. Brian reached for three packets of sugar and some cream. "I drink too much of this stuff," he said, "but I think it helps calm me down. Better than smoking, which I'm trying to give up."

"Jacob tells me your support group is exploring how you can find some positive benefit from all the stress symptoms you are experiencing. Why don't we begin with you telling me about what your group is thinking?"

"Well, this sounds sort of crazy, but the guys and I were talking at our Thursday night meeting about what had happened at your church a couple of weeks ago and the other church this past Sunday. We felt a little guilty saying it, but as one guy said, 'I've had more energy in the last several days than in the past year.'"

"We thought about it, and then we began agreeing with him," said Brian.

"I think I understand, but tell me more," said Frank.

"When you are in the field, every moment is full of danger. You each have your responsibilities, and you know that your buddies depend on you. You try to be alert all the time, and your adrenaline is always pumping."

"You are living life on the edge," Jacob suggested.

"You're right, bro." He stood up, and his eyes held a sparkle. "Even though you recognize what is happening is far beyond your control, your little part of life means something. Your buddies depend on you."

"Then you return," said Frank.

"And people seem like they are walking around in a bubble. They aren't aware of the dangers in the world, and they don't care."

"When you heard about the church shootings?" said Jacob.

"We'd been living in a dream, and all of a sudden we were back in the world we understand. We are familiar with shooting, and dying, and craziness. I mean, shooting in a church, how crazy is that?"

"Doesn't it scare you? Sure scares me," said Jacob.

"A soldier learns how to put feelings in different boxes for different times. Of course you get scared, but if you want to stay alive, you had better shove those feelings down so you can do your job."

"So you and your buddies felt like you were living on familiar territory again," said Frank.

"Familiar and crazy at the same time. This city is not supposed to be this way, and it's possible our skills can be of use. What we learned in Afghanistan can help people at home. We went over there to fight a war no one seems to understand, but now we can come home and protect our people."

"I don't know where this will lead, Brian, but thank you. I was crawling into myself this week, feeling guilty and not knowing what to do. Just having you make the offer opens up new possibilities. You've given me some new energy as well," Frank said.

"Not to get too philosophical on you two," said Jacob, "but your conversation reminds me of a quote from William James. I think it goes, 'The greatest weapon against stress is our ability to choose one thought over another.'"

Frank raised his left eyebrow as he said, "I think a rough translation is when we make choices, we break out of the endless cycle of despair and have hope and purpose again. I like it."

"The problem with being in a war," said Brian, "especially one with a new justification every time you turn around, is you lose hold of your moral compass. I did some horrible things over there. I don't think I'll ever forget them." He seemed to shrink, and he looked out the window as if seeking an answer that no longer existed in his world.

They all remained silent for a while. Then Brian reached for his cup and took a big sip of the coffee.

Frank said, "I'd like to talk to you more about that. One of the hardest lessons of Christianity is you can't earn forgiveness. You learn to trust God forgives you because God wants to love you into wholeness."

"If I can bring some good out of this mess, it's possible I'll believe that again," said Brian.

"Or perhaps if you can believe that again," said Frank, "you can bring some good out of this mess."

"If my buddies are open to it, would you meet with us and help us explore this further?" asked Brian. "I am eager to discuss this with someone who can understand.

Maybe we can help people prepare for whatever happens next," said Frank.

"What do you expect will happen this Sunday?" asked Jacob.

"It terrifies me," said Frank. "If the message hacked into the news services is true, we are seeing this spread beyond Lincoln."

"If I were the enemy, since my main goal is to paralyze the population with fear," said Brian, "I'd lay off a week or so and let them stew in their own panic."

"I'm hoping you're right, but there will be a lot of panic in Texas on Sunday. I just hope people don't start shooting at their shadows and innocent people get hurt."

"One of the lessons of a soldier," said Brian "is you can only fight the battle in front of you."

"Good advice," said Frank. "Can you talk to your group before their next meeting? If they give their OK, I'll join you on Thursday."

"I'll text them when I leave. I should know their response in a couple of hours. They knew where I was coming today and are expecting me to contact them."

BARBARA'S PLANS

CHAPTER 21

Barbara was excited about the panic that had flooded the church people in Lincoln. Daily the news media were reporting interviews with the terrorized populace. Many lamented that it was not safe to go to church until the shootings stopped.

"My family is too important to me to risk taking them to church," responded one man. "Why don't the authorities do something about this?"

"This is America," said a woman to another reporter. "It's not supposed to be that way here."

One response caused Barbara to laugh out loud. It was from a manager of the local Walmart. "It makes you begin to doubt God," said the man. "I mean, if God is real, why does he let people who have come to worship him get all shot up?" Then the man smiled, "I have to say, though, since this began to happen, business has picked up at my store. I guess they are looking for something to do on Sunday morning."

Barbara's husband, Bob, bewailed the sudden drop in attendance in just two weeks. "I've hired armed guards to protect people at all our services, and still my attendance is down by half. This has to stop or all the churches are going to fold. We can't exist if people stop coming. They are not going to contribute to a church that they don't attend. It's a nightmare."

Even as she consoled her husband, she delighted in tasting her revenge. *You'd faint dead away if you knew who was causing this panic.*

While Bob was meeting with the other clergy in the city trying to plan their response to this disaster, Barbara spent time trying to plan her next steps. She was searching the Internet trying to search out the most promising prospects for expanding her operation outside Lincoln. She felt some urgency to have a shooting beyond Lincoln, so it was clear that this was a national event.

She was pleased that the news of the two shootings had spread across the nation so quickly. Her hacker friends had taught her how to leave postings of her own that could not be traced back to the source. She immediately began posting on clandestine bulletin boards around the country.

IF YOU WANT TO BE PART OF THE REAL ARMY THAT WILL EXPOSE THE LIES OF RELIGION AND THE CABALS OF CORRUPTION AMONG THE ADULTS OF THIS WORLD, LEAVE A MESSAGE AND A WAY TO BE CONTACTED, said one message.

Another said, JOIN THE ARMY OF TRUTH AND BRING THE LYING ADULTS TO THEIR KNEES. LET'S CLEAN UP THIS ROTTEN WORLD. WATCH THEM QUAKE WHEN THEY SEE TEENS WHO KNOW THE TRUTH AND ARE NOT AFRAID TO DIE FOR IT. LEAVE A MESSAGE AND A WAY TO BE CONTACTED.

A third said, EXPOSE THEIR LYING HEARTS. THEY SAY THEY BELIEVE IN THE RESURRECTION BUT ARE COWARDS IN THE FACE OF DEATH. IF YOU WANT TO BE PART OF THE REVOLUTION OF TRUTH, LEAVE A MESSAGE AND A WAY TO BE CONTACTED. COWARDS NEED NOT APPLY.

Her postings bounced around the world and came to rest on different bulletin boards. Any attempt to trace their original source would prove fruitless.

Bloggers were going crazy, and there were many bulletin boards where a number of young people were indicating their support for what was going on. What began in the tens and twenties soon became hundreds of responses. There were the usual responses condemning what was happening, but there were also many who wanted to be in on this history-making event. She developed a small cadre of Internet friends who were willing to contact the most promising recruits. They sorted out the most alienated youth who were desperate to take some action that couldn't be ignored. She was intrigued by how many of them were fascinated by violence. It held a certain purity for them.

Many also volunteered to be involved in other ways. She was breathless when one hacker suggested the brilliant scheme of interrupting the nightly news with the announcement of further attacks. It was, she realized, a simple yet effective way of reminding those in authority how little power they had. Her target had been the churches, but she quickly realized she could reveal the underbelly of both the media and the government in one swift action and without much risk.

Her mind went into overdrive considering the possibilities. She believed that the one factor rulers used to cower the opposition was the projection of absolute authority. Authority can't stand mockery that reveals they, too, are helpless. She chose Wolf Blitzer in *The Situation Room* as her first target. She watched in amazement as a banner appeared at the bottom of the screen in the midst of Wolf's broadcast. The usually calm, cool reporters and aides began to run around the studios oblivious to the viewing public. From authoritative to confused, Blitzer suddenly looked like a little boy who had been caught with his pants down.

Then two days later, she interrupted Bill O'Reilly right in the middle of one of his self-righteous tirades on the *O'Reilly Factor*. She watched his face turn crimson as a banner went across the screen. "Really, O'Reilly, tell the truth. Listen to the youth. Stop being a shill for those who buy you off daily. Maybe you ought to go to Texas and take your gun with you."

The brilliance of the plan was that it spread panic around the nation while giving her more time before she had to execute the next attack. Bloggers from Texas reported to her that the testosterone politics of Texas went into overtime. Within days, the media reported hundreds of volunteers driving towards Texas packing their guns and vowing to protect the state against Muslim jihadists, Mormon missionaries, any suspicious well-dressed teenagers, and everyone else who looked threatening. The problem was that once they crossed the borders, they didn't know in which direction to go. They were a voluntary cavalry who weren't sure where the Indians were hiding.

Officials at the Texas borders lost complete control. Most of the highways had no checkpoints, and state troopers didn't know whether to question them or cheer them on. At the same time, many Texans resented the suggestion that they couldn't protect themselves. As one man said to a reporter, "We are locked and loaded, and no snotty-nosed little pipsqueak is going to scare us."

The governor placed the National Guard on alert and appealed to the President to declare Texas a national disaster area. At the same time, fearing chaos from the many untrained volunteers coming to defend Texas, he held a nationally televised news conference and appealed for calm.

Right in the middle of his news conference, a banner appeared on the screen. "Big town, little town, all in a row. The cowboys lined up but didn't know where to go. The governor huffed and puffed but couldn't blow the lies out of the churches. To the smirking reporters, he cried out, 'I'm in control, I just don't know what to do.'"

The governor went into a tirade right on national TV. Spewing swear words in every sentence, he cursed out the media who couldn't control their cameras. He threatened to pull their license if they didn't learn to behave. He started to turn on his handlers, when one of them pointed out that the cameras were still broadcasting. "Well tell them to turn the cameras off." Then he turned to the cameras, sweating profusely, lamely apologized, "I apologize for this confusion.

We will turn the cameras off until we get this straightened out. God bless Texas and the United States." Then he glared at the shocked camera operator until an aide went over and shouted at him, "Turn the damn camera off."

Barbara knew those unscripted moments and the banner would be replayed over and over again for the whole world to see. She barely acknowledged Bob's return from his clergy meeting. She did her best to remain composed as he shared the relief of his clergy friends and the city that the threat seemed to have moved on. Over the next several days, the national media sought interviews with many of the clergy about this threat to religion and why it had begun in Lincoln. With the threat on their particular churches not imminent, they were pleased to give their expansive opinions about the cause of alienation among the youth and the power of religion to provide answers to all of the questions being raised. They also pointed out that though this was a national tragedy, people in Lincoln could return to their churches and ponder the spiritual meaning of this tragedy.

She was relishing in this latest triumph and trying to plan her next steps when, for the second time in a week, she experienced the creative thinking of her blossoming cadre of Internet geniuses. One of those who were trying to help her identify potential shooters in the Texas region informed her of a serendipitous surprise. When he was vetting potential shooters, he discovered that two of them lived near the town of Texas, Wisconsin. He thought it was funny and wanted to pass it on, but Barbara saw a whole new possibility.

Jeb, in addition to training Jeremy and Natalie how to shoot, was a veteran of four tours of duty in Iraq and Afghanistan. At their second personal meeting, Jeb acknowledged that in addition to his disillusionment with the government he felt had lied to him, he also felt the hypocrisy of society because he was gay. While society was growing in its acceptance, Jeb carried many scars from his treatment growing up and in the military.

Barbara couldn't believe her good fortune. She was able to learn from Jeb's male perspective without having to be continually alert to the inevitable time when he would make a play for her. Both saw in the other a companion that could help them exact their revenge on society. While Jeb could care less about what he considered the malarkey of religion, he shared Barbara's disillusionment with the government and society. They shared a desire to make all authorities look like fools.

Now she texted him about a new twist in their campaign. "We told the world that Texas would be next. How foolish would they look if everybody focused on the state of Texas and it went down in Texas, Wisconsin?"

"You are evil, lady. If I were straight, I'd fuck your brains out for that beautiful idea."

"If you did, you'd never go back to men! How about finding a place in Wisconsin to train a couple of recruits I've identified?"

"I'll check with my buddies for a place and get back to you today. And, to match your brilliant idea, I have a thought about how we can fool them in Texas or wherever else we hit. I'll explain it later. We are on a roll, Barbara. I love you, in a most platonic way, of course."

BATTLE STRATEGY

CHAPTER 22

Jacob agreed to go with Frank to Brian's meeting. Several of the members knew Jacob, and they agreed that that would ease the introductions.

As they drove to the meeting, they discussed what might happen. "So, Jacob, give me a little background on this group. I've met Brian, of course, but how many others will be there?"

"If everyone makes it, and they usually do, there will be six of them. When they began, they were meeting almost every day and then a couple of times a week. Now they meet twice a month but are always on call for each other."

"It sounds like they think they are getting a better grip on life if they only meet a couple of times a month."

"As Brian will tell you," said Jacob, "that is a meeting of the total group. It's not unusual for a couple of them to team up every day or so. They also use the social media to keep in touch with each other."

"Any tips about how I should approach this? I'm very interested in their perspective on what is happening, but I don't want to come on too strong," said Frank.

"I've only met with them a couple of times as a group, though I see a couple of them on a fairly regular basis. My experience is that they are pretty intuitive."

"So whatever I say, they will also be reading my body and be pretty sensitive to what I am feeling."

Jacob smiled. "That pretty much sums it up. Fact is you're pretty good about being honest with yourself, so just be honest with them as well."

Frank glanced at Jacob as he slowed for a right turn. "You know, it has taken some getting used to, but I enjoy relating to you as an adult. Your decision to design your own doctorate combining spirituality and psychology has built on some of your best skills."

"Tell that to Brandy. Last time I spoke to her, just before she hung up she informed me that my spicology monster—that's what she calls my joint degree—lacked spirit and showed more psycho than ology."

"Me thinks she is feeling a little neglected," said Frank. "In my last FaceTime conversation with Mandy, she concluded by telling me that I might be smart, but I was really a dumb-ass."

Jacob barked a sharp laugh and said, "I hate to suggest this, but do you think my little sister could give us some pointers on how women think?"

"I think she would love the opportunity to try, but we had better be fortified for a long conversation," said Frank. "However, providing her that opportunity might be good for all of us. She feels the tension building around this investigation. Ragging us about women might bring her some comic relief."

"She did a great job in getting that information about Natalie."

"Yeah," said Frank, "but she feels guilty that she wasn't able to find the girl before she shot up that Lutheran church."

"No one could have done that, but she did pick up the clues that this is much bigger than a couple of out of control teenagers," said Jacob.

"Guilt is not rational," said Frank. "In my head, I know I am not responsible for the shooting at John Knox, but still I can't stop wondering if those people died because of something I did. I was in the middle of a sermon about finding hope in the face of chaos, and then all hell broke loose." Frank pulled over to the curb and bent over the steering wheel. "Oh, God, Jacob, what evil is loose in our city—and now maybe even beyond?"

Jacob laid a hand on his father's shoulder but didn't try to say anything until Frank stopped shaking.

"Dad, about two miles up the road, we are going to sit down with some young men who experienced violence and the death of their buddies all around them. They need us to hear their story, but we also need them to hear ours. As you have repeatedly told me, it is by the spoken word that we begin to bring order out of chaos. Let's go and see if we can help each other make some sense out of this madness."

Frank turned and gave Jacob a big hug. "Thanks for being my son and my friend, Jacob. You and Rachel were my lifeline after your mom was killed. Later you helped me figure out that serial rapist case. You've helped me bring a lot of order out of chaos."

"You just mentioned the other person who helped in that case. What is going on with you and Amanda, or should I say what is not going on?"

Frank looked out the window, took a big breath, and let it out. "Not now, but maybe we should have that conversation. You and I may be struggling with similar demons, and some very good women are suffering because of our blind spots."

Jacob grimaced. "Why is it I can see that with you and Mandy but screw it up with Brandy? Even more interesting, why do both of us continually have to distinguish whether we are talking to the women in our lives professionally or personally by giving them nicknames when it is personal?

By the way, before she blew up and slammed down the phone, she had asked if she could talk to the two of us and Rachel as Brenda Sides the reporter about this case."

Frank pulled away from the curb and headed towards the VFW

hall where they were meeting with Brian and his friends. "Was it Shakespeare who said, "Oh what a tangled web we weave . . . ?"

"Actually no," said Jacob. "It is often attributed to him, but it was Sir Walter Scott who said it."

"Well, Shakespeare should have said it. Anyway, I'll be glad to talk with Brenda the reporter. In fact, maybe we could make progress on both fronts if we set it up so that Amanda could join us on Skype. The Justice Department has charged her with spearheading this part of the investigation.

"Sounds good. Do you think Brandy would agree first to explore the subject with us and then come to a consensus about what is approved for publication?"

"Given your volatile relationship, maybe I should be the one to talk with her about the ground rules," said Frank.

Jacob stretched, rubbed the back of his neck, and then said, "I think that is an excellent plan. She might be a little more rational around you than me."

"I won't engage in the debate as to which of you is more rational, but I will call her later today and see if I can set it up," said Frank.

"There is the VFW hall up on your right," said Jacob. "When you enter the parking lot, pull around behind the building. We can enter through the rear."

As they parked, and exited the car, they walked towards the building. A door off to the side opened and Brian stepped out to greet them. "Hey, good to see you. You can come in through this door. It gives us more privacy, and no one will bother us while we are meeting."

Frank noticed that even as Brian was warm and open in his greeting, he carefully checked out the parking lot and gave them and their car a quick visual inspection. He also noticed a holstered gun attached to his belt.

Brian led them down the hallway to a small room on the left. Five men were standing or sitting around the room. Each turned and inspected their new guests. One wiry African-American man came forward with outstretched hand. "My name is Jalin." He shook

Jacob's hand and then turned to Frank. "We are glad you could meet with us. Come; let me introduce you to the guys."

While thin, Frank could appreciate that Jalin was well conditioned and physically fit. If Frank had to guess, he would estimate Jalin was about five foot ten inches. His Afro gave him an image of confidence.

"This here is Juan. He served three tours in Afghanistan and became quite an expert in bomb deactivation. You can tell he was good because he is still here, and his body is almost whole—though we think his brain has some missing links at times."

Juan grinned and greeted Frank and Jacob. "Mucho gusto de conocerles."

Next Jalin turned to a tall, thin man with red hair. He seemed very adept at using his prosthesis for one leg. "This here is Barrie. He served one tour in Iraq and two in Afghanistan. His red hair and freckles plus his height made it a little hard for him to blend into the population, so he drove a supply truck. Only hit three IEDs, though the last one blew up the truck and took one of his legs. The government is still trying to bill him for lost supplies."

"Jalin is at his best when he is bullshitting you. Nice to meet you—Reverend isn't it?"

"It is, Barrie, but I would be pleased if you would just call me Frank."

Jalin kept making his introductions. "These two are Phil and Julio." Both men had been sitting on stools at the bar, nursing a cup of coffee but clearly alert to what was going on in the room. Julio helped Phil stand on his crutches before reaching out his hand. Julio was a large man, at least two hundred and fifty pounds, and had a patch over one eye. Phil was around six foot and probably would have weighed about one hundred and sixty, except it was hard to tell how his two prostheses affected his weight.

"Phil just got these new legs adjusted, so I help him to stand, and he helps me to see."

"My goal is to get these suckers working and then I'm going to train for the Olympics like that fellow I read about a while back. Except, I think, I will avoid shooting my girlfriend like he did."

"Since when did you find a girl who would get near enough to risk being shot?" said Jalin.

"Hey, with these new legs, I'm going to start courting your sister. She is prettier than you, isn't she?"

The bantering continued for a few minutes, and then Brian suggested they all grab some coffee and take a seat in a circle.

"As you know from my text, the reverend here," Brian turned, and then corrected himself, "Frank is Jacob's father. He is also the pastor of the first church that was shot up —even got shot himself."

"Man you're a Purple Heart veteran the way I heard it," said Barrie.

"I heard on the Net that you went right at the enemy," said Julio. "Hadn't been for you, lots more might have bit the dust."

Others either mumbled support or gave him a sign of support. Frank knew at that moment that he was invited into the brotherhood of the wounded. "Thanks, but I only had to face it once. You fellows faced danger day after day. How'd you cope?"

"Once is one time too many," said Brian. "For many of us, it's not the getting shot that is so bad but knowing that it can come again at any time."

"And you never know from where or when," said another, "sometimes with bullets, but also IEDs and even hand grenades."

"Remember that time, Jalin," said Phil, "when that cute little girl came towards you asking for candy, and Sarge yelled 'Jump' just in time before she blew herself up?"

"I still see her eyes. She was scared but didn't know what else to do. I think all she wanted was a piece of candy." Jalin shook his head as if he wished he could shake the memory loose. "The hell of it is that you begin to look at all little kids differently after that. It ain't right. Kids are supposed to be sweet and innocent—not bomb throwers. What in the hell is this world coming to?"

"And now, with what Frank faced, people begin to look at teenagers the same way," said Julio. "The way I heard it, the kid that shot you didn't even look mean and scruffy. He looked like I would want my kid to look. Isn't that true Frank?"

"Suit and tie, good haircut, walked upright," said Frank.

"I heard that crackpot, Eric Ivory, describe him as looking like one of those Mormon missionaries," said Barrie.

"What you listening to that idiot for?" asked Jalin. "He's as bad as those stupid congressmen that sent us to war."

"I heard," said Juan, "that some thugs in Texas accosted a couple of those Mormon missionaries. Dios Mio, next thing you know everyone will have to start dressing with the barrio look to stay safe."

"Jalin's right, though," said Frank. "It's only been a few days for me, but I do look at young people differently. And with the shooting at the Lutheran church, it's not just boys but girls too."

Just then a door behind the bar opened, and all the men tensed until they saw it was a young lady with a tray of donuts. She had a bright, pleasant smile and said in a cheery voice, "My parents told me to bring these over for you. It was their way of saying thanks for all you've done."

She was in the midst of her speech when she noticed how tense they all had become. "I'm sorry, I didn't mean to interrupt."

"It's OK," said Jacob as he rose to receive the donuts. "We appreciate you bringing them. Tell your parents thanks too."

When she left and all had some donuts, Barrie spoke. "You see, Frank, most of us saw all that violence over there, and we learned to live with it, but now that we are back, the adrenaline continues to pump. We are always on the alert for that sweet little girl asking for candy. I almost cautioned Jacob when he approached that pretty girl to get the donuts, and that's just crazy.'"

"And right now," said Brian, "I'll bet it's hard for you to walk into a church service without surveying all the youth present looking for signs of danger."

"And replaying the shooting asking myself how I could have prevented all those people from being killed," said Frank.

"Yeah," said Barrie, "sometimes I wake up and see some of my buddies who were standing near me when they bought it. I keep replaying this one scene when Sally shoved me out of the way and took one right in the neck. It could have been, maybe should have been, me. I'll never forget that gal, and I barely even knew her."

"Barrie talks about always checking things out and being on the alert," said Juan, "but the problem, when we returned, is that most of the population not only isn't alert, they don't give a damn. Until these recent shootings, I was getting bored. I hate to say it, but these church killings have made life more normal for me. That's crazy."

"Pardon me for acting like a professor," said Jacob, "but that's not crazy. When you live in constant danger, your survival instincts are triggered, and each moment of life seems precious. When you returned, people didn't understand. The biggest challenge for them was calling AAA to get their car started on a cold morning."

"At least they don't have to live with having killed a bunch of women and children," said Phil. "I was in the grocery line the other day, and this fucker was whining because the clerk wouldn't accept his coupon that had expired. I lost it. I screamed right in his face. 'You scumbag, people died for your freedom, and all you can do is complain because your turd brain couldn't read the expiration date on the coupon.'"

The group broke out in laughter. "I'll bet he shit in his pants," Jalin said.

"I don't know," said Phil. "Everyone got very quiet, and I realized I had blown up again, so I just threw down the groceries I had and ran out of the store. He was an idiot, but I didn't have to lose control like that."

"That's what we are here for—to help each other with our confused feelings and find a new way to normal in this screwed up world," said Brian. "Frank and Jacob have brought us in on a different problem. How do we help a whole society—our home community—cope with their confused feelings."

"Sounds like some of our war experience might have use once again," said Barrie. "OK, Frank and Jacob, tell us what you know at this point, and let's think this through together."

"As we have already said," Frank began, "a couple of weeks ago this teenager stood up in the middle of my sermon and started shouting something about a lie and began shooting people. I came down into the aisle to try to talk him down. When he shot old Mrs. Nagle, I sort of lost it and started charging him. He turned back and shot at me."

"He was saved," said Jacob "because he was carrying a Bible, and the bullet hit the Bible first. The impact bruised his heart, and he lost consciousness. Then the police arrived and took out the shooter."

"Let's back up a little," said Juan, "what were some of the things he said?"

"Well he knew my name," said Frank, "and he kept babbling about the church being full of lies. He said he was a prophet, and then he started shooting people."

"What made you think he wasn't just some crazy who you had offended in the past, and he was getting revenge?" asked Julio.

"That's what the police thought at first," said Jacob, "and then my sister, Rachel, who is a cop, went to his high school looking for a girl he hung out with. The girl wasn't there, but they found a message in her locker. The police began to put it together that this was something bigger than one crazy kid."

"Then she shot up that Lutheran church," said Barrie.

"That's right," said Frank, "and she kept shouting about it being a lie and some confused words about Mary Magdalene. She said that Mary stole the body of Jesus and made up a lie about the resurrection."

"What's that mean?" asked Phil.

"It's probably based on the theories of some skeptics over the years that the resurrection never happened but was just made up to keep the movement going after Jesus was killed on the cross."

"That's not true, is it?" asked Juan.

Frank turned and looked at his puzzled face. "No, but the fact that a young and, from her high school record, not too bright a girl could talk that way suggests that someone was coaching her."

"So we have more than a couple of crazies in this city," said Barrie.

"It would be nice if we could at least say it was confined to this city," said Jacob, "but it gets worse."

"You've heard how hackers broke into the computers of major stores like Target and even one time into the Pentagon," said Frank.

"I don't have much sympathy for the Pentagon," said Jalin, "but it makes you wonder if anything is safe anymore. I hear the government listens to all your phone calls as well."

"Better be careful flirting with your neighbor's wife on the phone, Barrie. The government might tell your wife, and you would have real shit to pay."

"I ain't never flirted with my neighbor's wife," said Barrie, getting red in the face. "She is a cute little button, though."

"We can take care of Barrie's marital problems later," said Brian. "Let's let Frank continue with his story."

"Somehow the hackers have gotten into this, and they broke into CNN news a few nights ago and left a very scary message."

"Oh yeah, I heard about that," said Juan. "They gonna pick on Texas next. Wahoo, those cowboys going to be shooting it out at the old saloon."

"I see what you mean about being a lot bigger than Lincoln," said Phil.

"And if it is churches, how do you protect every church in Texas?" asked Frank.

"Now we are into real guerrilla and terrorist fighting, boys, and that's our territory," said Brian. "When Jacob and I were talking about this, he asked me to talk to his father, Frank here. That's what led to my suggesting that we might have some ideas that would help."

"Even if we did, who would listen?" said Jalin. "Now it's a national issue. The FBI and CIA will be into it. They ain't going to listen to a bunch of grunts like us."

"I disagree," said Frank, "and here's why. First, it started in Lincoln, and for reasons I can't figure out, I was named specifically, so they are going to want to talk to me."

"I'm not trying to be a cynic," said Phil, "but even if you have something to say, will they pay any attention to it? The way I see it, they always think they're so much smarter than the rest of us they don't have to listen to anyone else."

"Listen to his second reason," said Jacob as he smiled at his dad.

Frank raised his eyebrow at his son and continued, "Second, I have a friend, Amanda Singletary, at the Justice Department, and she is in charge of coordinating this investigation. She will listen to whatever we have to say and, knowing her, if we have something worthwhile to say, she will make sure it's heard."

"So what have you got to say?" Brian asked and turned to the group.

Juan spoke up. "When I was trying to deal with the IEDs, I was always trying to think like the terrorists and guess where they might plant them."

"When Jacob, Frank, and I were talking at his office a couple of days ago, I told them that if I was a terrorist and my goal was to paralyze the community, after the second shooting I would lay off for a week or so and let people feel the fear for a while. What do you guys think?"

"Makes sense to me," said Phil. "Course I got two legs blown off, so what do I know?"

"Hey, you almost made it through two tours, and you were driving a truck. That was like driving around with a bullseye painted on you. Besides, that last time they told you it was a dangerous run, but you wanted to get supplies to your buddies. If you'd played it safe, you'd still be dancing with the stars," said Jalin.

"I think you are right," said Julio, "so we have at least another Sunday, but where do we look? Texas is awfully big, and they have a lot of churches in every town."

"And they could be lying about Texas just to throw us off," said Barrie.

"These are American terrorists. I'll bet they not only want to terrorize the population, but they want to make the authorities look like idiots. If they do that, no one trusts anyone, and the whole society falls apart," said Jalin. "I'm guessing that they are telling the truth but in a way that will make us look like fools. It's a trick, but it's like a puzzle that when you know the answer you'll say, 'Oh, yeah, I should have seen that.'"

"Hey, Juan, did you bring your iPad?" asked Jalin.

"Sure, what's up?"

"See if you can find any town or city named Texas but not in the state of Texas," said Jalin.

"Man, that's evil," said Juan. "I wish someone had brought a six pack. This is starting to get interesting."

Jacob rose. "I just happened to bring a couple of six packs in case they were needed. They're in a cooler in the car. I'll be right back."

"I knew all that seminary training was good for something," said Julio, "I'll help you bring it in."

The group broke up, but all stood near Juan as he worked on the iPad.

Jacob and Julio brought in the beer and passed it around. Each took a long swig and smiled in appreciation.

"Bingo," said Juan, and everyone crowded around.

"It took several searches, but there is a Texas, New York, and a Texas, Wisconsin. The one in New York only has about 50 homes in it. It is connected with a town named Mexico. That's probably too small. Even if there is a church there, a stranger would be spotted right away."

"What about the one in Wisconsin?" asked Frank.

"It has a population just under 2,000. I'll bet there are several churches there. Says it's by the Wisconsin River, and the river gives the county lines unusual shape like the state of Texas."

"If that's it, we have a real clever terrorist and with a sense of macabre humor as well," said Jacob.

"Even if that is the location of the next attack, what can we do about it?" asked Frank.

"If we guessed right, at least it's a small town. Now let's think further. If the teen terrorist were to pull off an attack, how might he or she do it?" said Barrie.

"Before the attack on the Lutheran church, they put up signs on the door to try to scare people away," said Frank.

"If they are trying an end run and hit outside the state of Texas, they might put up some signs on some churches in Texas to draw attention, but they won't put up any in Wisconsin, because they won't want anyone to think they are coming," said Phil.

"So we might alert the police in the State of Texas to keep a careful watch on Saturday night," said Julio, "to see if they can catch one of the young people alive to question him, but that is a long shot with so many churches all across Texas."

"The FBI can send a notice to all the police departments and see what they come up with," said Jacob. "We could get Amanda to get that moving."

"But what about Texas, Wisconsin? Even if we could stake out most of the churches, we don't just want to scare them off," said Barrie. "Our goal is to send a little chill back down the line that maybe their operation has been compromised."

"These are American teenagers and white ones at that," said Jalin. "What's the motivation behind what they are doing?"

"I remember trying to engage Jeremy, the first shooter, in conversation to break the killing spree. I asked him who he was and what he wanted. I remember his words: 'Until today, I was nobody. Everyone will know me now. I am Jeremiah the prophet.'"

"Rachel told me that Natalie didn't have much going for her either," said Jacob.

"So we are dealing with a bunch of misfits who would rather go out in a blaze of glory than be ignored?" said Phil.

"The way that Rachel got into the high school to ask around was to pose as a college student doing a survey. Rachel says that even as the class talked about it, a couple of the students said that they understood why Jeremy did it. It's almost like there is a human yearning to be noticed, and sometimes it can become a really sick hunger," said Jacob.

"So how do we spot these kids before they shoot the place up?" asked Brian. "From what you report, Frank, instead of looking like losers, they dress like they are winners."

"They are dressing to fit into a congregation's expectations so as not to draw attention to themselves before they are ready to act," said Frank. "People look at them and begin to think *I wish my kid looked that proper,* and then the bang, bang starts. Not only are a lot of people killed, but also our biases are thrown upside down."

"It's like Jalin's little candy girl. You can't begin guarding against every well-dressed teenager in society. We have enough generation gap as it is. Those kids are supposed to be our future," Barrie said.

"How many churches would be in a little town like that?" Jalin asked.

"Maybe ten either in the town or just outside it," said Frank. "What do you have in mind?"

"Would they all have ushers or officers or deacons, or something like that?" Jalin got up even before Frank answered and began pacing around.

"Yeah, I suppose so." said Frank.

"So what if someone official contacted the pastors or head deacon and alerted them. You tell them that this probably won't happen, but we want to be prepared. They are to have several men gather at the entrances to the church, and when any youth comes in that they don't recognize, a man offers to show that person to a pew. Then he sits down with the young person and begins to talk with him or her like they are somebody."

"I get it," said Brian. "First, there is a man near the kid in case he or she decides to act. Second, the kid is treated like a real human being, which undermines the reason for shooting up the place. Third, if this teen isn't a shooter, he or she still gets treated as someone with value. I like it."

"Man, treating people like real human beings," Juan said. "What a concept? Maybe that could become a national strategy—no teen goes unfriended. I know some barrio kids that could be turned around if that became a reality."

"Of course, we still don't know if it will happen in Texas, Wisconsin," said Frank. "And even if it does, we don't know how big this conspiracy is."

"Right," said Phil, "but even if we are wrong, some teenagers in one small town have a great experience in church. That's a plus in itself."

"How do we set it up?" asked Jacob. "We have to explain this to every church in the area and not totally freak them out in the process."

"I think Amanda can help us with that," said Frank. "Is there a place where I can make a private phone call?"

"Sure," said Brian "there is an office right over there."

BUILDING A COUNTER PLAN

CHAPTER 23

Frank entered the small office, closed the door behind him and took out his iPad. He felt the urgency of the call, but he was a little nervous. Officially Mandy was the person to call but, given their rocky relationship, he was never sure what type of reception he would receive. Still he decided first to try the FaceTime App rather than a straight phone call. He had to admit that he looked forward to seeing her face. He just hoped that she would receive the call.

It rang three times, and he was beginning to have doubts that this was a wise decision when the connection was made, and he saw her smiling face appear. The slightly Asian cast to her eyes always gave him pleasure. She lifted her hand to brush back the hair from her face.

"Well, well, am I to believe this is a social call or are we all business today?" she said.

"I'd like it to be a social call, but I'm afraid we have an emerging situation that I'd like to get your reaction to and some help if possible," said Frank.

The smile left her face, and her eyes narrowed slightly as she leaned into the screen. "I'm alone in the office. What have you got?"

"Jacob put me in touch with some returned veterans who have a PTSD support group, or as they like to call it, a post traumatic growth group. The idea was that maybe the veterans knew something about how to handle panic that would be useful as I tried to help people in this city."

"Makes sense to me," said Amanda. "If they can make use of their prior experience to help someone else, it will probably help them as well."

Frank grinned. "I admit that that crossed my mind when I agreed to meet with them."

"Always the pastor," Mandy said.

"In our conversation, they began to talk about how terrorists operate and how we should respond," said Frank. "We started talking about the latest feed into the media declaring this terror would spread to Texas next."

"We have every law enforcement agency we can lay our hands on spread out all over Texas, but there are so blooming many churches that it is impossible to cover them," said Amanda. "It's at times like this that I wish Christianity hadn't spread so well."

"I wish we had done a better job in explaining the faith to those churches so that the accusation that they are full of lies wouldn't stir so many doubts among people," said Frank.

"Some of my people have raised doubts" said Amanda, "and wonder if their threat is just another lie meant to throw us off."

"Well, that is part of what I'm calling about," said Frank. "Mandy, what if it was both true and meant to throw us off at the same time?"

"I'm listening," said Mandy as she grabbed a tablet and pen prepared to take notes.

"We were talking about the threat to the state of Texas and the possibility it was a lie when one of the veterans came up with an intriguing idea. He thought the whole plan might be a unique form of American terrorism. Not only do terrorists want to spread panic but they also want to make fools out of law enforcement, the church, and the government."

Amanda bent over as she took notes. Frank tried not to be distracted by her dark hair falling in front of her face. "So how do they make fools out of us?"

"This may be farfetched, but what if after the attack was over everyone could see that the terrorists had told the truth, but the authorities had been too stupid to recognize what was right in front of them?" said Frank.

"Society depends on people having at least some trust in the structure that holds them together," said Amanda. "You think you may have figured out how they plan to do that?"

"We still have to do what you have already set up in the state of Texas," said Frank, "but what if it occurred in Texas but not in the state of Texas?"

Amanda stopped writing and slightly tilted her head as she stared at the screen. Frank could see her trying to process the idea even as she waited for him to continue.

"There are at least two towns outside the state of Texas that are named Texas. There may be more," said Frank.

"Damn," she said. He saw her reach for an iPad. "Tell me where the towns are," she said even as she began to enter her query.

"There is a Texas, New York, and a Texas, Wisconsin."

"Tell me more about them as I look them up," said Amanda, even as her fingers danced across her keyboard.

"Texas, New York, is a small community associated with a town called Mexico, New York. It has only about 50 residents, and our group thought it would be too easy for some strange teenagers to be noticed," said Frank.

"And Wisconsin?" Amanda asked as she looked up at the screen.

"It has about 2,000 residents," said Frank. "We would need to watch both towns, but the guys think the larger town would be the most likely target."

"Hold on a second," said Amanda, "I want some other people in on this conversation. She reached over and pressed a button. "Church Task Force, in my office stat."

"Now that is what I call authority," said Frank with a wink.

Almost before he had finished speaking the door behind her burst open and five people crowded around her. Amanda quickly filled them in on her conversation with Frank. "Laura, I want you to do a thorough search of the Internet for any community, town, county, or division outside of the state of Texas with the name Texas.

"Eric, I want you to find out who the officials are in both Texas, New York, and Texas, Wisconsin. Then arrange for a conference call to both sets of officials. Don't make the call yet. Just get it ready."

"Amanda," Frank said, "and Amanda turned back to the screen. Make sure they also find the contact numbers for all the pastors or lay leaders of religious communities in those towns."

"Add that to your list, Eric," Amanda said.

"The rest of you gather around the table. I'll put Frank on speaker phone, and we will project the picture up on the larger screen."

Frank heard the scraping of chairs and the sounds of electronics being connected. "While you are getting that set up, I want to bring in the men who helped me identify this idea. They are in the other room. We won't have the fancy setup that you have, but at least they will be able to hear and respond."

Frank walked back to the men from the support group. "OK, guys, we are now connected with the task force of the Justice Department that focuses on this issue. The director is Amanda Singletary, a personal friend. I've explained our idea about Texas, Wisconsin, and they want to explore it in more depth."

The six vets and Jacob gathered around the desk where the phone was.

"I'll put us on speaker phone, but it is a small speaker, so you will have to listen closely," said Frank.

"Au contraire mon ami," said Juan. "I have two small speakers that can plug into your iPad, so all of us can hear." Juan proceeded to connect some speakers that had been sitting in the corner of the room.

"Did you hear that?" said Jalin. "We have a French-speaking immigrant from Guatemala who has gone high tech on us."

"Watch it, ghetto man," said Juan, "remember I'm also an expert on small explosives. If you move off that chair, you might fly straight up."

"I hesitate to interrupt this stimulating conversation but allow me at least to share your names with Amanda and her group. Amanda, Jacob is here."

"Hi, Jacob, glad you are part of this."

"Also, for simplicity sake, I'll just give you the first names of our six veterans. They are Jalin, Juan, Barrie, Phil, Julio, and Brian."

"Hello, fellows" said Amanda. "If this develops as I think it will, my task force and I will be having several conversations with you. Thank you both for your past service and for helping us on this puzzle as well."

"To save time, I'm going to lay out some of the ideas this group generated," said Frank. "And by the way, it was Jalin who first thought of the idea, and Juan found the two towns we mentioned."

"Great thinking guys," said one of the male voices in Amanda's office.

"So, the question is, how do we go about this in a way that doesn't broadcast we are there. If it is planned for one of these towns, we don't want them to see us coming and just run off and plan for another day," said Frank.

"Also," said Jalin, "we want to break their mystique. Terrorists strive on being both cruel and invisible. They want people scared of them, but also they want to look more in control than they are. At least that's the way they worked in the Stan and also in my ghetto when I was growing up."

"But even if it is in this town, how can we cover all the churches without being noticed?" said a female voice in Amanda's office.

"That's where the phone call from you comes in," said Frank. "We figured if we could talk to both the police and the pastors, we might develop a plan but also convince them to keep quiet about it."

"OK," said Amanda, "in a small town like these two, that might work, but what are we going to tell them when we talk to them?"

"No teen goes unfriended in that town," said Barrie.

"Say that again," said Amanda.

"I was thinking about that first shooter," said Frank. "He said something about no one knowing who he was, but now he would be remembered. When you think about what little we know about Natalie, she also seems to be a neglected child. We're thinking that someone is recruiting alienated teenagers with the prize of being a part of something that will make their names go down in history."

"They could even be teens that their neighbors know," said Julio. "When we had trouble in the barrio where I grew up, the gangs were often made up of kids we knew. In a small town like Texas, New York, it might be smart to recruit someone that no one would notice because the kid was familiar."

"Yeah," said Phil, "small towns can make you feel like you're nobody and no one cares."

Frank saw Amanda take a piece of paper from one of her aides. She glanced at the paper and then back at the screen.

"OK, we have a list of officials and several names of pastors, but we can't find the pastor's name for all the churches that we have identified. Some have something called a 'lay pastor.' What's that?"

"If it is a small church or between pastors, a trained lay person might fill in as a pastor," said Frank.

Another voice behind Amanda spoke up, "In both communities, it looks as if they have a church or so with in the town limits but also several just outside the town. Do we need to cover all of them?"

Jacob spoke up. "We need to cover all those nearby, just to be on the safe side. However, since they are trying to make us look like complete fools, my money is on churches that are within the official town limits."

"OK," said Amanda, "but if we are trying to cover them without being noticed, how are we going to do that in these small communities? Any stranger will stand out like a sore thumb."

"That's where the phone calls come in. Our first layer of defense will be the church members themselves. We'll have the pastor identify some trusted members and tell them what to do."

"We'll be putting untrained civilians at risk," said a female voice in Amanda's room. "Is that wise?"

"It's like in the Stan," said Jalin. "The civies are already at risk. By recruiting them ahead of time, they at least have some idea of what to do when the shit hits the fan."

"Jalin is right," said Frank. "If our idea is right, one of those churches has people whose lives are in danger. Our hope is that we can lessen the damage."

"The other possibility," said another voice in Amanda's office, "is this is all fantasy, and we will look like idiots anyway."

Amanda glared off to her left side and then turned back to the screen. "If we are wrong, two little towns will have a weekend of excitement but live peacefully while we have a bloodbath somewhere in the state of Texas. Let's hear the rest of your plan."

"There is plan A and plan B. Plan B is easiest to explain," said Frank.

"We have the cavalry hiding behind the rocks," said Brian.

"Say what?" asked Amanda.

"Netflix strikes again," said Barrie. "You've been watching too many of those old Westerns."

"But he is not far off," said Frank. "While we can't have a lot of strangers roaming the streets of these towns, we thought we could have them stationed outside of these towns and start driving into town about the time these worship services are taking place. The police force will also be alerted, and we might sneak a few guys into their station during the night."

"I suppose it is obvious," said Jalin, "but our posse can't be waiting outside of town in black SUV's and the drivers wearing sunglasses. We need them to look like normal people from nearby communities, so we need to spread them out and give them old cars and pickups."

"All right," said Amanda, "that can be arranged, but what is plan A. That has to be up close and personal if we are going to prevent a blood bath."

"That's right," said Frank. "Our idea is a little sketchy here, but this is the best we can come up with. I'll let Barrie explain it."

"When I was growing up in church," said Barrie, "the church always had a bunch of male ushers and deacons present at every service. Our idea is to have the pastors round up several men in their church. These men will hang around the entrances to the sanctuary."

"But won't it seem strange having all these men hanging around? Now days a lot of the ushers are women."

"First of all, they won't gather until right before the service. Second, Jalin came up with an idea about how to make it look strange and normal at the same time. Tell them, Jalin."

"In my parent's church, they always had special Sundays—women's day, father's day, missionary day, and even youth Sunday. My idea is to have the pastors declare this *Befriend a Youth Day*. On this Sunday, every young person that enters the church is treated as special."

"Part of that special treatment," continued Brian, "is that every youth will be escorted to a seat by an adult who will sit with them and begin a conversation about the youth's life, future, and dreams."

"We figure that will be a good experience anyway," said Frank, "and all the time the adult will be watching the hands of the youth. If the youth begins to make a suspicious move, the adult will immediately hug the youth while talking about how special that person is. That way, if there is a gun present, the young person will not be able to get it out and start shooting, or if a shot is fired the person can be quickly subdued."

"And the pastor," said Jacob, "will be supplied an alarm signal that can be pushed to alert the cavalry that it is time to move and where to come. Of course, if there is more than one church, the police will have to be prepared to split up."

"That's so simple," said a voice on Amanda's right side, "that it might work."

"And even if it doesn't," said a female voice, "a lot of young people will experience what it is like to be seen as important. That's sheer genius."

"So, Frank," said Amanda, "when we set up this conference call, I think it would be good if we patched you into it and let you explain the church part. Not only are you a pastor, but you were also the first church to get shot."

"I'm ready to do that. Just let me know when you are ready."

"I'd say in about a half-hour."

"Contact the pastor of the biggest church in town," said Frank. "Fill him in on the reason for the phone call and ask for his or her help in identifying the churches without pastors.

"Don't they have some type of association that can contact all of them?" asked Amanda.

"For the most part, those organizations disappeared in recent years," said Frank. "Impress on the pastor that you need contact with the independent churches as well as the mainline churches. We won't be able to reach all of the pastors, but we can get those we do reach to find out how to contact those we are missing and have a second call to them."

Amanda rolled her eyes. "I'm glad to know that you all work so closely together. Where's this love your neighbor stuff I've heard about?"

"It went the same way as all the law enforcement agencies communicating with each other," said Frank. "Fortunately this is a small town, so we should be able to reach most people."

"All right, we will be back in touch. Tell all your guys thank you. This may be the first break we've gotten."

Frank saw Amanda lean forward and click the disconnect. Did she wink? He couldn't tell, but it stirred some old feelings in him just the same.

PREPARATIONS FOR THE WEEKEND

CHAPTER 24

Frank knew that the conversation with the pastors in Texas, Wisconsin, was crucial to their plan. Even in a small town, there would be a variety of religious perspectives and not a lot of trust between the churches. In about fifteen minutes, he had to convince them that their diverse religious perspectives would not be compromised by working together and working with the government would not violate their understanding of the separation of church and state.

He turned to his group. "Why don't you take a break with some of those pastries? Let Jacob and me discuss my best approach to the pastors."

As the group began to gather around the pastries at the bar, Frank and Jacob pulled off by themselves in a corner.

"Even though it is a small town, my guess is that some of these pastors will be more used to competing than cooperating." He sighed,

"I'm afraid that some of their theological differences will immediately make them suspicious. We need immediate cooperation from the beginning," said Frank.

"It's ironic," said Jacob, "but Jesus had it right from the beginning. The issue is the love of neighbor, not agreement on doctrine. I suggest that you focus on how their cooperation can save lives and let them know how important they are to the process. That's love of neighbor at ground level, but it also appeals to our need to be at the center of the action."

"OK, we impress on these pastors the critical nature of their participation and their silence. They'll need to recruit at least ten to thirty men depending on the size of the church." Frank paused, scratched his head, and looked towards the ceiling. "It would be a whole lot easier if we knew whether the shooters will hit a large or small church."

"All of this is guesswork," said Jacob, " but I think we can bet on their naive cleverness."

"What do you mean?"

"These are not pros. The organizers are planning by the seat of their pants. They get this brilliant idea about how to make everybody look like fools."

Frank felt his forehead wrinkle and his right eyebrow lower. "I'm listening."

"Whoever is organizing this thinks the shooters will catch everyone by surprise. If they hit a small church, it would be tragic but a little surprise. If they hit a larger church, there will be more deaths, more panic, and a bigger news splash around the world."

Jacob turned to the veterans at the bar. "Hey, guys, if you were going to make a surprise hit on Texas, Wisconsin, would you pick a small or a big church?"

Julio was the first to respond. "No one knows you are coming, so you hit the biggest fucking church in town. Causes the most damage and spreads the most terror."

"Yeah," said Barrie. "If you hit a small one, all the big churches would say there is safety in numbers."

The other vets added their voice in agreement.

Frank's lips puckered and he nodded. "So we put all of them on alert, but we add additional emphasis on how the big churches respond."

"But Dad, make sure that you make the pastors know how important they all are. There could always be more than one young person sent on this mission."

Barrie stood and spoke to the group. "If I were planning this surprise, I'd send two or three. Not too many to get noticed, but when it goes off, I'd want havoc everywhere."

"Might even stagger it," added Juan. "Remember how some of those rag heads would set off a bomb in one place, and just as everyone was rushing there, they'd set off another bomb. Pretty soon everyone was paralyzed. The civilians didn't know where to run."

"Damn," said Phil, "if the terrorists do this right, they could have the whole town running in circles."

"Which is why," said Jacob, "your experience is going to help us be better prepared."

Just then Frank's iPhone buzzed. He glanced at the screen and saw that it was Amanda.

"Mandy, I thought we were going to do this by FaceTime?"

"My engineers think it might work better on Google Hangout. They contacted Google and got special permission to do an enlarged meeting format. Do you have a laptop that can tie into the speakers you have?"

"Yeah, we have two or three in the group."

"OK, I'll shoot you instructions. We are contacting the clergy now. We've asked them to be ready to access us in a private location. We're having some trouble locating some of the pastors or lay pastors of the small churches. We are still trying . . ."

"Mandy, that may not be necessary. As we have thought it through, it seems much more likely that it will be in one of the large churches. It would get the most press there—spread the terror."

"You're probably right. Though we might as well alert as many as we can, just to be safe."

"I agree, but to keep the rumors down, we might let the pastors we talk to on the first call alert others after we are done talking. It's going to be pretty important that someone doesn't leak this while chatting in a local diner or gossiping on the phone."

"Sounds wise, I . . ."

"Mandy, Jacob and the guys came up with an additional wrinkle that we need to be prepared for. It's possible that the organizers might send out two or more shooters to different churches, so our officers need to hold back some units when the first alarm goes off, just in case."

"That's scary. I'll alert the teams. Why don't you set up your computers and be ready to log on in about another half-hour."

"We'll get ready. Talk to you then."

Frank gave instructions about connecting the computers, and Juan hooked the speakers up as well as a projector that they found in the back storeroom.

Twenty minutes later, instructions came from Google on how to connect into the group conversation. Naturally it didn't work at first, but a Google engineer was quick to guide them through the necessary adjustments.

When the screen lit up again, about fifteen small squares surrounded the screen, and Amanda was on the enlarged screen in the center. She immediately took control of the conversation.

"Ladies and gentlemen, I appreciate all of you entering into this electronic conversation on such short notice. Because this is very important, I need to ask each of you if you are in a secure location that is not likely to be interrupted by unexpected visitors. If so, since I can see all of you in your little boxes around the screen, if you will just raise your hand, I will take that as an affirmative."

Frank could see each of the pastors raise their hands and nod their heads. They looked solemn and tense.

"Ms. Singletary," said a voice, and the picture of a uniformed officer took the center screen. "I'm assuming that it is OK, but I have invited my assistant chief and the sheriff to sit in on the conversation. That way we can coordinate and not have any jurisdictional issues."

"That was good thinking, chief. Thank you for making it clear. I have two others here with me to help me answer any questions that might arise."

Amanda took a deep breath and breathed it out through her mouth. "OK, I'll try to be as clear as possible about why you have been asked to gather in this rather dramatic way." She cleared her throat and leaned forward.

"You are all aware of the tragic shootings that have taken place in Lincoln, North Carolina, and the threat put out on the networks. The news media interruption suggested that this violent act might spread beyond Lincoln. For several reasons that we will explain, we think it is possible that whoever this group is may have targeted your town.

"I have here The Reverend Frank Sessions, who was the pastor of the first church shootings and who was shot himself. He will try to give you some of the reasons that have led us to this conclusion."

Frank came on the screen. As he glanced at his image projected on the screen, he noticed that he looked tired, and his clothes looked like he had slept in them. He looked intently at the screen. "Ladies and gentlemen, as Ms. Singletary has said, we think it is possible that the next target of the shooters may be in your town, and we need your help to make sure this does not result in another tragedy."

He noticed every one of his listeners sit forward. He proceeded to explain to them how they had reached this conclusion.

"I'll just cancel church," said one of the pastors.

"I'm hoping that you will not do that until you hear my proposal," said Frank. "If churches start canceling services, the people who planned this horror will be alerted and just disappear until another opportunity arises. If we are right, they think they are very clever, and, hopefully, they will make some mistakes that will help us break this wide open."

"By the way," interrupted Amanda, "as you speak, will you identify yourself and your church so that we can keep track of who is present."

"I'm Reverend Troy During from Community Gospel. I appreciate your explanation, but it seems pretty farfetched to me. We could end up being the people who look like fools."

"There is that risk," admitted Frank. "But having been the target of the first shooting, I know the tragic results of our not being prepared, and I am willing to risk looking foolish if there is any chance that I can help prevent a bloodbath in one of your churches."

"Ralph Emerson of First Methodist here. I understand where Troy is coming from, but that crazy logic sounds just like the kind of thinking that might appeal to some youngster looking to make an impact. Do we have any clue as to who these insane people are?"

"I'm afraid not," Frank said, rubbing his jaw and looking again at the screen. "My daughter is the police officer who interviewed some of the people who knew the first shooters. What she heard is confirmed by some traffic on the Internet that we have picked up. It seems that someone with a vendetta against the church is seeking to recruit alienated youth to do their violent bidding."

"But why would anyone in their right mind fall for such an evil scheme that only gets them dead?" asked one of the pastors.

Amanda spoke up, "A lot of people have been trying to figure that out. The reality is that there are a couple of hundred youth who have tried to go and fight for ISIS and more than one incident in our schools where a youth has walked in and opened fire without ever planning to walk out alive. It's sad, but they see violence as dramatic, a way to make an impact that can't be ignored."

"In those few cases where we have been able to talk to youth bent on such an act, the common denominator seems to be a total breakdown in their orientation in life. The universe holds no logic for them," said Frank.

"But why do they choose to strike out in violence?" asked another pastor.

Frank felt the hand of his son Jacob rest gently on his arm. He glanced at Jacob who gently shook his head indicating that Frank should not get sucked into the conversation.

Frank turned back to the camera. "That is a good discussion for us to have at another time. Right now, if they do strike in your town, we want you to be ready for them in a way that will lessen their impact."

"What do you propose?" Emerson asked.

Frank noticed that many of the pastors had a pad of paper and pen at the ready. "What we propose is this. In your own words, you inform the church that in light of the tragic shootings in Lincoln, the churches in Texas have decided to declare this Sunday a "Befriend a Youth Sunday." As part of your preparation, you will recruit several men, the number determined by the size of the church, who will stand at your entrances to receive whatever youth arrive."

An Episcopal priest spoke up. "Are we just looking for youth who are strangers?"

"Not necessarily," said Frank. "To make this look authentic, we want every youth that enters your door to be greeted and ushered towards a special section set aside for youth and their male accompaniment. The man taking them towards the seat will stay with him or her and immediately engage them in a conversation. Where possible, have the man sit next to the aisle."

Jacob spoke up. "The idea is to ask the young people questions about their lives, their values, goals, sports, schools, etc. Most young people think that adults don't understand them. We want them to feel as if they are the center of these men's undivided attention, and that they are of value."

"That could be valuable regardless of whatever else happens," said Troy.

"Our hope is that even if nothing happens, the youth will have been listened to in a way that makes them feel important," said Frank. "However, if a youth appears to be reaching for something that might be a gun, the man will be present to respond. The first clue may be if the youth tries to stand. If that happens, the man will immediately put his arm around the youth and give a hug pulling the young person back towards the seat. If the man does see a weapon, he will cry out for help."

"And what are we supposed to do?" asked a pastor.

"You will each be given an electronic signal that you will push to send a signal to the police, who will immediately come to your church," said Amanda.

"What if we push the button by mistake?" asked another pastor.

"There will be a second button that you can push three times to indicate that all is clear," responded Amanda.

"How will the rest of us know where the attack is taking place?" asked the Episcopal Priest.

"Our concern is that if the group is really clever, they might send more than one shooter so that they can spread panic all through the town, so we will wait until your services are all over before we send word that all is clear," said Jacob.

"Is there any clue as to which churches will be the most likely targets?" asked a Catholic Priest.

"Remember that this is insanity, so there is no real logic," said Frank. "Based on our assumption that they want to spread the terror as far as possible, we guess that they will likely pick on one of the larger churches in town. However, we want everyone to be on alert, just in case we are wrong."

"May I make one additional request," said Emerson. "My church is one of the larger churches in town, so it will be one of the scarier Sundays in my ministry. We've not always worked together as closely as we should in the past. I'm asking all of you to have the churches in this town in your prayers and also the youth of this nation."

"Emerson," said Troy, "you and I have not always seen eye to eye on many issues, but I not only promise to pray for your church and the other churches, but I invite all of us to come together next week and continue our prayers for this nation and its many churches. If, the Lord willing, my church is spared this Sunday, I will provide the lunch for a meeting on Wednesday at Community Gospel. If we are not spared, I pray that another church will issue an invitation of their own. Regardless, we need to gather."

The conversation continued for another half-hour making sure that someone was in charge of contacting the pastors of those churches not present on the phone call.

When it was over, Frank felt himself wilt from all the tension his body had been feeling. As he sat back in his chair, he heard a burst of applause coming from the veterans.

"All right, preach."

"You did good, rev."

"I don't even believe all that stuff, and you almost made a believer out of me," said another.

"Jacob, you have a righteous father. What do we do next?'

"We'd better get prepared," said Julio. "Bin Laden didn't ever try to put all his eggs in one basket. He was always trying to think about several ways to cause havoc. I think we had better begin thinking about other possibilities."

"I agree," said Barrie. "If this works, that's great, but it is only one small part of the war. There will be more battles."

"Why don't we think about it, and regardless of what happens this weekend, we will continue this discussion at our meeting next Thursday," said Brian. "And Frank, Jacob, we would be honored if you could meet with us."

TEXAS, WISCONSIN

CHAPTER 25

Fifth Sunday in Lent

Ralph Emerson felt his gut tighten. He convinced five trusted men to leave work early and meet him at the church on Friday evening. Though they were curious, for once they had sensed the urgency in the pastor's voice and not questioned him when he told them that they needed to come to the church for the explanation. They were shocked when he explained to them what they were facing. If there was a hint of skepticism in any of their thoughts, it was quickly wiped away when he reported on the conference call on Friday from the Justice Department. Shaken to the core, they immediately offered their support. The church held two services on Sunday morning, and he needed to prepare for both. They carefully identified twenty men to be present for both services. His plan was to have each of the five contact four other men from the list and have them meet him at the church at eight a.m. for a preworship meeting.

He also sent out a special bulletin to his congregation declaring that all of the clergy in their town agreed to focus their worship service on a response to the tragedy in Lincoln, N C. As part of that emphasis, the Sunday service would focus on celebrating the youth of their congregation and praying for the youth around the nation. While they were far away from these events, he told them, they were all part of the Body of Christ. He then quoted the admonition of St. Paul in 1 Corinthians 12:26: "If one member suffers, all suffer together with it." He knew that the other pastors in town were sending similar messages to their congregation.

He spent a restless Friday evening reconstructing his worship service and rewriting his sermon. He didn't consider himself a good preacher, but, more than ever before, he felt a power flow through his body and his brain as he prepared. His support group was to report on Saturday afternoon. He paced the sanctuary Saturday morning trying to picture how these events might take place. Frequently he found himself falling to his knees and praying for God to give him strength and to protect all the churches in the town.

Saturday at 3 p.m., his chosen cohort of five men arrived in the sanctuary. There was a gravity to their demeanor like soldiers preparing for battle. He was both surprised and pleased to hear that each of them had recruited their requisite number, and all of the recruits had pledged secrecy and willingness to be at the church Sunday morning at 8 a.m.

They walked the sanctuary together as he explained the idea of having a man accompany each young person who entered the sanctuary. They agreed that all of the youth, male and female, would be accompanied by an adult and would be ushered to a reserved set of pews near the front of the sanctuary. The celebration of youth theme would provide an acceptable reason for separating youth from their families. They rehearsed how to explain to their selected adults the importance of having an adult sit on the outermost seat of the pew to prevent anyone from leaping up and gaining extra room in the aisles.

They talked about the strategy of being ready to subdue a youth and hoped it would never become necessary. They prayed together that no violent incident would occur and that all the youth who entered their sanctuary would be made to feel special.

"Well, pastor," one of the men said as they were preparing to leave, "I hope we can all meet in a couple of days and have a good laugh about what didn't happen, but I want you to know how much I respect you for the courage and planning you have given to this."

"Texas, Wisconsin," said another. "Who'd of thought that would be a dangerous name for a town? The weird part is that it is just crazy enough I'm afraid something might just happen. I hope the other churches have a pastor as wise as you are proving to be."

Strange, Ralph thought as the men left the sanctuary, *I've thought about leaving the ministry several times in the last ten years, but I've never felt a deeper sense of satisfaction than right at this moment.*

He thought about the other pastors in town. He especially wondered about St. Mary's Episcopal and Holy Trinity Catholic. These were the three biggest churches in town. If someone wants to create a big splash, we are the places to attack. He was touched by The Reverend Troy's invitation to come together next week. That will be good, regardless of what happens tomorrow.

As he prepared to leave the sanctuary, he glanced up at the cross that hung on the back wall of the sacristy. *Interesting. You came in violence, and you left in violence. I sure hope it is true that God so loved the world. There are times I wonder what there is to love.*

Sunday morning came all too soon for all the pastors in Texas, Wisconsin. Each went nervously towards their church to prepare for worship. This time it wasn't how prepared they were for worship, the quality of their sermon, or whether they would have a full sanctuary that concerned them. Several of them passed other churches as they made their way to their church. Later they would confess that they found themselves praying for the other churches and a little ashamed of themselves that they had never done it before.

Ralph arrived at First Methodist at 7 a.m. He carefully opened the doors to the church and walked through the sanctuary towards his office. He stopped in the little kitchenette and prepared a pot of coffee, setting out some cream and sugar.

By 7:30 a.m. his five leaders had arrived and several of the men they had recruited began to arrive soon afterward. By 7:50 a.m. all that had been asked were present and nervously drinking some coffee and making small talk.

Ralph looked at the men assembled and invited them to share in a brief opening prayer. When he looked up, they were all watching him closely. "When you were baptized and later confirmed, you committed yourselves to the way of discipleship." He paused and allowed his eyes to look at each one of them. "You have never been more faithful than you are today."

He proceeded to describe for them the potential for violence that might occur today and the plans that he and his five recruiters had made. Several glanced away, trying to gather their thoughts. They would like to dismiss this as a crazy idea, but they had too much respect for the men who had called them.

After describing the plan again and answering the few questions that they had, he asked them to enter the sanctuary and go to their assigned entrance point. "Make sure you are comfortable with your assignment and then grab another coffee if you want. Find a seat near your assigned entrance. The first service, the contemporary one, is more informal, and many others will bring their coffee. The pews for the youth have been marked off. Remember that 98 %, and hopefully 100%, of the youth who will be here are just good wholesome young people. Take advantage of the opportunity to get to know them, affirm them, and thank them for being part of this church. Let them know that this Sunday is a beginning of what you hope will be a continuing friendship. If you are willing, offer them a way to contact you if you can be of support."

Two hours later, Ralph Emerson breathed a sigh of relief. He glanced at the electronic device he had kept close to him and didn't see any indication of trouble in the other churches as well. I'll bet the blood pressure of every pastor in town will go up several notches this

Sunday, he thought. May God bless them with a peaceful Sunday. He glanced around at the twenty men spread around the sanctuary, was pleased to see some of them still engaged in a conversation with one of the young people. He noticed others glance towards him and give a thumbs up sign.

Amanda had arrived at the police station around 6 a.m. She had recruited twenty additional agents and stationed them near but not in the city limits. Some of them were in pickup trucks, a couple of guys in a bakery delivery van, and three Chevys, two Toyotas, and a couple of Fords. She called each of them to make sure they were in position. Some of them had stopped at a gas station, others at some crossroads along the highway leading into town. Some others had found an unobtrusive camping site outside of town. The earliest worship service was at 8 a.m., a mass with minimal attendance. Others had services beginning at nine or nine-thirty. Everybody agreed that the most likely scenario would be during the 10:30 a.m. or 11 a.m. services. The police and sheriff deputies were at their normal posts, although extras had been called in and congregated at the police station. The traffic was light, typical of a Sunday morning.

Frank and Jacob had insisted on accompanying Amanda and were now conversing quietly with some of the officers at the station.

At precisely 11 a.m., the organist at First Methodist began ringing the chimes to announce the beginning of the service. When the choir finished singing the introit, Ralph stood behind the choir and joined the procession down the aisle. He had chosen the robust hymn, "The Church's One Foundation," to open the service. The third verse began as he climbed the chancel steps. The words became his prayer, "Though with a scornful wonder this world see her oppressed, by schisms rent asunder, by heresies distressed. . . . and soon the night of weeping shall be the morn of song." Oh, how he prayed for that to be true.

He glanced around the sanctuary and particularly towards the section that had been set aside for the young people. He had watched carefully prior to the service as the men ushered young people to their seats. Most thought it a little strange but were willing to participate. A couple rebelled. If they were with their parents, the man assigned to the youth asked if he might sit with the young person and the parents. If they were alone, the man asked where he might sit with them.

The early part of the service went smoothly. The nation felt tense because of the shootings, and the congregation seemed pleased to see their church making an effort to reach out to the young people. As Ralph rose to read the Scripture, he noticed some movement in the third row of the section set aside for the young people. At first it seemed just to be some loud chatter, but soon he heard the chilling shout "It's a lie, and some of you are going to die." He gripped his electronic signal but paused to make absolutely sure of what was happening. The young person who had shouted was struggling to rise. He was nicely dressed in a blue suit. Ralph guessed he was about one hundred and fifty pounds and a little pudgy. The man who was with him, an older man, was not nearly his match, but he was clinging to him with a strength generated by desperation. "No, Daniel, don't do it," he shouted.

Ralph pushed the call button and then ran down the chancel steps to assist. As he neared the pew where the young person was, he heard the gun explode and the man wailing in pain. Ralph was in his late 50s and overweight, but adrenalin pushed him forward, and he launched himself towards the youth who was trying to climb over the man he had shot. His momentum struck the youth knocking him back over the pew even as the gun went off a second time. The bullet grazed Ralph's arm and then struck the communion cup at the base of the chancel steps. As Ralph and Daniel went over the pew into the laps of some other youth, an athletic young man grabbed the gun in one hand while a blond girl at his side sunk her teeth into the shooter's arm. Within less than a minute, Daniel was subdued and weeping. "It's not fair," he cried. "You are supposed to die like the other times."

Several men helped subdue the young man called Daniel. Others helped Ralph off the pile. One ran to get the first aid kit to attend to his wound. The sanctuary doors opened, and the agents who had been alerted by the signal entered. The wounded man was shot in the fleshy part of his thigh. A nurse, who was part of the congregation, quickly applied a tourniquet and attended to him until the ambulance arrived.

While there were some screams and a couple of people fainted, it quickly became apparent that the shooter was in custody. Assisted by two men at his side, Ralph stood and grabbed a microphone. "Please sit down and allow the officers to take charge. I assure you that I am all right—just a little excess blood that I probably didn't need anyway."

People began to lower themselves into the pews. It was clear that many of them were in shock. "I want you to begin repeating the 23rd Psalm," said Ralph, "and keep repeating it until you feel calmer." He began, "The Lord is my shepherd . . ." And soon the whole congregation began to pray the psalm with increased energy.

As Ralph would learn later that afternoon, a similar scene had taken place at St. Mary's Episcopal Church, only this time the shooter was a young lady. The difference was she had resisted being seated in the special section and began an argument. As a couple of men were talking to her, she was clearly very nervous. She began to reach for the gun in her purse while making her prepared speech. While one of the men grabbed for her arm, the gun went off striking him in the foot, but otherwise there were no other overt injuries.

The other churches did not experience any disruption.

Amanda turned to Frank. "Thanks to you we were lucky this time, but I'll bet we don't get much information from either shooter. What is happening, Frank? How does this end?"

"I wish I knew," said Frank. "Whoever is behind this is going to be frustrated. We won a small victory, but I suspect our enemy is going to be energized to prove the worst is yet to come."

NO VICTORY IS COMPLETE

CHAPTER 26

Daniel, the shooter at First Methodist, and Shirley, the shooter at St. Mary's Episcopal, were both taken into custody. The small town police were uncertain about what to do next. Since it had national implications, they seemed quite willing to let Amanda coordinate the next steps.

"The first thing we need to do is prepare for the media onslaught that will begin within the next hour," Amanda said. "I talked to the rector at St. Mary's and the Reverend Emerson at First Methodist and asked them to refer all inquiries to us here at the station."

"That will work for the pastors, but if I were a reporter, I'd be going for the church members, and they won't be easy to rein in," said the police chief. "People are pretty independent in this town, and, no offense, but they don't hold the federal government in high esteem."

"I'm under no illusion that we will be able to control what people say, but I do want to set up an official response that doesn't exacerbate our problems," said Amanda. "We are dealing with something we don't fully understand."

"So what do you want us to do?"

"To begin, I want to address all of your officers and the sheriff and his deputies. Can you arrange a meeting in the next half-hour? I figure there is less than an hour before the national media figures out where Texas, Wisconsin, is."

"The one advantage to a small town," said the chief, "is we can set that up in the conference room in fifteen minutes. I'll contact the sheriff. Paul's a good man. He'll cooperate."

"Thanks, chief. Let me huddle with Frank and Jacob. I'll talk to your people, and, if it's all right, Jacob, who has a background in psychology, can begin conversations with the shooters."

The chief hesitated.

"Believe me, Jacob knows his stuff. You can have an officer in the corner, if you want, but I'd like him to have first crack at these kids."

"OK, I guess this is on you." The chief proceeded to set up the conference with his officers. Amanda turned to Frank. "My fear is this is going to unleash some craziness all around the country. We have to convey the impression we know what we are doing, even if we don't."

"So what are you going to tell them?"

"I'm going to remind them of the national importance of how the media interprets whatever they say as reporters. They need to be reminded we are entering what could be a major crisis. Everybody is tempted to say something that will make them standout, put them on the national news. It could contribute to an increasing hysteria in our country or be used by whoever is behind this to advance their objectives."

Frank ran his fingers through his hair and blew out a breath. "I wish we could identify what the objective is. I keep wondering what I'm missing and why my church was the first target?"

"We need to think about that," said Amanda, "but regardless of what triggered this, hysteria tends to build on hysteria, and we have to find a way to dampen this down."

Frank grabbed a chocolate covered donut and smelled the aroma of freshly brewed coffee. As he bit into the donut, he watched some police officers move towards the conference room along with two or three sheriff deputies. "Your meeting is about to begin. Do you want me with you, or should I sit in on the interviews with Jacob?"

"I can handle the officers. See if you can pick up something from what the youth say in their interrogations."

"OK. Oh, I did think of one promising angle we can take with the media."

"What's that?"

"From what Ralph said at the church, a couple of young people acted promptly to help him. May have even saved his life. Since this whole thing seems focused on youth feeling no one listens to them, we should give the media some young heroes. Why let the shooters get all the attention?"

Amanda stared at him for a couple of seconds with a quizzical look on her face. "Sometimes you amaze me, Frank Sessions. I'll lay the groundwork for that, but you keep thinking about how we can interpret that to the reporters. I'm sure one of the persons they will want to interview is the pastor who seems to get himself mixed up in the strangest mysteries of our time."

"I don't seek . . ."

Amanda reached out and patted him on the shoulder. "I know, Frank, but you might think about how you want to present yourself because soon it will be one question after another."

"You're right, Mandy. By the way, you're pretty quick on your feet as well." He winked and turned as he said, "Good luck with the officers. We'll compare notes over supper."

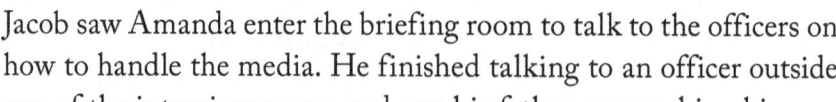

Jacob saw Amanda enter the briefing room to talk to the officers on how to handle the media. He finished talking to an officer outside one of the interview rooms and saw his father approaching him.

Frank said, "At least there are some live shooters this time. I wonder what we can learn from them."

Jacob said, "The boy is in room one and the girl in room three.

Both have two-way mirrors. I'll go in alone, and you watch through the mirror to see what you can pick up from body and tone as well as whatever they say. My hope is that, being closer to their age, I might be less intimidating."

"Sounds good to me. Which one are you going to talk to first?"

"I think the girl. The way I heard it, she panicked early at St. Mary's, so we can build on that. We'll let the boy stew in silence and see if it softens him up."

Frank entered the observation room as Jacob opened the door to room three. Shirley sat in the chair provided, rocking back and forth, and twisting the strands of her dishwater blond hair. She was slightly overweight but was dressed in an attractive light blue dress. Her eyes expanded into big circles, and her lips were quivering.

"I'm not scared, you know?" she said as she watched Jacob take a seat on the other side of the small table.

"I can see that," Jacob lied. He smiled as he watched her. "I'll bet you are thirsty, though. Would you like a soda or something else to drink?"

"Coke, I guess."

As he rose to get it, she added, "In a can, and I get to open it."

Jacob nodded. "You are pretty smart. I'll make sure they bring unopened cans." He opened the door and told an officer what he needed. In a few seconds, he received two Cokes through the door.

As he approached the table; he extended one to her, and she immediately reached out for the other Coke.

"Shirley, may I call you Shirley?" He paused.

"That's my name."

"Shirley, it's your right to have your parents here with you and even a lawyer if you want."

"I watch TV. I know my rights. Wouldn't do any good, though. My parents are idiots. As long as I leave them alone, they leave me alone." He heard a roughness in her small chuckle. "Won't be able to ignore me now, though."

"Is that why you wanted to shoot up the church—to get them to pay attention?"

"Not just them," Shirley looked down. "It was supposed to make everyone pay attention like it did in that North Carolina town." She squinted her eyes, and her bottom lip began to quiver. "They said no one would know we were coming, and we would fool them all. Then we were to shoot ourselves like the others."

"It takes a lot of courage to be willing to die for your cause, Shirley."

"Guess so, but they grabbed my gun before I could pull the trigger. It was as if they were prepared for us."

"Who told you that no one would know you were coming, Shirley?"

"The Leader and the soldier who trained us how to use the gun."

"A soldier taught you how to shoot?"

"Yeah, in a cabin in a woods out by the lake. He never let us see him. Always kept a mask over his face."

"How'd you meet him, Shirley?"

The Leader contacted us over the Net and told us we should call a special number. Daniel and I were excited to have been picked. We met and called the number. It was a recording, but it told us where to go and what to bring. We spent a couple of days there, learning about guns, and how to shoot."

"Didn't your parents miss you when you didn't come home at night?"

"I told them I was spending the night with a friend. They didn't care."

"And was there just one soldier at the cabin?"

"No, there were two, but the other one kept watch while we were there to make sure no one followed us."

"How did you know they were soldiers, Shirley?"

"I guess because they wore uniforms—you know the kind with the camouflage. Sure looked like soldiers, and they had the guns and bullets for us."

"And they taught you how to shoot. Did they provide targets to shoot at?"

"No, they said we would be so close all we needed to do was point and pull the trigger. They had some dummies, so they could show us what part of the body to aim at. We tried it several times so we were used to firing the gun and how it kicked back."

"I think it would be difficult to shoot another human up close. I'm not sure I could do it."

"They had some special dummies that exploded and something like blood shot out when we hit them. It was strange at first, but, after a while, you get used to it."

"When you weren't shooting the guns, what did you do? Did they say anything about what you were doing?"

"They talked about how we were going to stick it to the church and the government, and how we would go down in history. Most of the time, though, we watched the videos."

"The videos?"

"Yeah, the ones from the Leader who told us all about the lies the church and the nation were telling us. You know what the church is telling people are a bunch of lies, don't you?"

"What makes you think they are lies, Shirley?"

"I watch TV. I hear about those preachers who build big churches and do those dirty things to little children. That's not right you know?"

"No, it's not right, Shirley. Did this Leader tell you the church lies about other things?"

"Bout the resurrection and Jesus. When you are dead, you are dead. That's what the Leader said. They shouldn't lie to people and then ask them for their money to build those big churches. They should be feeding the hungry and helping people who need it."

"You want another Coke or something to eat, Shirley."

"I saw a vending machine out there with candy bars, peanuts, even ice cream bars."

"What do you want?"

"I'll take another soda and a candy bar—maybe a Snickers."

"OK, you rest here, and I'll go get them for you." Jacob rose, stopped, and patted her hand. "You are being helpful, Shirley. Maybe we can teach the churches a lesson."

He walked out the door. When the door closed, Jacob felt his knees go weak. He went over to a chair and sat down.

Frank came out of the observation room and took four quick steps over to where Jacob leaned his elbows on the table with both hands on his face. "Are you all right?"

He raised his head; his face drained of blood. "I've read a lot of psychology, but this stuff is crazy. Did you hear how someone convinced her she is part of an army to cleanse society? Whoever is behind this is demonic, Dad."

"You are doing a great job. She visibly relaxed as you talked to her. It's like she is so starved for someone to hear her that your listening acted like a powerful drug."

An officer brought three candy bars and two sodas to the table. "Thank you," Jacob said. "I guess I need to finish this so that we can get to Daniel. How's he doing in that room?"

"He's pacing the floor," the office said. "Tried to throw a chair, but it was bolted down. One of the female officers brought him a Coke and sandwich a little while ago. She told him someone would be in to talk with him soon."

"OK, let me deliver these snacks to Shirley and see if she has anything more about the Leader, and then we'll tackle Daniel."

"I know it's draining," said Frank, "but you are doing a good job. I'm proud of you."

"Makes me wonder how you ever survived all those counseling times and did all the other things in the ministry."

Jacob took the candy and sodas back into the room where Shirley sat. She gave him a small smile and said thank you.

He asked some questions about the Leader, but all she could tell him was she made contact with the Leader on the Internet. She recited some of the messages the Leader sent, but she seemed to know little about anything that would help with making an identification.

Finally, Jacob said, "Shirley, this is serious, and you will spend the night here at the police station. Will you give me your parent's telephone number so we can inform them you are here? I know you think they don't care much, but I'm sure they will want to come and see you."

"Sure, now that I'm in jail. They'll be embarrassed and want to come and see if they can straighten everything out."

Shirley gave him the number, and Jacob told her someone would come soon and show her where she would spend the night.

"Will you come and see me again?" Shirley asked.

"I go back home tomorrow, but I promise I will come and visit you before I go." Jacob extended his hand to shake Shirley's hand and left the room.

"OK," he said, "Let me take two Tylenol, get a cold drink of water, breathe deeply, and then we will tackle Daniel. Is there a damp towel I can use to wipe my face off?"

A few moments later, Jacob handed the towel to an officer, ran his hands through his hair, took a deep breath, knocked, and entered the interrogation room.

"What the hell took you so long?" Daniel shouted, red-faced and breathing hard.

"I'm sure you are frustrated. I'm sorry for the long wait."

"You're damn right I'm frustrated. This two-bit town doesn't know how to do anything right."

Jacob shoved his hands in his pocket and tried to look sheepish. "I'm sorry. Can I at least make it up a little by getting you another Coke and maybe a candy bar?"

Daniel's left eye narrowed as he looked at Jacob. With a slight sneer on his lips, he put his hands on the table between them."How about a pizza? I'm starving."

"Do you want anchovies or just pepperoni and cheese?"

Daniel drew his head back, and his eyes widened. "Are you shitting me? You're really going to get me a pizza?"

"If you're willing to help me understand what happened this morning, I think that can be arranged."

Daniel plopped down in his chair and rocked back a little. "Go for it, man. I ain't afraid to talk."

Jacob held up one hand with a finger raised. "Just a minute." He opened the door and spoke to the police officer outside. "Officer, would you ask someone to get me a medium size pepperoni pizza with extra cheese?"

Then he closed the door, but not before seeing a deep scowl form on the officer's face.

He pulled out the chair across from Daniel, sat down, and tried to be friendly. "OK, why don't you tell me about what happened at First Methodist?"

"Not until I get my pizza," Daniel said with a stern look on his face.

Jacob changed his body posture. He sat up straight and leaned within an inch of Daniel's nose. "Listen, shithead, I tried to be nice, but if you want to see who can make your life miserable, just try me."

The color went out of Daniel's face, and he shrank a little. "Hey, don't get upset. I was just poking at you."

"This is the way it goes down. You talk, and if I like what you say, you get the pizza. No talk and you can starve in this room till Tuesday. Get my drift?"

"All right. Don't get all steamed up. What do you want to know?"

"Now, tell me what happened out at the cabin by the lake where you trained to shoot."

He saw Daniel's eyes widen, and his face thrust forward. "How'd you know about the cabin?"

He wanted to throw Daniel off balance and cause him to wonder what Jacob already knew. "I know lots of things."

Daniel began to speak, and Jacob held up his hand. "And remember, I want the truth. If you lie, not only is there no pizza, you could go to an adult prison where some of those killers like to do things to young boys."

"All right, I'll talk. It all started a few weeks ago, after that church shooting in that town in North Carolina. I thought that was a cool way to make people take notice. I searched the Net, some of the back portals where lots of people never go."

"What were you looking for?"

"I don't know. I was just browsing the Internet, seeing what other young people were into. So I found these announcements on a bulletin board. Talked about screwing up the system by scaring the hell out of a group of churches. Hey, that's sort of funny—scaring the hell out of churches."

The inanity and superficial thinking that led to the death of several people was tearing at Jacob's guts. He tried to keep his face calm and give the impression that Daniel was an important spokesman for a new truth. "You wanted to be part of forcing adults to admit the lies that were being told in their churches?"

"You got it. When the second church was shot up, I knew that this was the beginning of a new movement, and I wanted to be a part of it."

"So you responded."

Daniel scowled. "Yeah, but I never thought anyone would get back to me. I mean who cares about what happens in this dump?"

"But you were contacted?"

Daniel's face lit up like he'd won the lottery. "Who'd of figured it, but Texas, Wisconsin, was part of the Leader's plan. Everyone was thinking they were going to hit some place in the state of Texas, and we'd fool them all by shooting up churches here." Then he paused, and his face fell. "But it didn't work. Someone knew. How'd they figure it out?"

"I don't know, Daniel," Jacob lied. "Tell me about what happened at First Methodist."

"After our training, they gave us some sharp clothes and told us where we were going to hit."

He could tell by the change on Daniel's face that a piece of the puzzle just came into place.

"Shirley! That's how you found out about the cabin. That bitch Shirley told you. I knew you couldn't trust that girl. Is she flipping for a deal?"

"She's talked to us. Told us some interesting stuff. Not sure about a deal. Depends on which of you is most helpful. Let's get back to what happened at First Methodist this morning."

"So I have my Glock hidden in a clever place in my jacket that I carried over my arm. I'd been to that church with my parents a few times. But when I entered, they were all set up with this "Be Friends with a Youth" crap. There were men at the door who greeted all young people and took to a special section."

"So a man took you to your seat?"

"This old man, I think he was called Ben, took me down. I tried to sit on the outside like I'd been told, so I could get in the aisle and start shooting, but he wouldn't let me. And all he wanted to do was talk to me about me—who I was, what I liked, what I wanted to do, what I thought about what was happening in the world—bullshit like that."

"And so you told him about yourself?"

"Yeah, it wasn't so bad. At least he listened."

"So then what happened?"

"That fat old preacher got up to read from the Bible, and I knew that was my signal. The problem was that Ben saw me reach for my gun, and he grabbed me. I had to struggle, but I got it free enough to shoot him. I thought I was going to get it on then, but the preacher was faster than I thought. I looked up as he was diving at me. Knocked me over, but I held onto my gun."

"Then what happened?"

"Some jock yelled something about protecting the preacher and grabbed for my gun. I would have shot him too, but his bitch bit me in the arm. Man, did she bite hard. I dropped the gun."

"Daniel, tell me about this person you call the Leader."

"Don't know much about him. Mostly got text messages except for the training videos at the cabin."

"What was on those videos?"

"Told us the truth about the lies that the church is telling—and other religions too. Keep people filled with lies about the resurrection, and how you have to obey if you are going to make heaven. Told us how the government uses the church to keep people in line. It's like a dictatorship where everybody pays their dues and behaves while the rich people have all the fun."

"So it's a pretty rotten system?"

"Got that right. Just like my school. If you are in, you get everything, but if you are out, you don't get squat. That bitch that bit me, she was one of the cheerleaders." He held up his bandaged arm. "Do you suppose she has rabies? She bit deep, like a cannibal or something."

"I'll get a doctor to check you. How is shooting up some churches going to clean up our rotten system?"

"That's where the Leader has a cool plan." Daniel began to get excited. "It's not just a few churches. He, or maybe she, I don't know, has teenage soldiers all around the country just waiting for the signal."

"Wait a minute, you say you don't know whether the Leader is a he or a she?"

"The voice was tinny but a little high at times. In this one tape, the voice went on and on about Mary Mag . . . something, about how she had faked the resurrection. In another video, the voice talked about the first born being the right sacrifice. What man talks about first-borns and all that crap?"

"I see what you mean. Tell me more about the plan."

"Well, the Leader,—it must be a man because it is a cool plan—anyway the plan is to use the same tactics as the Jihad something or other in that war we are fighting. Those guys are really righteous. They don't mind dying for a cause."

"And you want to be like those guys?"

"Well, they are going to bring down all the corrupt adults who are running things. And, like us, they don't have any real power. But if enough of them are not afraid to die, and they learn how to make explosives, they can keep poking those in power, and they look like fools. Soon no one trusts anyone, and it all falls apart."

"And so the Leader is making everyone look like fools?"

"Sure. This one messed up, but as the Leader says, the beauty is that there is no army to bomb, and you got to lose a few battles if you want to bring the structure down. Once in awhile, the police will get lucky, like this time, but they can't stop it everywhere."

"So the idea is the Leader keeps sending teenagers into churches all over this country, taking their losses, but keeps spreading the terror until the bad guys lose all power and the good guys take over. Is that the plan?"

"Pretty cool, huh? All the armies and rich people in the world can't stop anonymous people who aren't afraid to die. That'll teach the authorities to treat us like idiots."

Jacob reached out and touched Daniel's arm. "But you will be dead, Daniel. What good is that going to do?"

"It's like the Leader said. We are all going to die sometime. So do you want to die a nobody, or do you at least want to be part of a movement to wipe out the sick politicians and preachers and start over?"

"But what if you are wrong, Daniel? What if the Leader isn't telling you the truth? What if he is just a rich guy who's figured out how to use gullible teenagers to bring down his competition? Or what if she is a rich bitch who was screwed by one of these sick preachers and wanted to get revenge on all churches?"

Daniel seemed shaken. "That's not true. The Leader tells the truth and uses the Net to do it because the Net is the only way to talk to the little people. I read it myself."

While he was saying this, Jacob looked at the mirror and nodded. In just a few moments, there was a knock on the door. When he opened the door, the same scowling officer handed him a box with a medium size pizza in it. "Could you bring Daniel another cold Coke, officer?"

When Daniel tore open the box, the pizza was still steaming. He grabbed a piece and took a big bite. "Wow, that's great. I'm starved."

Then he looked at Jacob. "You want one? It's good."

Jacob took a small piece and took a bite. "It is good. Thanks for offering."

"Sokay. You kept your word and listened to me."

There was another knock on the door, and the officer brought another can of Coke in. Through clenched teeth he asked, "Will there be anything else, sir?"

"We're about done here officer. When Daniel has finished his pizza, he will be ready to be taken to his cell. You might arrange for someone to call his parents as well."

When the officer left, Jacob turned back to Daniel. "I won't lie to you. You did an awful thing, and there are going to be consequences. I think it will be obvious that you were lied to by this Leader, and that is who we will go after. I'd advise you to be as helpful as you can, and maybe it will go a little easier on you."

"We're going to win, Jacob. Then things will be different. You'll see."

"I doubt that. I don't think you are a bad kid, but you are going to spend time in prison. You may not want to hear this, but I will give you one piece of advice."

Daniel's head came up, a half slice of pizza dangling from his mouth.

"The resurrection is not a lie and no evil you committed can defeat God. I'd use your time in prison trying to get in touch with God and see what God can do for you."

Jacob turned and walked out of the interrogation room.

Amanda was standing outside the door. She came up and gave him a big hug. "That was brilliant," she said. "We still have a long way to go, but thanks to you, we have some ways to get started."

THE MEDIA REACTS

CHAPTER 27

While Jacob interrogated the youth, the national media was speeding to Texas, Wisconsin. By late afternoon, the streets of the small town were filled with large vans with extended disks on top. Numerous cars arrived carrying reporters as well. Despite the tragedy, there was an atmosphere of excitement. They had never had this much attention. Imagining being on one of the national news programs, several people tried to position themselves on the downtown sidewalks, hoping to be noticed.

When approached, one middle-aged woman willingly consented to be interviewed. "From what I heard, the churches had gotten wind of this possibility ahead of time and were prepared."

"How did they prepare?"

She turned to the man standing next to her. "You tell them, Harold. You were one of the brave men who volunteered to protect our church."

The reporter turned to the man.

"Well, let me give credit to our pastors. They were pretty smart.

They all declared a special youth Sunday. We roped off a section for our young people. Then, when any young person came to our door, one of the men would take him or her to the section and sit with that person. That way the youth felt special, but if there were any troublemakers, a man was next to each one to help out."

"So where did the shootings take place?" asked the reporter.

"Way I hear it," said the lady, "there were problems at St. Mary's, and First Methodist, but not many people were hurt because we were prepared."

"'Cept the preacher at the Methodist church. He was shot up pretty bad," said the man. "Guess he's going to make it, though."

Similar interviews took place up and down the main street.

Some people said we ought to have stricter gun laws, while others suggested every pastor should encourage people to bring their guns to church. One said pastors should get special training and keep a pistol in the pulpit.

Both First Methodist and St. Mary's had posted large signs on their doors instructing all media to proceed to the courthouse where a news conference would be held at 4 p.m. CST. They hoped this would allow the stations to make their evening broadcast, although they would be cutting it close for those in the east.

Several reporters had heard the pastor and a deacon from First Methodist had been shot and were in the hospital. Both were briefed to say they would only be open to brief questions after the news conference, and the media would choose three pool reporters to ask the questions.

Amanda had arranged for the young man and girl who had intervened at First Methodist to be present with their parents at the courthouse. She asked Jacob to talk with them about what they might say while she coached the others who would be present at the news conference, including the rector of St. Mary's Episcopal.

She approached the tall austere man with thinning hair and a pinched face. "Father," she said, "they are going to want your opinion on many things in addition to the actual event. They will ask for your response to the accusation the church is full of lies and the resurrection never took place. They will ask you why you think youth chose violence against churches. They may ask why you think St.Mary's was a target. They will go on and on because they want to catch you saying something unusual that will make the news."

The events had deeply shaken him. "So what am I supposed to say?"

"You can say what you want, but if I were you, I would resist being drawn into speculation about the causes or getting defensive about the church. You could just say the church's faith is quite clear, and you see nothing helpful about debating it on the national media. We need to focus on how to bring healing to all the people of our country."

"What about poor Ralph Emerson? How badly was he hurt? Oh God, this can't be happening."

Frank spoke up. "Father, this is deeply tragic, and the people of this town are going to need strong spiritual guidance to get through this. Reverend Emerson was wounded, but he will recover. All the churches need to support each other."

"You're Frank Sessions, aren't you? You've already been through this. I guess if you all made it through in Lincoln, we will too. We may need your help, though."

"I'll do what I can, but first we have to get through this news conference without saying anything that will increase the hysteria in the country."

The rector nodded. "That is what you and I are all about, isn't it?"

"What's that?" asked Amanda.

"Our whole faith is about bringing hope out of tragedy and order out of chaos. Isn't that right, Frank?"

Amanda felt her body relax. "OK, you stick with that, and you'll do fine. Now I'll get this show on the road."

The courthouse conference room was filled by 3:30 p.m. Numerous reporters and camera technicians were seeking personal interviews with anyone who looked interesting. At 4:00 p.m., the police chief, a portly man with reddish thinning hair, accompanied by the sheriff and Amanda, stepped to the podium and asked everyone to sit down. Frank and Jacob were discreetly off to the side. Jacob sat by a young athletic appearing man who nervously cleared his throat and a teary-eyed young girl.

The chief called the meeting to order. "Ladies and gentlemen of the press. I will open with a brief statement. Then Amanda Singletary from the Justice Department will conduct the rest of the meeting."

Several hands went up in the air, and some questions were shouted out.

"As you might imagine, in a small town like this, we are not used to large press conferences, but we take polite behavior seriously. Please wait until we share the information we have, and then we will take your questions."

Amanda watched nervously while the chief made a brief statement about the two churches that had become victims of the shootings. He concluded by saying, "We were incredibly fortunate we had been forewarned this might take place, and, with the help of the Justice Department, we implemented a defensive plan that kept injury to a minimum. I have been in touch with the hospital, and both The Reverend Emerson and Deacon Thompson, though they sustained injuries, are in stable condition."

His voice cracked, and he paused for a deep breath and then continued. "You all know what happened in Lincoln, North Carolina. This could have been even worse, but the good Lord blessed us with some courageous pastors and deacons as well as some brave young people. Before I turn this over to Ms. Singletary of the Justice Department, I want to emphasize in contrast to the evil acts of some youth, we here in Texas have some young people who showed us what true young people are made of. We'll introduce them to you in a minute, but first the Justice Department will bring us up to date with the information they have gathered."

He stepped aside, and Amanda assumed the mike. "I want to second what the chief said about the young people. We've had some scary events take place in the last couple of weeks, but it would be a mistake to paint the youth of this country with a broad brush."

"Tell us what they did," a voice shouted.

Amanda glanced off to the side of the stage where the two young people, Bart and Ellen, were sitting. "Maybe that is where we should move the story. Let me introduce you to Bart Baker and Ellen Fisher. Be kind to them now. They are still a little shaken by the events, but I want you to hear their story. I'd ask their parents to come up with them."

The two young people, who were clearly nervous but trying to be strong, came towards the mike accompanied by their proud parents.

"We'll let Bart tell his part of the story first. You town's people know Bart as the right guard of your local football team, and Ellen plays field hockey and is a cheerleader. Go ahead Bart, just tell them what took place."

The stocky, well conditioned young man with short dark hair stepped forward. "Well, it all sort of happened real fast. We were all in the pews reserved for young people. You see, our pastor called for a special Youth Sunday. I don't know who this dude was, but he was sitting next to Deacon Thompson, and the first thing I knew, he started to stand up, and Deacon Thompson was trying to hold him down."

Bart wiped his arm across his face to get the sweat out of his eyes. "I wish Deacon Thompson could be here. He's the real hero. Anyway, while this dude was struggling with the deacon, I guess our pastor was running down the aisle. The next thing I knew, he had head-butted this dude, and he fell back into the pew where Ellie and I were sitting."

He glanced at Ellen, who was standing next to him. "She was pretty brave too." The young woman with auburn hair woven into a French braid smiled weakly. He reached out and touched her.

"Anyway, when our pastor head-butted him, he shot the preacher as well. That made me mad. It's not right to shoot preachers. So I grabbed the gun, and Ellie bit him on the arm and made him let go of the gun. She took a bite out of him. She should tell you that part."

Ellen stepped forward but was clearly hesitant. Her father placed a hand on her shoulder to encourage her. "I . . . I just saw Bar . . . that's what we call him, grab the gun and pull the shooters arm down. The arm was right there. I didn't think about it. I was scared. I bit him, and the blood came out. It tasted awful, yeach! . . . But he dropped the gun. Then some men grabbed him." She looked a little perplexed. "I guess that was it, 'cept the police came and took him away."

The whole room, including all of the reporters, burst into applause. After a few minutes, Amanda guided them back to their seats and came back to the mike.

"This is going to frustrate you, but I can't tell you a lot about what tipped us to this event. Holding on to that information will, we hope, help us track down the monsters that are behind this. I can tell you these are not random acts of a few crazy young people. They are being led, wrongly, to try to sow panic among the churches of our country."

"Why did they choose here for their attack?" shouted one reporter.

"You will recall the banner that went across the national news channels threatening the next shootings would be in Texas. I think they thought they were being clever and would fool everyone by picking churches here in Texas, Wisconsin."

"Will there be other shootings in other places?"

"I fear they will try, and we must be on alert. Our hope is this debacle might serve as a warning to young people across the country that the people who are behind this are not as clever as they thought. It is an evil day when some adults are willing to sacrifice young people to achieve their selfish ends."

"Who is behind all of this?" a reporter from CNN asked.

"We are gathering information on that, but we don't have anything definitive yet to report."

Amanda and Frank had agreed if possible, he and Jacob should remain on the sidelines. Since the strategy was to calm fears and emphasize the positive note of the young people as an inspiring model, both were pleased with how the event was unfolding.

Rector Bill Young caught Amanda's attention and indicated he would like to say a few words. Amanda brought him to the mike.

"Most people in this town know me. I've been rector at St. Mary's for the last ten years. I think I've aged another ten years in the last twenty-four hours."

An understanding chuckle flowed through the room.

"My church, along with First Methodist, were the two targets. The shooters in North Carolina shouted that the church was corrupt and our faith was a lie—particularly our faith in the resurrection. By God's grace, the alertness of law enforcement and the courage of some of our members, we did not suffer the same violence as those churches in North Carolina.

"I just want to say to the young people across the nation who might be tempted by such violence; the real lie is from those who urge you to sacrifice yourself. Violence is easy, especially if you are sending others to sacrifice themselves. It takes courage to stand up for faith, hope, and love. Our churches are imperfect, but like the early church, our faith is in a God, not in our perfection. God will not be defeated by death."

He seemed encouraged by his own words. "That's all I have to say." He sat down.

At first the reporters just stared in silence and then slowly they began to applaud.

Amanda knew how to quit while she was ahead. She stepped quickly to the microphone and said, "This concludes our press conference. Thank you all for coming."

The shift in the tone of the news stories was almost instantaneous. "Courageous Teenagers Take a Stand Against Violence," said one headline. "Rector challenges young people to stand up for faith, hope, and love."

Wolf Blitzer, who had been the target of one of the banner incidents on national media, began his broadcast with these words: "Two young people and an Episcopal rector in Texas, Wisconsin, have shown the world what real courage is about. A clever plan implemented by the clergy of this small Wisconsin town demonstrated the way for the churches and our nation to counter this latest terrorist threat." He proceeded to describe the efforts of the congregations to surround the youth who entered their sanctuaries and befriend them.

The other media took a similar approach to the story, although many also cautioned that the leaders behind this violence had not been identified and would undoubtedly try to find other targets. Bloggers and columnists debated the significance of what happened in Wisconsin and why the youth were attracted to this type of violence in the first place.

Bill O'Reilly, who also had been a target of the banners, fumed that violence could only be countered by an equal or superior power. He congratulated the people of Texas, Wisconsin, but he quickly transitioned to his own analysis of what was happening. He suggested adults needed to cease pampering the youth as if they held some unexplored truth. Those miscreants had been seduced by what appeared to him to be a jihadist plot to destabilize the country, and he urged his listeners to fight back. "Take your guns to church and be prepared to defend your faith and your family," he said. "I can understand why those cowards behind these attacks chose not to come to Texas. Real men in Texas will defend themselves."

Amanda headed back to Washington, and Jacob, after keeping his promise to say goodbye to Shirley, joined his father and drove back to Lincoln, North Carolina.

"I think the rector made some good points," said Frank. "I hope the media helps spread his challenge to people all over."

"He's right in what he said," Jacob said. "My concern is this Leader will feel the pressure to do something dramatic to recapture the momentum. Unless we can identify who the Leader is, this thing is far from over."

"Did you get any clues from the kids you interviewed? By the way, that was masterful. I loved watching you play good cop and bad cop with Daniel."

"Thanks. As I thought about both conversations, two things stand out. When Shirley talked about the soldiers teaching her how to shoot, I about fainted."

"Yeah, that means this is bigger than just some nut-case on the Internet. Somebody has more plans than just a couple of scary incidents to get some publicity."

"Do you suppose they are active soldiers?"

"I can't believe that there are rogue soldiers out there willing to risk their whole careers and prison by training some teenagers how to shoot a gun."

"When we get back to Lincoln, I think we should talk to Brian and get the vet group together. Maybe they can help us think this thing out."

"Good idea. If they trust us, I'd like to bring Mandy into the conversation. These guys know the military and can help us think this through."

"They'd trust Amanda. It's what she represents that might cause a problem. They don't have a lot of love lost for the government. We should probably talk to them first."

"Sounds wise. You said two things stood out for you in your conversations. What was the other one?"

"The chilling idea that this Leader has recruited "teen soldiers" and can strike at multiple sites at once. How can we possibly defend against that? There are teenagers, alienated young people, everywhere in this country. They might even choose some small rural churches next time. No one can cover them all."

"That's why we have to cut the head off this monster before it gets too late. We've slowed it down for the moment, but a couple of successful attacks would re-energize them. There are many teens ripe for the picking. Something else intrigued me about what Daniel was saying."

"What's that, Dad?"

"The possibility that the Leader is a woman rather than a man."

"Yeah, I didn't know whether to take that seriously or not."

"When you think about it, some of the propaganda the Leader is putting out may be thin theology, but it appeals to those who think men are oppressing women."

"You mean that stuff about Mary Magdalene and the resurrection being a story she made up?"

"That might make for a fun debate sometime," said Frank, "but if you believed such malarkey, it would justify whatever you could do to bring down the church that has been so unfair to women over the centuries."

"Whether the Leader is a man or a woman, how do we get a clue to tracking him or her down?"

"In addition to the conversation with the vets, lets touch base with your sister, Amanda, and, if you are game for it, even Brandy. Let's brainstorm, and see what we can come up with."

"Brandy? Do you think she would come?"

"In addition to your somewhat strained relationship, she is also a crackerjack reporter and a good thinker."

"You're right, of course. I'm game if she is. Say, I have another great idea."

"What's that?"

"That sign up there says a McDonald's is up ahead. I know it is not the healthiest of meals, but I could really use a sandwich and a large frappe."

BARBARA REGROUPS

CHAPTER 28

Barbara had always been good at hiding her feelings and presenting herself the way other people wanted to see her. She had learned as a child what it was that her beloved father wanted. He was devoted to his faith, and to please him, she put on her religious costume. Her mother was more skeptical, so in private Barbara would raise questions and pretend to have great doubts when, in fact, she could care less about what people believed. As she grew to be an attractive teenager, she learned what boys and later men wanted to see. It was rare that she lost it and revealed her true feelings.

This Sunday was more difficult than usual for her to appear at church as the perfectly composed pastor's wife. She went to the early service and made sure that many who were attending the later service saw her, but then suggested she had an upset stomach and was leaving early. Bob and those she spoke to seemed properly concerned and urged her to return home and get some rest.

She fought to maintain her composure until she was far enough away that no one would recognize her. Then she let out a yell and pumped her fist in the air as she sped towards her home. She knew that the churches in Texas, Wisconsin, were in the Central time zone, and the shootings would not take place until about 11:30 CST or 12:30 EST. She did a little dance as she entered her office and turned on both the TV and computer. She used her remote to move between several stations on the television. It was the usual Sunday morning talk show drivel, and there were several church services in progress. One news show had several commentators ponderously speculating on which Texas city and which church might become a victim on this Sunday.

She flipped her center finger towards the screen and said in a singsong fashion, "You don't know what the fuck you're talking about. This Barbie doll is going to make you all look like complete idiots."

While she knew that Bob wouldn't approve, she decided that a Bloody Mary was in order. She'd clean it up before Bob returned, and, by that time, the whole world would be focused on Wisconsin anyway. All she would have to do is to feign a slight wooziness. She practiced a shocked look on her face when it would be announced that the news departments were pulling their reporters out of Texas and sending them off to Wisconsin. She figured that a double portion of vodka and a strong dose of Worcestershire sauce might make it easier to appear a little woozy.

About 12:15 p.m. she cleaned up her glass and settled down in her special comfortable chair to focus on CNN news on her computer and CBS news on her television. She could hardly wait for the *Breaking News* banner to break across the screen. About 12:35, when she could barely stand it, the first hint of breaking news appeared first on CBS and then on CNN.

"CBS beat you, Wolfie. They were 15 seconds ahead of you," she announced to the screen.

"We have just been informed that a shooting has occurred in a little town called Texas, Wisconsin," the CBS weekend commentator announced. "While we were prepared for something to happen in the state of Texas, apparently the teen-terrorists tried to fool everyone by showing up in a little town called Texas, Wisconsin."

While CBS was describing the town, CNN broke into their breaking news broadcast with a new announcement. "We are getting reports that while the news media and most of the nation was fooled by this switch to Wisconsin, some very alert members of the terrorist division of the Justice Department had picked up hints of this possibility and demonstrated some cleverness of their own."

Barbara almost dropped the Coke she was sipping. She grabbed the remote control and raised the sound as she leaned into the screen on her computer. How could they have gotten any clue to this? So few people knew.

"We'll have further developments as they come to us," the reporter announced, "but it sounds like some very alert law officials may have frustrated this first attempt to take the attacks outside of North Carolina."

Barbara was about to hurl her glass against the wall when she heard her husband come into the house. "Barb, have you got the TV on, honey? There's been another attack."

He knocked on her door and asked, "Can I come in?"

She smiled at his hesitancy and put on her shocked face, which actually fit how she felt but for different reasons. She called out. "Yes, yes, come in. I have it on both the TV and the Internet. There seems to be a lot of confusion."

"It's both good news and bad news," he said as he came in. "According to the radio, there were some injuries, but the attack was largely foiled."

She had a pained look on her face. "All this violence is so horrible, Bob. Now that it's spreading, no one will be safe going to church."

They continued to watch and make comments to each other throughout the afternoon as more reports came in.

During the news conference, the camera panned the participants near the speakers. Bob suddenly sat up. "Isn't that Frank Sessions and his son Jacob over there to the right of the speakers?"

Barbara shifted toward the TV, but the camera moved on to sweep the reporters who were trying to make their questions heard.

She didn't see Frank Sessions, but when she heard Bob mention his name, she felt her gut tighten, and she knew that her face felt hot.

"I guess since his church was the first one hit, he probably knows more about this than most. I wonder if they have called him in as a consultant," said Bob.

"I wouldn't trust that bastard if he were the last person on earth," Barbara said. She recognized that she had revealed more about her feelings than she wanted to.

"Barbara, I realize he was part of that mess that David got into, but remember, his daughter was at risk, and he was defending her."

Barbara felt herself pulling the reigns back in. She didn't want to do anything that would make Bob suspicious. "You're right, Bob. It's just every time I get a letter from David and think of him rotting away in that prison, I sort of lose it."

"I understand, Barbara. We should plan to visit him again next week. I'll check my calendar, and we'll find a good day."

Barbara just nodded. "It is all so horrible. It makes you wonder about the fate of our nation."

"I know we both want to watch this to see what else they find. How's your stomach? Can I get you something to eat?"

"I'm feeling better. The Coke helped settle my stomach. I'm not very hungry, though. Perhaps just some cereal and a cup of hot tea."

Bob brought them lunch, and they watched the developments as the news broadcasters reported them. When they broadcasted the rector's statement affirming his belief in God and the resurrection, Bob cheered. Barbara seethed inside. *As soon as I can get away from Bob, I' have to contact Jeb and plan how we can get the fear moving again.*

It was clear that the media thought that this might be a turning point. The story about the youngsters and the rector played repeatedly. Barbara watched, but mostly to see if she could get a glimpse of Frank Sessions again. *Bask in your small victory, Frank. It will be your last for a long time to come.*

About eight in the evening, when it was clear that there probably wouldn't be further developments that day, Bob announced that he was going to his study to prepare an article for his church's newsletter trumpeting the rector's remarks. "Then, I think I'll go to bed early. This has been an exhausting day, and tomorrow I want to gather some of my colleagues and see where we go from here. Maybe I'll give Frank Sessions a call as well and see what he is thinking."

"You go right ahead, Bob. I'll do a little more work here, and then I'll be up to join you."

As soon as Bob left the room, Barbara texted Jeb. "Need to meet soon. Hope your training of our new recruits in the other states is going well. We can't afford to let the bleeding hearts get the upper edge."

Within an hour, she got a reply.

"Training going well. Have new tactics to discuss. Bummer re TW, but not all strategies work. What about Tuesday at the cabin?"

Knowing that Bob had a church board meeting Tuesday and wouldn't return to the house until after 9 p.m., Barbara texted back, "Cabin at three."

She drove down the gravel lane towards the cabin in the woods. She knew she was driving too fast, sending a cloud of dust in her wake, but she was too worked up to slow down. Yesterday she played out in her mind all the events leading up to what happened on Sunday in Texas, Wisconsin. There were so few people involved. She couldn't imagine how the authorities got wind of the plans. Who could have betrayed them?

When her Internet recruiting team shared their list of potential soldiers with her, she had spotted the two that were near Texas, Wisconsin. It felt like divine intervention, which she didn't believe in. It seemed like the perfect switch that would make everyone feel like fools and create a myth of brilliance for the mysterious leader behind the movement. The only one she talked to about it was Jeb, and he was almost ecstatic when he heard her plans.

He had teamed up with a buddy of his to provide the training, and, except for the two teens, no one else knew what was going down.

Yet the authorities were waiting for them with a plan of their own. How could that have happened? She was certain that Jeb wasn't the leak, so that only left his buddy or possibly one of the teens who tried bragging to friends. Even that seemed impossible. Neither the teens nor the buddy would know who to call and be taken seriously.

And the plan, the "Befriend a Youth Day," having the men adopt all teens at the door and place them in a special section where they could be watched, was brilliant. Who could have thought of that in such a short period of time? They had even accomplished another miracle. Apparently all the churches had cooperated with each other, and, even more miraculously, they had done so quietly. Barbara had been around church people all her life. There were always too many egos involved for that sort of teamwork. They may preach love of neighbor, but the preachers never lived it out.

As she mused about what happened, the cabin suddenly appeared in front of her. She had to slam on her brakes to prevent the car ramming the front door. She was still fuming and confused as she threw the door of the car open and ran up the steps. As she was about to grab the door nob, the door opened, and she looked down the barrel of a gun in Jeb's hand. She was so consumed by her thoughts that the gun didn't even frighten her. She simply reached up and pushed the gun aside as she entered. "Always the cautious one, I see."

"When I heard that car come barreling up my lane, I wasn't sure whether I was being attacked or just in the way of a couple of teenage drag racers."

She didn't even engage in the banter but went straight to the point. "Jeb, who could have betrayed us? I've reviewed every possibility, and I can't come up with anyone."

"We were screwed, that's for sure, but I can't figure out how they did it either. You, me, and my buddy were the only adults involved, and I know it didn't even come by accident from us. The only good news is that the teens won't have anything to tell them. My buddy chose an abandoned shack for the training, so we are untraceable."

"We have to get the momentum back on our side. I hope the new idea you said you had is a good one, because we don't want them thinking they have turned this around." She threw her purse on the table, marched over and grabbed a beer from the cooler, popped the cap off and took a long swig.

"Thanks for offering. I thought I'd join you in a drink while we plan." He got his beer and returned to the table and sat down. "The first step in my plan is that we do nothing for several weeks and let them think they are winning. The rag heads used to pull that on us all the time. When we began to relax, they would strike us again."

She took another swig of her beer, still standing beside the table. "Go ahead, I'm listening."

She was wearing tight fitting jeans, white tennis shoes, and a red sweater that nicely contoured to her body. Her makeup emphasized her eyes and lips and her hair was softly combed back but still hung loose. She saw him look her up and down, smile, and shake his head.

"What?"

"You know, if I was straight, all that effort to look seductive might pay off, but since I'm not, you are wasting your effort. Unless you have a date with another man when you leave here?"

She blushed, pulled out a chair, and sat. "I'm not sure I'll ever get used to being near a man who is not at least partially interested in getting his hands on me." She looked down at the table and then chuckled as she looked back up. "How do I manipulate and gain control over a man who doesn't want to bed me?"

He raised his right hand, palm upward and looked at her. "You don't. Get used to it. We can make a good team, but that's it."

"Agreed. Now tell me about your plan. I hope it works better than my last one."

"Don't beat yourself up over that. It was a brilliant plan, but something went wrong. Let's move on."

"So we wait a couple of weeks and let them get lazy?"

"Which gives us more time to plan and train so that it goes right. You got the list. In which states do we have the best soldiers?"

She reached for her purse and pulled out a carefully folded piece of paper. "We have four or five possibilities in California."

"They still go to church in California? I thought they were all into that Eastern mystical shit."

"There are still plenty of churches, big and small, there. We also have a couple of good possibilities in New York, both in the city and in other places. Indiana is a possibility. I still like doing it in Texas, though, and we have several potential soldiers there."

"Not a good choice for the next strike."

"Why not? Those are big states. They'll make a big splash. And I got a list of potential recruits right here."

"Two things to think about," said Jeb. "First right now the law is on high alert. Those states you mentioned will come eventually, but they also have some of the best security details—maybe with the exception of Indiana. Second, those recruits need to be trained, maybe even a little more thoroughly than the first ones."

"So?"

My buddies hang out in the wide-open spaces. They don't like all those crowded cities. They like the mountains. Besides, New York and California are all hung up on monitoring who is buying the guns."

"So what states do you suggest?'

"Think about the wide open west where men are men and guns are available. Anybody can get a gun in Kansas, Wyoming, Nevada, and possibly Colorado. They believe in freedom in those states. And I know some good contacts out there. Texas is not bad either. We can see where you get the best recruits."

"Don't worry, I can find some young soldiers that will be glad to come to whatever camps I indicate."

"You always refer to your teenage recruits as soldiers, and that gave me an idea. Since even after a few weeks, people are going to be suspicious of strange teenagers, let's buy some army outfits from a used clothing store, get a few medals and ribbons to hang on them, and have them pretend they are coming to protect the church."

"I like it. Then people will be scared of both teenagers and soldiers."

"And in Texas, where all the real men carry guns to church, we'll send in two different youth to sit in different spots. Then when one gets up to shoot, and the great defenders rise to shoot back, the second plant gets up and picks them off. Pretty soon there will be people shooting everywhere. We can have a whole massacre, and our guys won't have to do all the shooting."

"Brilliant and during our several week hiatus . . ."

"Our what?'

"Our break, while they think they are winning. During that time, do we do any more with the banners on the TV and Internet, or do we just lie low and make them think we have gone away?"

"That is your area. What do you have in mind?"

"I was thinking of teasing them and getting them all riled up. Like we could run a banner that said "Texans are wienie's . . . Lean to the left, lean to the right, pull out your shooter and fight, fight, fight."

"What you got against Texan men? They're just trying to stand up for their rights."

"OK, then we could have a banner that said, 'Bet you can't do in 50 states what you did in little Texas, Wisconsin.'"

"I'd say leave them alone for several weeks. Save your banners for after the hit."

"You ever go to church, Jeb?"

"I have my own religion out among the trees. I don't need a bunch of uptight preachers messing with my mind."

"Well, I've gone to church all my life, and they are always shouting 'Jesus saves,' and 'Jesus will come to take you to heaven if you are a good little boy or girl.' It is all based on a big lie that they call the resurrection. My daddy did all those things they say, and then some wino plowed into him with his car. Jesus didn't do diddly to save him."

"So you're going to prove them wrong?"

"I'm going to prove God wrong.

First we'll paralyze the whole nation and make them scared to go to church.

Hey, let's plan a shooting for Easter. "

"Easter, I like it, lots of people go to church on Easter."

"Right in the middle of Easter Sunday," she was getting enthused now, "when even the lazy ones get up and come to church, we'll send our soldiers into four states at once. They'll get a chance to test out the theory of resurrection all across the land."

"You're crazy, Barbara, but I think that just might work. And it will teach the government a thing or two as well."

"If we pull this off, Jeb, they will pull out all the stops to try to find us. Maybe we ought to vacation for a year or so in Tahiti. Maybe I can find you a pumped up stud to entertain you."

"Sex, sex, sex, that's all you think about, Barbara. You have to get that Barbie doll crap out of your mind. You are worth a lot more than a couple of tits and a tight ass."

"Sorry, I've always kept my brain to myself. I am concerned, though."

"What about?"

"You, really. If I die in all of this, at least I'll go out in a blaze of glory—or infamy as the case may be. But what about you? If we pull off this Easter showdown, they will pull out all the stops, and they'll shoot first and ask questions later. Are you prepared for that, Jeb?"

"I was born on a small farm in West Virginia. The banks screwed my papi out of his land and broke his spirit. He ran away, and my mom kept us alive by cleaning other people's homes and occasionally whoring herself for some extra bucks."

"Then you joined the army."

"Yep, and for the first time in my life, I was important to somebody else. My buddies counted on me, and they had my back. Every day we'd go out knowing if we weren't sharp, it could be our last. Some of my buddies didn't make it."

"A horrible way to live."

"No, you don't understand. It was a great way to live. Each day was a rush. I smoked some weed, but I didn't need it to get high. I was tough, and my buddies looked up to me."

"And then you came home."

"I came home to a world of lies and boredom. The government lied, the rich people screwed you and went scot-free, the Internet was full of a bunch of scam artists, and no one gave a crap about me or each other. I joined up with a bunch of survivalists, but mostly we just run around in the mountains and pretend we'll make a difference. And then you came along, and I saw a way to get back into the action."

"But what if it crashes. We blew it in Wisconsin. Even if we succeed, they'll just hunt us down."

"Those terrorists in Iraq and Afghanistan took on the most powerful military in the world, and they are making fools out of our best generals. You are going to have our bloated government tied in knots. Even if we only do it for a few months, we'll have changed history."

"And you are willing to die for that?"

"We are all going to die, Barbara. A hillbilly like me usually dies in a mud puddle, and no one gets dirty. This way I'm at least going to have a chance to make a big splash, and a whole lot of self-important idiots are going to get mud in their eyes."

"Thanks, I knew you weren't the Judas, but I had to make sure."

"OK, let's pick our targets, and I'll get my buddies to start identifying training sites."

GATHERING THE TRIBE

CHAPTER 29

Frank and Jacob arrived back home on Tuesday. They chose to drive to give them time to mull over the possibilities. They tried to imagine what they would feel if they were the ones behind this operation. The idea of having the attack in Texas, Wisconsin, rather than the state of Texas was brilliant. Since the purpose of terrorism is to convince the public they are vulnerable and the authorities are helpless to protect them, the surprise attack in Texas, Wisconsin, should have accomplished its purpose. The fact it failed must infuriate the Leader.

As they drove and talked, each tried to think like the madman behind this. What would they do to get the plan back on track? Mile after mile, as they drove down through Illinois, Indiana, and Kentucky, they rolled the possibilities over in their conversation. Several times Frank would stop for a coke and call Rachel to play out different possibilities. Would they hit in the middle of the week next time, perhaps at a church supper? Would they return to Texas or pick a church in New England or Colorado?

Jacob finally interrupted his father's endless speculation. "Dad, this is getting us nowhere. I'll call Rachel and a couple of the veterans from the group. Together we can come up with a plan."

"That's good. We'll be home Tuesday. Do you want to meet at my house? What about Tuesday evening?"

"Better meet on Wednesday so you can catch a little sleep first. I'll call Brian and see if that will work."

"Shall I invite Mandy? She'll be able to marshal the resources if we come up with a plan."

"Tell her about the meeting but ask her not to come. The vets are a little skittish around government folk. Find out where you can contact her in case we come up with anything."

"What about Rachel, she's police, will that spook them?"

"They're men, Dad, and your daughter, my sister, is young and beautiful. If she doesn't wear a uniform, they'll fall all over themselves trying to impress her."

Frank and Jacob arrived home Tuesday late afternoon. Frank called Amanda while on the road to tell her about the plan. She was not happy to be disinvited but said she understood. Later in the day, she called him back and suggested he arrange a Skype connection so, if the group agreed, she could be skyped in.

By late Wednesday afternoon, Jacob and Rachel arrived bringing both food and drinks for the meeting. The vets were scheduled to arrive about six.

"Let's set up in the living room around the big table. We can put the food on a side table and the drinks in a cooler," said Rachel. "Jacob, help me move Dad's chair into the bedroom out of the way."

"Dad, what do you want us to do with the files on the table?" asked Jacob.

"And the floor?" added Rachel.

"That's what spare bedrooms are for," said Frank.

They cleared the living room. Frank began to pace. "Where do we begin?"

Jacob opened his briefcase and unfolded a large map of the United States on the table. "Think like you were the mastermind behind this, and your brilliant idea failed. What would you do?"

They all three stared at the map.

"I'd want to strike quickly and in a big way to show I'm still in control," said Rachel.

"Except you don't want to take a chance on blowing it twice in a row," said Jacob. "They, I'm assuming there is more than one of them, they are a little on edge."

"Why's that?" asked Frank.

"Remember, before they were in charge of anything that happened, but now someone out-thought them. It's evened the playing field. Neither side is sure how the other one is figuring the next move."

"Yeah," said Rachel. "Someone discovered our last plot in time to stop it. What else do they know? Are the authorities moving in to arrest us? Is there a spy among us? Should we plan the next attack or should we run for cover?"

"Clearly they need to strike again somewhere," said Frank. "If they fade away, they lose everything."

"If I were them," said Jacob, "I'd plan the next shooting outside North Carolina. The target should be far enough away that people would be convinced this is a national event. Texas might still be a good choice."

"According to police reports," said Rachel, "there were three attacks on youth last Sunday by vigilantes who thought Texas was the target."

"What happened?" asked Jacob.

"Sort of ironic," said Rachel. "This time people aren't nervous about Blacks, Hispanics, or Middle Easterners. Now when someone sees a well-dressed Caucasian teen walking near a church, people get uptight. In Dallas, a young couple came on Sunday to talk to the pastor about a wedding. They thought they would attend worship and talk to the pastor after the service."

"Don't tell me," said Jacob, "some super studs decided they would protect the church and accosted them."

"You got it," said Rachel. "Same thing happened in Laredo. Except in Laredo, you'd think we were having a repeat of the shootout at the OK Corral.

"A self-appointed posse tried to stop a group of teens walking down the street. The problem was young people made up the posse as well. Along came some older volunteers in a pickup. Seeing young people with guns drawn, they figured they might be the enemy. Bullets started flying, and three people were injured before cooler heads prevailed."

"Pretty soon the terrorists won't need to do anything," said Frank. "They can just hide out while we all grab our guns and shoot each other."

The doorbell rang. Frank opened the door. Brian, Jalin, and Julio from the PTG support group stood on the steps. They wore shorts and light shirts. Brian had a smile on his lips.

"Jacob mentioned you might want a few of us to help you brainstorm the possibilities," said Brian.

"Welcome, we can use your thinking. Be nice if we could get ahead of them like the last time."

"I'm afraid we were pretty lucky last time, but we will be glad to give it a try."

As they entered the room, they quickly greeted Jacob but became shy when they saw Rachel.

"Fellows, I want you to meet my sister Rachel. She is the one who first smoked out Natalie, the second shooter."

"Not that we were able to track her down in time," said Rachel, "but it did help clue us into the larger pattern."

"You're that cop? The one who went undercover to the high school?" said Jalin.

Rachel smiled as she extended her hand. "I'm with the police and part of the task force trying to figure this thing out."

Julio came across the room to shake her hand. "Jacob tells us you're pretty sharp." He chuckled and turned his head so that his one eye glanced back at the others. "I think Jacob may be right; on the first part at least."

"Cops aren't our favorite company, but you might be an exception."

"Let's gather around the table in the living room. Food on the side table and drinks in the cooler," said Frank.

"Now you're talking," said Brian as he greeted Rachel and headed for the table.

Jacob tried to summarize some of the things they discussed. "The problem is we aren't sure when or where they'll strike next."

For the next hour they ate, drank, and discussed possibilities.

Lifting his Coors and taking a swig, Jalin said, "If I were the genius behind this, I'd lay low for a few weeks. People are hyper-alert right now. I'd want them to get bored with waiting and begin to relax. Americans have no patience."

"Gives the Leader more time to recruit the next soldiers and give them training," added Julio.

Brian grabbed a hot dog flowing with mustard. "I think we should leak to the media the suits have an inside informer, and they are trying to pin down the location for the next hit."

"The suits?" asked Frank.

"The Feds," said Brian. "They always dress like they're going to a bank meeting."

"I get it," said Rachel. "We feed the Leader's paranoia. Let them spend some energy looking for their Judas, cool."

Brian's face colored a little as he stood up taller. "If we can ramp up the pressure, one of them might turn on the others."

"Eh, Brian, you may be a genius at strategy, but your table manners suck. You got mustard everyplace 'cept the hot dog." Julio handed him a napkin. "I only have one good eye, and I can be neater than that."

"While you guys are trying on new mustard designs, we still need to figure out where they will strike next," said Jalin. "Maybe we should start not with where but with who."

"Say more," said Jacob.

Jalin popped the cap off a Budweiser and started walking back and forth as if gathering his thoughts. "Something Julio said before he started playing Miss Manners with the mustard bit."

"I'm sure it is brilliant, but what did I say?"

"You said this Leader might use some time for more training. These snot-nosed twerps who are shooting up the churches knew what they were doing when they pulled those guns."

Julio slapped his thigh. "That's right, and if they are going to hit more than one state, they either do a lot of traveling or have some buddies helping them out."

"Traveling slows down their range and also raises the risk they might be spotted," said Jalin.

Frank, Rachel, and Jacob stood there twisting their heads back and forth between the speakers like watching a tennis match.

"Now we're cracking," said Brian. "What group do we know that is spread across the country; trained in the use of guns; and if approached right, would like to embarrass the government, and could give a shit about the churches?" He stopped and turned to Frank. "Sorry about that preacher, but if it's the guys I'm thinking about; the church is just another club."

"Well that club is a target right now, so I can't waste time being defensive about how it's described. Who are these guys you're talking about?"

"The media calls them survivalists," said Jalin. "They are vets who came back from the wars but never fit back in. They love their guns, and they love their freedom."

Frank was getting excited. "Jacob mentioned them after the interrogation of the shooters in Wisconsin."

Brian pushed the last of his hot dog into his mouth and wiped the mustard from his face. "They hide out in the mountains, practice for the next big battle, and above all believe those in charge aren't to be trusted."

"So if someone can recruit alienated teenagers and has a strategy to paralyze the government, they might be interested in helping out," Jacob said.

Rachel grabbed a hot dog and smothered it with mustard. "I think this may be genius food. These soldiers of fortune are spread out across the country, so there are natural bases of training anywhere you want to strike." She almost danced with excitement.

Brian handed her a couple of napkins. "I think you are beginning to fit in. There is a spot of mustard where I wouldn't dare try to wipe it off."

Rachel glanced down at her blouse and blushed. "Thanks for the napkin and your caution. I wouldn't want to test out whether police or veterans have better jujitsu training."

"Whoa! Watch out Brian," said Jalin. "I think the sister is locked and loaded."

Frank was amused at the banter but wanted to direct the conversation back to the subject at hand. "How does this help us pin down the next place of attack?"

"Those vets feel crowded easily. They want space and freedom. That's why they like the mountains," said Julio. "If you can choose anywhere, then look at places where they hang out."

"Near a city," said Jalin." To make a big splash, you will need a big church in a large city."

"Like with Wisconsin," said Jacob, "we make our best guess and hope we are lucky. It's like a giant chess game. We are going to make some bad moves but, hopefully, so will they."

"To use your analogy," said Frank, "we also keep an eye out for the king or the queen as the case may be. If we can checkmate the king, I think we can begin to get some control over this."

"OK, brothers," Jalin glanced at Rachel "and sister, let's study the map on the table and find places vets might hang out near a juicy city."

They all crowded around the table and began to examine possibilities.

"I vote for wide open spaces like Kansas, Wyoming, and Colorado," said Julio. They have loose gun laws, moves the center of attention out west, and you can set up training spots where you won't be noticed."

"OK, we'll miss some places, but those might be good beginnings." Frank picked up the cooler and placed it on a table for others to access. "We'll probably add some later, but even if we choose right, how are we going to protect the churches in those states? We aren't even sure what city to watch."

"Let's think like a terrorist who wants to frighten those in charge," said Barrie. "We avoid DC right now because they are too good at security, but we do want to shake the government."

"Gotcha, brother," said Jalin. "We pick on the state capitols to show the government is ineffective."

"This can be all wrong," said Frank, "but let's assume you are right. How do we protect the churches in those cities?"

"We invite the esteemed governors in those states to call out the National Guard to patrol near the largest churches," said Jalin. "Then you convince the pastors to employ some version of the strategy you used in Wisconsin. That was brilliant, by the way."

"You mean the befriend a youth approach?" said Jacob.

"If we can get them to cooperate, that might be a good plan even in the cities we overlook. What if all the churches all over the nation gave special attention to any youth who came their way?" said Brian.

"I'll take that bet and up the ante," said Rachel. "Let's invite young people across the nation to help us combat the plague. We put out the word that all young people who care about this country start attending church and standing up for the faith. The youth themselves will be part of our front lines."

"Rachel, that's brilliant," said her father. "We get a triple win. We invite the youth to be part of something larger than themselves; we invite the churches to take the youth seriously and address their hungers; and we demonstrate to alienated young people there is a future worth living for."

They continued talking for another hour.

Frank decided it was time to bring Amanda into the conversation. "Fellas, Amanda, from the Justice Department, knows of our meeting, and she asked if we developed some good ideas, she could be Skyped into the conversation."

The vets all looked at each other. Julio picked up another Coors. "We are not part of the survivalists, but we have our own issues with the government. However, this lady played straight with us in Wisconsin, so if she is your main squeeze, I say let's talk to her."

Rachel was just taking a swig of a Coke when Julio talked about Amanda as Frank's main squeeze. She spewed the Coke all across the table as she saw her father's face turn bright red. She struggled for control and said, "Yeah, Dad, let's talk to your main squeeze."

Frank tried to look stern. "When we get her on Skype, let's remember she is representing the Justice Department, and our rumored relationship is not part of the conversation."

There were several hoots and hollers as Frank set up the Skype connection. Almost the moment he pushed the connect button, Amanda responded.

"Amanda, I think you know most of the people here. You met them in the Skype conversation prior to the Wisconsin event."

"Hi, fellas. Have you got another miracle to pull out of the hat for me?

Frank spun the camera around while the vets along with Jacob and Rachel greeted her.

"Let me fill you in with our thinking at this point." He described the reason for them focusing on the survivalists and how that idea led them to make some educated guesses about what will happen next. "We are hoping, whoever this group is, they will take a couple of weeks to regroup and to plan. We can only guess which states will be next, but since they need a victory the next time, and if we are right about the survivalist involvement, we think some states are more likely than others."

"The deployment of the National Guard around several big cities shouldn't be a problem," said Amanda. "Most governors are really on edge and want to take some action. The idea of involving the youth is a little more complicated. I'm not sure about how to set that up."

"Amanda," said Jacob, "what about speaking to the President about the possibility of a national address to the youth of our nation? What we want to do is to flip this conversation around from looking at the youth as a source of fear and suspicion to seeing them as a resource."

"I can't guarantee what he will decide, but I'm sure the President will be glad to be part of the conversation. This whole nation is nervous."

"Do you think the press leak is a possibility?" asked Brian. "What we want to do is plant some seeds of doubt and even disunity among the Leader and whoever he is working with."

"Sure, but we don't need to leak the news. I can hold a press conference and phrase it in such a way as to leave the impression we have an inside source. I mean how else can anyone explain our incredibly good fortune in Texas, Wisconsin." Amanda lifted her arms as if to embrace those on the screen. "Let me say again how fortunate this nation is you guys came up with that option. If I were the Leader, I'd be banging my head against a wall trying to figure that one out. They should be ripe for a little paranoia."

"We thought if the goal is to paralyze the whole U.S., they will probably want to move further west," said Frank. "Our guys are going to try to make some contacts with vet buddies who might know more about the survivalist groups, but we chose about four states as possibilities—Kansas, Wyoming, Colorado, and Nevada. They all have loose gun laws and lots of wide open spaces in which to hide during the training."

"What cities and what churches?" asked Amanda.

"We think state capitols would be a good way to embarrass the government. We're not so sure about the churches, but likely they will pick on the big ones," said Jalin.

"Makes sense, but what if we guess wrong?" asked Amanda.

"We probably will guess wrong on some of them. People will be killed," said Jacob, "but if the congregations buy into the befriend the youth emphasis and the young people start flocking to the churches, together with the Guard, maybe we can minimize the damage."

"At least we have a strategy and hope of disrupting some of the plans," said Amanda. "We're in a better place than before. I'll talk to the President and get back to you. Again, thanks, people. I'm not sure what we would do without you."

Brian winked at the others and turned towards the camera. "We had some good leadership from your main . . ." He hesitated as Frank sent him a sharp look . . . "from our main man, Frank, here. We are glad he knew you, so we had access to your resources."

Amanda got a large smile on her face. "When you get him in the right mood, he's OK."

They laughed.

"Seriously, there isn't a better man to be connected with. He almost causes you to want to reconsider the value of faith." She folded her hands in a prayer stance. "I'll talk to you all soon."

She winked out on the screen.

NATIONAL CAMPAIGN

CHAPTER 30

"I hope and pray we are right about the delay," said Frank. "What if we are wrong, and they shoot up some church this coming Sunday."

"Dad, if that happens, it will be tragic, but what could we possibly do to stop it? We got a good break in Wisconsin, but we are no closer to pinning down who this leader is than anyone else."

"Rachel is right. If they strike this Sunday, we'll hope they make a mistake that will give us some idea what is behind all of this."

"I keep thinking about the message I found in Natalie's locker. There has to be a clue there."

"How did it go again?" asked Jacob.

"'It's a lie.' 'Others must pay 127OMN.'" Rachel held her head in both hands. "I can't get it out of my head."

"It looks like a children's code to me—not very sophisticated," said Frank.

The doorbell rang.

Frank glanced at Jacob. "Could you get that, son?"

BLESSED ARE THE PEACEMAKERS

Jacob rose to answer the door.

Frank poked Rachel and whispered, "Watch this."

When he answered the door, they heard him stutter a second and say, "Brandy, what are you doing here?"

Brenda took her baseball cap off, releasing her fiery red hair, and looked past his shoulder. "You may not remember me, but I used to be a close friend. So are you going to stand there, or are you inviting me in?"

"Of course, come in. I just didn't expect you. I'm pleased to see you."

"Relax, Jacob. Your father invited me, and I come as a friend, not as a reporter. I know the rules."

As Jacob bent to kiss her on the cheek, Frank called out, "Brandy, good to see you. We can use another good mind to help solve this puzzle."

"I am glad to see you," said Jacob. "I've meant to call you. I really have. It's just that things were so crazy lately."

"We'll talk about it later—maybe." She placed a hand on Jacob's arm and moved around him. "Hi, Rachel, Frank. Thanks for inviting me. So what are you working on?"

"We are trying to break the code we found in the locker of the second shooter," said Frank.

"Oh, I love puzzles," said Brandy. She reached out and grabbed Jacob's hand pulling him beside her. "That's why I started dating Jacob."

"Ouch, nice zinger," said Rachel. "Let me bring you up to date. When I searched Natalie's locker at her school, I found a note with this message on it."

She showed a piece of paper to Brenda that said, "It's a lie. Others must pay 127OMN."

"We are dealing with teenagers," said Rachel. "We are trying to think like a child to decode it."

Jacob reached across the table and grabbed a notebook and a pen. "If a child wanted to make a secret code, what is the most logical way he'd do it?"

"Substitution," Brandy said, as she placed her purse on a chair and came around to look over Jacob's shoulder. "You remember those dumb codes we used to make up as children. Every letter or number stood for its substitute."

Jacob wrote out the alphabet and over it the numbers. "Let's see, 1, 2, 7 would stand for a, b, and g. Substitute numbers for O, M, and N, and it comes out 15, 13, 14. I don't see anything there."

Frank stood up and began to walk around the room. "Remember, this all started with a focus on the resurrection." He scratched the back of his head as he walked.

"Maybe it's Adam, the Bible, and God are a lie," said Brandy. "An angry young person would think that was a rather bold thing to declare."

"That's good," said Rachel, "but what about the rest. Besides, suppose those are the words, how does it help us?"

"Since it's teenagers who are doing the shooting," said Frank, "let's keep trying to think like a young person. Jacob, is there a psychologist over at the university whose focus is on teenagers? She or he might be able to assist us."

Rachel poked Jacob and grinned. "Maybe we ought to bring your main squeeze into this conversation. She's pretty good at sorting out clues."

Brandy looked up from studying the paper. "Who's that? Oh, you must mean Amanda?"

Frank turned red in the face and tried to cover with a scowl.

"Oh come on, Dad," Rachel said. "It was pretty funny when Julio said it."

"Besides," said Jacob, "the Coke that came through Rachel's nose did a good job of clearing her sinuses."

Frank waved his hand in dismissal and cleared his throat. "Amanda is going to call about finding a time when we can discuss some next steps with the President. I know the whole country is feeling this fear, but I don't have any brilliant plan to share with the President."

"That's both exciting—talking to the President—and rather

unnerving," said Brandy. "I wish I could put my reporter hat back on. This story gets bigger and bigger."

"Not now," Frank said. "Like the last time, once this is resolved, you will be on the inside track."

"Sounds good to me," said Brandy.

"Let's get back to trying to think like a terrorist," said Jacob, "and maybe we can come up with some ideas."

"Hey, look at the time. Didn't Amanda say they were going to hold a press conference at the Justice Department this afternoon about five?" said Rachel. "It's four-forty-five now. Where's your remote, Dad?"

"How should I know? You guys cleaned up this room. Now I can't find anything."

"Let's see, if I were my fastidious sister, where would I place the remote for the TV?" Jacob began to survey the room. "Oh, I have an idea, how about in the little basket that holds the other remotes?" He walked over to the TV. "Voila, my sister is so predictable." He raised the remote above his head in triumph and then pointed it at the TV. "What channel?"

"This is big news," said Frank. "I suspect any of the major channels will do. Try CNN on 29."

Rachel was already opening the refrigerator. "I'm having a cold beer. Can I get you one, Brandy? Dad?" She shifted her gaze. "I may be predictable,"(She stuck out her tongue at her brother.) "but I'm also marvelously forgiving. If you say pretty please, I may even get you one, brother dear."

Soon they were all seated and watching as Wolf Blitzer came on the screen and was beginning to provide some background in preparation for switching to the news conference about to begin at the Justice Department. "We are about to hear from Amanda Singletary, the head of the Violence Task Force tracking these events."

The cameras focused in as Amanda approached the podium. She was dressed in a severe business suit, and her hair was tightly wrapped in a bun on her head. She thanked the reporters for coming but did not greet them with a smile.

"I will make a brief statement bringing you up to date with our investigation. I will only take a few questions. I am informed the President will be addressing the nation within the next forty-eight hours."

"As you are aware, there were two shooting incidents in churches in Lincoln, North Carolina, over the last several weeks. In both cases, the shooters were clearly disturbed teenagers who entered the buildings under the pretense of attending worship and opened fire on the congregation. There were multiple injuries and some deaths, including the pastor of the second church."

"Was the pastor of the first church a specific target?" one of the reporters called out. "The shooter knew his name."

"We are investigating that possibility. Please let me finish before we have other questions."

Amanda continued. "At first we focused our investigation on Lincoln and the fact the first shooter did, as was mentioned, call out the pastor's name—Frank Sessions. Now, with the further incident in Texas, Wisconsin, we know this is more than a local issue. "

"Did you have an informer that tipped you off to the new location?" a reporter shouted.

Amanda had found a friendly reporter who agreed to shout out the question without indicating to anyone he was cooperating with the Justice Department. Amanda turned and stared at him as if he had violated her request to hold the questions until she had finished.

"We were fortunate to gather some info before the incident that allowed us to be prepared. I cannot go into any more details as to how we came into our intel." There was an immediate buzz among the reporters. Several attempted to ask more about a possible informer and whether the source would help in identifying future incidents. Amanda deflected the questions but allowed them to surface the possibility the Justice Department had some inside information. Within a few minutes, she ended the press conference with a reminder to stay alert to further announcements about when the President would speak to the nation.

Frank clicked the TV off. Jacob raised a fist in the air. "That was beautiful. Whoever they are, that ought to throw them into some confusion and paranoia."

In another part of the city, Barbara was watching the news conference in her office. When it was over, she gritted her teeth and pounded her chair with her fist. "Who the hell could have ratted us out?" She pulled out a bottle of Jonnie Walker and a glass from her bottom drawer. She and Bob occasionally shared some wine in the evening, but lately as the pressure built, she found an occasional slug of Scotch calmed her nerves. She kept the bottle in her office because she didn't want Bob to begin to wonder what was upsetting her.

She and Jeb had agreed to wait a couple of weeks and let the nation stew in anxiety. When people began to relax, there would be shootings in four different states at once, which would throw everyone into a complete panic. What she didn't like was the President and Justice Department suggesting they were getting things under control. How could they possibly know about Wisconsin?

If there is a rat on the inside, maybe if she makes a sudden switch in the plans, it will smoke him out. She opened her computer and entered her password to a locked file of potential candidates for shooters.

As she was searching, the Fox station she left on after the news conference began an interview by Bill O'Reilly with Eric Ivory. She shifted her gaze towards the TV as she heard Ivory's name mentioned.

"Eric, I think it might be helpful for our listeners to know you have a little closer connection with these shooting incidents than being, I must say, an outspoken and rather courageous commentator. You are from Lincoln, North Carolina, where all these events began, and you had previous interactions with Frank Sessions, who is pastor of the first church to be shot up. Tell us a little about your background."

An acute observer might see Eric's chest expand slightly as he turned towards the camera to respond to O'Reilly's introduction. "Well, Bill, as you said, I'm from Lincoln. For several years, I've tried to spread the truth in that area of North Carolina in my "Out of the Ivory Palaces" broadcast. Yes, I am acquainted with Frank Sessions, a rather liberal pastor in the city."

"It's been reported," O'Reilly said, "the shooter, not a member of Frank's church, not only knew his name but seemed offended by him. Do you think Frank had some role in triggering this tragic series of events?"

"I want to be fair, Bill. I don't know how the boy knew Frank's name or whether Frank was part of what triggered this rampage. I do think the type of liberal, watered-down Christianity Frank and his ilk represent contributes to the emptiness of life and the breakdown of the family that allows these teenage hoodlums to act out in such destructive ways."

"As you know, Eric, I've been pretty involved in the study of religion, even written a couple of books in that area." He paused as if expecting a response.

"Yes, I've read them. Valuable work."

"Uh, thank you, but to return to our subject at hand, do you think these shooters and their mysterious leader have a vendetta against religion—might they even feel betrayed in some situation or other, and are seeking some deranged type of revenge?"

"I'm not sure, but I think we don't need some weak-kneed, bleeding heart response. Whatever their motivation, our churches are under attack, and we need to defend the faith."

"Well, that raises an interesting question. A couple of years ago, there was a lot of talk about whether Christians should bring guns to church, particularly concealed ones. I think one pastor in Texas was defending concealed carry as a constitutional right. What do you think about that?"

Eric leaned forward and extended his arm with a closed fist. He stared directly into the camera. "Let's get this straight, once and for all. Turning the other cheek was for personal interaction where you might save the sinner. Turning the other cheek was never about stopping a deranged killer from shooting down the faithful."

"So," O'Reilly said as he sat up in his chair and focused on the camera, "you'd encourage worshipers, especially in this tense time, to come prepared to defend the defenseless and protect the faithful."

"Any man worthy of the faith would take such a position." Then he smiled and chuckled a little. "To show you what a liberated man I am, I'd encourage the women to come with guns in their purses as well."

"So Texas has it right?"

"Listen, Bill, you mark my words, the shooters, who are mostly scared teenagers, will choose any place but Texas for the next time. Their crazy leader, whoever he is, was shut down in Wisconsin and won't risk challenging men who are prepared to defend themselves."

The interview continued, but Barbara turned her attention back towards the computer. She reviewed the list of teenagers who had already received some training in Texas and especially those near Dallas. "Let's see what real men," she raised her voice, "will do when they are looking down the barrel of a gun." She giggled. "If they are like the real men I know, they will probably pee in their pants."

The next day she arranged for a quick meeting with Jeb in a McDonalds on Duke Street. He arrived, looked around to be sure no one was watching, and ordered a Frappé Mocha. Having paid for his drink, he walked towards the booth in the rear where Barbara was sipping on a Coke.

"Hey, Babe, what's up?"

"I am not your babe." She glared a warning and said. "Did you see the news conference? Somebody ratted on us. I've decided to make a change in our strategy."

"OK, general, what's the plan?" There was a slight smirk on his face as he sat down.

"That idiot, Ivory, was bragging on the Bill O'Reilly program that Texas men know how to put a stop to all of this by bringing their guns with them to church."

"Oh, Lordy, we're out to cut the balls off some Texas cowboys and show them who's really in charge." He gave her an intense look, but she didn't turn away. "I'm impressed, Barbara, you're going to take it to the man. If we can frighten Texas men, the rest of the nation will shit in their britches."

"That's the idea, and I like your suggestion of sending in two or even three shooters so we can pick off some of the defenders and confuse people as to who is doing the shooting. I reviewed our list, and you have two shooters in training outside of Waco."

"Waco?" he shook his head. "You do have a sense of the macabre, but yeah, a couple of buddies told me they had two who were mighty disappointed when we told them to draw back and wait."

"OK," said Barbara, "but with this issue of a mole somewhere, let's tell them it may be San Antonio and in a megachurch—one of those that think they are God's gift to the faith."

"Sort of like your husband's church?"

Her fist closed around a bottle on the table. "Careful, Jeb, you are about to cross the line. But, yes, now that you brought it up, like my husband's church. Only at the last moment, we will choose a more modest congregation in Dallas and observe who scrambles to change the message."

"I'll go you one better. You pick the place and don't tell me until the last moment. I'll tell my buddy to pass the word it is San Antonio but to keep it a secret that it might shift back to Waco. Then we'll see where the defenses gear up."

Barbara carefully put the bottle back on the table and smiled. "I think we understand each other. Let's try for a week after Sunday but pay attention to the President's address and see if we need to make any last-minute adjustments."

Jeb took a draw on his Frappé and rose. "Most of the crap they serve in here is pure poison, but their frappes are delicious." He tilted his head to the left and up and smiled. "I wish I'd had a tough broad like you at my side in Iraq." He smiled and pulled his lips in. "After I leave, wait five minutes, and then you leave. I'll observe in case anyone is following you."

BRIAN HAS AN IDEA

CHAPTER 31

Brenda left after the news conference. Frank suggested the rest of them order some pizza and continue to process what was happening. "Amanda said she would try to call about 9, and I want all of us in on the conversation."

About 7:30, Rachel's cell phone rang. She read her call screen. "I don't recognize the number, but it's local so I think I will find out." She pushed the button and said "This is Officer Sessions. Can I help you?"

Frank and Jacob heard Rachel hesitate and say, "Hold a second." She turned to them and said, "Save me a piece of pizza. I'll be right back." She moved into another room leaving them to continue their conversation.

When she returned, Frank noticed a slight flush on her cheeks. "Uh . . . that was Brian. He had a question he wanted to run by me."

"So my old friend, Brian, wanted to consult with my sister. How interesting."

"Cram it, Jacob."

Jacob folded his hands and was about to speak when Frank held up a hand to interrupt the teasing and said, "What did he want, Rachel?"

"He and his buddies have been putting out feelers about this issue of the survivalists. He's heard a couple of rumors that makes him suspicious.

He wanted to know if the government would spring for a couple of airplane tickets so that a couple of the guys could check them out. I told him about being here waiting for Amanda's call and told him to come on over."

"Rachel, I'm your brother, and I will tease you whenever I get a chance, but that was a good decision. Brian may help us make some more progress in solving this problem."

"Do you think we ought to order another pizza?" said Frank. "If I recall, Brian is thin, but he doesn't have any problem eating."

Rachel lifted her phone. "I'll do it. Brian likes extra cheese and anchovies." She began to dial.

"So this may not be the first pizza he has shared," said Jacob with a big grin on his face.

Rachel made a face at Jacob and continued ordering the pizza.

Brian and the pizza arrived about 30 minutes later. "Wow, my supper came the same time I did. It's amazing how that Pizza Hut read my mind."

With the pizza delivered and drinks refreshed, Brian explained to them about some of the rumors he was picking up. "Nothing is ever direct," he said. "You have to read between the lines, but the word is there are several different soldier groups working around the country. It's amazing how these guys are fiercely independent, but with the Internet, they are beginning to connect with each other."

"No matter what our politics, we have a hunger for community," said Frank.

"That's true among the teenagers too. That's why cults form," said Jacob. "Do you hear any rumors about this mysterious Leader? Is he one of the survivalists too?"

"Don't have any information on that," said Brian. "Don't have much on this, but I do have some contacts in various parts of the country. I was thinking— if a few of us could take a trip, we might smoke out some more info."

"Dad," Rachel said, "Couldn't Amanda find some money to help Brian and a couple of friends scout out this thing?"

"She's calling soon. Let's ask her. I think she will find this very interesting. Brian, we'll share some of your pizza, but we've already had some, so eat your fill."

"Don't mind if I do." He lifted a piece to his mouth. "Um, this is good—extra cheese and anchovies, an excellent choice."

Brian didn't notice Jacob's smile and Frank's wink at Rachel, whose cheeks colored slightly.

They continued to talk and speculate about next steps until Frank's computer indicated a call was coming through. "Gather around, folks, this should be Amanda."

Amanda's face popped up on the screen, and Frank told her Brian, Jacob, and Rachel were with him.

"Hey, guys. Good to see you all. Brian, the President wanted me to mention how grateful he is for your group's help. Veterans are a real asset to our country."

"Actually, Mandy," Frank said, "Brian came up with some new information that may be helpful. I'll let him explain it to you."

Brian told Amanda what he had heard about activity among some survivalist groups. "I want to emphasize these are rogue groups and don't reflect the attitude of most veterans, but the rumors are there is some extra activity among some of them."

"So you think those guys who trained . . ,"She paused to look through her notes, " . . . trained Shirley and Daniel in Wisconsin might be part of one of these survivalist groups?"

"Someone trained these teens to shoot. There is some buzz to suggest there might be several similar soldiers willing to train more of them in different parts of the country. They often hang out in remote places where they can run war games and practice shooting. These would be perfect spots to bring the teens for training."

"Good grief, how many of these estranged vets must be hiding out all over the place, and who is connecting them with these lost teenagers?"

"Amanda, this is Jacob. We don't have a clue to the second question, but if what Brian heard is true, it might provide us with a thread we can trace back to the Leader. Many vets are only willing to open up to another vet, so Brian was wondering if it were possible to let him and a couple of others travel out to some of the known sites and see if he can find out more."

"Sure, Brian, I'd fly you first class if it can help us get a lead on this."

Brian gave a small laugh. "Another time that would be great, but if a survivalist travels, it will be incognito, so economy class will be fine. There might be three of us going to a couple of places out west and maybe in Arkansas. It shouldn't be obvious we are traveling on government subsidy."

"You get me the names, and I will set up a code word with a couple of airlines so you can get the tickets you ask for." She paused and shook her head. "You guys are all amazing. OK Frank, you got any more surprises for me before we talk about your conversation with the President?"

"Amanda, this is Rachel. I'm going to let you get started talking with Dad and Jacob while I show Brian out, and I'll be right back."

Rachel and Brian stood up and moved towards the door.

Frank and Amanda had just begun to explore some of the talking points they thought should be included in a Presidential address when they heard a shout, a shot, and a scream.

Jacob was up first with Frank not far behind him, leaving Amanda shouting into the screen. "What's happening? Frank, what's happening?" She got no response and could only see a couch and a wall with a Guatemalan cross hanging on it.

When Jacob threw open the door, he saw a dark Ford Focus disappear around the corner and some lights coming on in neighboring houses. Then he looked to his left and saw Brian lying on top of his sister in the bushes.

Frank leaped off the steps into the same bushes as he shouted

Rachel's name. He noticed a dark red spot forming on Brian's right shoulder as he reached down to help them both. Brian was trying to rise as Jacob reached out to help him.

"Rachel, speak to me, honey. Are you all right?" Frank got down on his knees near his daughter.

Her eyes were a little glazed, but she quickly focused and began to speak. "Thanks to Brian, I'm fine." Then she looked over and saw Jacob holding Brian in his arms. She got to her knees. "Bri, you're shot. Dad, call 911 and get an ambulance."

"I'm on it," said Jacob as he pulled out his cell and punched in the numbers.

"We need an ambulance at 400 Carver Street, home of The Reverend Frank Sessions. There has been a shooting, and people are injured. Please hurry."

"An ambulance is already on its way," came the response. "We had a call from the FBI about two minutes ago. Didn't know there was a shooting. Police are also on the way. Ambulance should be there in less than a minute."

At first Jacob was confused, but then he realized Amanda must have called when they ran from the Skype conversation. He clicked off, and his phone rang again.

"This is Jacob."

"Jacob, thank God I connected." Jacob could hear the mixture of the professional voice and the near panic of someone not knowing what had happened. "This is Amanda. I've alerted the police and ambulance. What happened?"

"There was a drive-by shooting. A dark Ford Focus. Too busy to get the license number. Brian's been hit. I'll call back when I know more." Jacob pocketed his phone. "Amanda already called the ambulance," said Jacob.

"Bri, speak to me. We have an ambulance on the way."

Brian opened his eyes and looked at Rachel. "You OK?"

"Yeah, thanks to you. I'm normally pretty alert, but I didn't see that coming. What tipped you off?"

"Car coming too fast and then it screeched its brakes. Used to be cycles in Iraq, but the same idea."

Just then four police cars with their lights blazing and sirens at full strength came down the street, closely followed by an ambulance. Not knowing what had happened, the police exited their cars with their guns ready.

Rachel rose and quickly shouted to her police colleagues. "I'm Rachel Sessions, Badge 5268. A man's been shot. Shooter was driving a dark Ford Focus headed North on Beacon Street. Radio an alert. See if you can cut him off before he reaches the interstate."

Seeing the site was secure, the EMT crew approached Brian on the run. His shirt was cut open and a light was provided to assist in examining the wound. The EMT looked up from where Brian was laying. "Upper right shoulder, entered from the rear. How'd he get you from that angle?"

"He turned to place his body between me and the shooter as we were flying off the steps into the bushes," Rachel said. "How bad is the wound?"

"Doesn't look like there will be any permanent damage, but it's going to be painful. Let me get some morphine to help out." He turned and sent his companion to the ambulance.

An attendant turned towards Rachel. "Let's check you and the others for any hidden problems."

"Check Rachel first," said Frank. "We came out after the shooting."

"Dad," said Jacob, "if you don't want half the Justice Department in your front yard, you'd better call Amanda. She sent the ambulance and police, but she is waiting to hear what really happened."

Assured that Brian and Rachel were safe, Frank exited the bushes and walked towards the street while placing a call to Amanda. "Sorry to leave you hanging," said Frank. "It got a little crazy."

"Jacob told me there was a shooting. Do you have any idea who it was or why?"

"It's going to take me a little while to process this," said Frank, "but I think we can conclude there is a reason why my church and I were the first targets of this nightmare."

"Come to Washington, Frank. I'll charter you a plane for the first thing tomorrow. We need to think this through before we talk to the President and his advisors. We need to know whether this is a national event or a local vendetta. Bring Jacob and Rachel too. We can make use of their brains while providing them a measure of protection at the same time."

"Rachel won't leave until we make sure Brian is OK. He took a bullet for her." Frank glanced back seeing his daughter hover near Brian as they put him in the ambulance. "Schedule the plane for 9:30 a.m. at Andrews. At least Jacob and I will be on it."

WHAT TO TELL A NATION

CHAPTER 32

Frank watched as they began their descent into Andrews Air force Base. He had taken Jacob and Rachel to the hospital to make sure Brian was out of danger. It was clear Rachel had developed an interest in Brian, even before the shooting. Frank had a father's concern. The overwhelming gratitude his daughter felt for Brian saving her life, and the sacrifice he had made in the process might move that relationship along more rapidly than was wise. Still, he had saved her life, and they were all grateful to him for that.

Frank had been impressed that her professional role as a police officer surfaced when the other officers arrived on the scene. Her quick description and command had been acted upon without question. There might even be a chance to catch the shooter, which would give them one more clue as to what was happening.

Even as he offered support to Rachel and Jacob, his mind kept puzzling over what had happened. He had begun to think beyond Lincoln and how the nation should respond. This attempt on Rachel's life jerked attention back to where it began. How did Amanda phrase it, "We need to decide whether this is a threat to the nation or some local vendetta?" If he was the real target and not the nation, a Presidential address might unnecessarily raise the nation's anxiety rather than be helpful.

But why was Rachel targeted? Was she just the unlucky one who had first opened the door? There was Texas, Wisconsin, which suggested this was far beyond something personal. Yet, the first shooter had called out his name and accused him of spreading a lie. Now the shooting had returned to Lincoln. We are approaching Easter. Are the nation's churches threatened or just he and—O God, and my children? I can't lose another family member to violence; I just can't.

He hadn't gotten much sleep last night. It was midnight before Rachel was convinced it was safe to leave Brian, and they had returned from the hospital. They were all so exhausted it didn't take much persuasion for them all to fall into bed. Within a couple of hours, Frank was wide awake rehashing all his old ideas and hoping something new would occur to him.

Jacob was up first and had the coffee and some eggs and toast ready when both he and Rachel stumbled out of their rooms. After calling the hospital and using some official language to persuade them to provide the latest update on Brian, Rachel's professional side emerged, and she agreed to go with them to Washington. Each was deep in thought as they made the flight.

Frank heard the landing gear being lowered on the plane. He had a quick view of the area as they made their final descent. *I can understand how having a private jet available on call might swell your head a little*, he thought. *Not a habit I'll need to get used to, though.*

He watched the plane taxi to a space removed from the normal terminal. A large SUV approached. Even before the door was opened for them to deplane, he spotted Amanda emerge from the car and step towards the stairs. She was dressed professionally, but Frank couldn't help but be struck by how attractive she was. *What is wrong with me? Here we are facing a national crisis, and I'm thinking about how Amanda looks.*

"Are you coming, Dad, or are you going to sit there and stare out the window?"

He came out of his daze and saw Jacob and Rachel moving towards the plane exit. As he rose to join them, the weight of what was facing them struck him. Although he accepted the fact he was somehow personally connected with what was taking place, he knew this was far bigger than him. What could he possibly tell the President?

Amanda greeted each of them with a friendly hug. It was clear to everyone she also felt the strain and wondered about the next steps.

"The President asked me to bring you directly to the White House. We are all convinced this is going to get bigger before it is over."

They all got into the dark van that waited for them and headed out. Under other circumstances, Frank knew he and his family would be thrilled to be invited to the White House to talk to the President, but their thoughts were focused on fears for their country. They exchanged some small talk but mostly sat in silence.

"What can I tell him?" Frank asked.

"Trust your gut. No one has an answer, but you have always had an inner compass that led you in the right direction. What the President and his advisers want are some fresh angles from which to view this."

Within 20 minutes, they saw the White House. Frank had heard about a special side entrance, and now he was entering an underground driveway. Even with the seriousness of the agenda, he couldn't help but be a little awed. He looked at his children and saw they also were impressed. Only Amanda appeared to be unaffected by their surroundings.

"You've obviously been here before. Any tips on how we should behave or what will be happening?" asked Frank.

Amanda smiled and patted his arm. "We will probably be taken to the oval office. Just be yourself, "she chuckled "or perhaps a tad humbler."

Jacob snickered. "Well put, Amanda."

It's almost like in the movies, Frank thought, as the door to the van was opened by a tall man in a suit who also was talking into a lapel mic announcing the guests had arrived. Without any hesitation, they were led to some elevators and taken upstairs. When the elevator doors parted, again they were met by a member of the Secret Service and ushered to the President's outer office, where an administrative assistant greeted them.

"The President will be available shortly. Would you like a cup of coffee or a cold drink while you wait?"

She turned to Amanda. "The President would like to see you first, Amanda, and then your guests will go in."

She nodded, smiled at the others, and moved towards the door. Another man standing by the door knocked softly and heard someone say "Enter." He opened the door for Amanda.

In less than ten minutes, she emerged from the room and invited them to come in with her. She had a strained look on her face but didn't say anything to them.

Frank was struck by how familiar the room looked, even though he had never been there before. There were two men and a woman sitting on couches, each with a cup of coffee before them, and the President, leaning on his desk facing the others. Amanda stepped forward. "Mr President, may I present to you The Reverend Frank Sessions, pastor of John Knox Presbyterian in Lincoln, North Carolina, his son, Jacob Sessions, who has a degree in the area of psychology and spirituality at the Seminary in Lincoln, and his daughter, Rachel Sessions, with the Lincoln Police Department and with the special task force investigating the church shootings in Lincoln."

The President reached out his hand to each of them. "While I wish it was under other circumstances, I am pleased to meet all of you." He smiled a depreciating smile and added. "A Presbyterian pastor, huh? I used to attend a Presbyterian church but haven't been very active lately."

"I fear former Presbyterians may be a majority among Presbyterians in this country, so you have many allies," said Frank.

"I guess I belong to that group," said the woman sitting on the couch. The two men chuckled with her.

"Let me introduce Dorothy Baker, Greg Simmons, and Ralph Smart, who are part of my task force working on this matter," said the President.

They all shook hands, and when everyone was seated, the President spoke. "So what have we got here, Frank? May I call you Frank?"

Frank nodded.

"Is this a new terror tactic by some Muslim fanatics or what?"

Frank felt his facial muscles tighten; he drew in a deep breath and exhaled. "That is not accurate," he said, "and if you even allude to that possibility in public, you will contribute to the terrorist's agenda among all the fanatics around the world."

There was a sudden silence as some studied the floor and others looked at the President to see how he would respond.

Amanda held out a hand towards Frank. 'Uh, Frank, I don't think . . . "

The President silenced Amanda and stared at Frank for a moment. "Present company excepted, I have plenty of Yes-Men around me, and I like it that you are not afraid to challenge me, Frank." The others began to relax. "What we are dealing with is far too serious to hide behind being nicey nicey. Go ahead, Frank, I want to hear your take on this."

"First, I apologize if I offended you, but the American temptation to always scapegoat their latest opponent is one of the contributing factors to alienation among our youth. As Jacob can explain better than I, we are dealing with a small set of deeply frustrated young people who are willing to strike out in extreme ways to be heard."

"Psycho babble," said Ralph. "You can't tell me these psychopaths who are shooting up our churches are just some kids who weren't listened to by their parents. That's pure bullshit."

"Ralph," the President said, "I listen to you every day, and frequently you have much wisdom to offer, but for now, as politely as I can, I want to ask you to shut-up and listen to our guests. We can ignore what they say later, but I want to hear them out first.

They saved our butts in Wisconsin, and the reverend's church and he, himself, were the first to be shot in this mess."

The President turned towards Rachel, "According to Amanda, you nearly missed being killed yourself, and you also were one of the first to help us identify the larger scope of these events. On behalf of the nation, thank you, Sergeant Sessions."

"Oh, sir, I'm not a Sergeant. I took the test, but I haven't heard the results yet."

The President grinned. "I have. I even called your chief. I have the pleasure of presenting you with your Sergeant's badge."

There was a round of congratulations. Rachel's face was flushed. Frank rose and pulled her to her feet. "I'm proud of you, Rachel."

"Thank you, Mr. President. I don't know what else to say."

"No need to say anything. It's good to have a moment of celebration in the midst of our trauma. We still have a long way to go in this nightmare." Then the President turned back to the rest of them. "Admit it. We don't have a clue how to stop this. At least these people have firsthand knowledge of these events." He pulled a chair out from under a table, reversed it, and straddled it. "Jacob, you don't need to have all the answers, but drawing on your studies, experience, and most of all your intuition, I want you to talk to me about what your best guess is as to what is happening."

Jacob bent over and studied the floor for a few seconds. "This is a lot of guesswork, but let me give it a try."

Ralph interrupted. "Jacob, forget what I said. I was an asshole. Any ideas you have will be appreciated. That goes for all of you."

He nodded briefly at Ralph. "Many students feel a level of despair and hopelessness at this point in their lives. They see what they describe as hypocrisy at all levels of society. Politicians selling their souls to get elected; pastors diluting the gospel till it is little more than psychobabble," he nodded to Ralph, "Wall Street caught in their version of pyramid schemes and skimming off the top; manufacturers risking the customer's safety to make a few more bucks." He paused, "Name a major institution that hasn't been caught with their pants down in recent years. At the same time, youth are sensitive to the suffering from poverty, bigotry, and greed happening all over the world."

Rachel spoke up, "And don't forget the violence by police caught on videotape and judges taking bribes."

"That, too," said Jacob, "and they feel no one is listening. They are utterly helpless to make a better world. The majority of youth absorb those feelings and hope the darkness will someday disappear. Some, however, are so alienated they are affected mentally. In the past, we saw examples of a lone deranged person shooting up a school, church, or business. It's a devastating incident, and people are horrified, but after a while nothing changes. My father can speak to this more than I can, but now something has changed."

Everybody turned to Frank. "You may ask yourself, why some teenagers would deliberately put themselves in a situation where they will die. In fact, in many cases, after they shot several people and see the police arrive, they shoot themselves."

"Never made sense to me," said Dorothy.

"Yet soldiers do it all the time," said Jacob. "They willingly die for something bigger than themselves."

"That's different. That's patriotism and to protect their loved ones," said Greg.

"It's different," said Frank, "because they believe in their country. There is nothing sadder than these returned veterans who have lost all faith in their country and leaders, and all they know how to do is use tools of violence. We are going to get to that in a little while."

"Even soldiers," continued Jacob, "believe if they die a heroic death, someone will be proud of them. But what happens if you think no one even knows you exist. We know in psychology some people will cut themselves just to feel the pain and know they are alive."

"Now consider this," said Frank, "what if someone could figure out how to organize those alienated youth and convince them that in going out in a violent cataclysm, they could make a mark on the world, and no one would ever forget them. They would be soldiers for a greater cause, and the world would never be the same."

"Why the church?" asked Dorothy.

Rachel spoke up. "The police are often called to protect vulnerable places. We hire security guards at airports and other places of large public gatherings. However, think about churches. The large ones may be able to afford extra protection, but even they don't want to hassle worshipers with metal detectors, and there are thousands and thousands of tiny churches who could never pay for extra security."

"Besides," said Frank, "think about what communities of faith represent and what they talk about. However poorly we do it, we at least declare life has meaning and there is reason for hope. Even casual participants, or ostensibly inactive-believers," he smiled at the President, "benefit from what Karl Marx's called the opiate of the people to maintain some sense of community. If you can paralyze the churches, you strike a blow at the very structure holding our society together."

"If there are enough foot soldiers," said Rachel, "the shooters can keep popping up all over the place, and you will never know where the next shooting will occur."

"As the terrorists discovered," said Jacob, "you don't need much money or a major weapons system to destroy the power of a government. All you need is a group of people who are absolutely unafraid to die. You might recall that more people are killed by our homegrown fanatics and zealots than were ever killed by foreign terrorists."

Everyone sat in dumbfounded silence as they thought about the implications of what had been described. The President got up, walked over, and looked out at the Rose Garden. A gardener was tending some roses that had recently emerged. "Roses are so beautiful and yet so fragile. They need constant care if they are going to lift our spirits. So do our youth." He stared a few more minutes and then walked back to the group.

"Let's assume what we heard is right, and I'm inclined to believe it is at least in its broad outlines, what is our next move?"

Amanda spoke up. "Jacob put us in touch with a support group for veterans who were struggling with PTSD. They were the ones who spotted the possibility of the attack in Wisconsin."

"When we questioned the two shooters," Jacob said, "they told us they were trained by people who they thought were soldiers."

"Soldiers!" Ralph began to sputter. "Now we not only worry about well-dressed teenagers but our armed forces as well?"

"Maybe ex-armed forces," said Amanda. "Our friends, who have a better connection than we do, picked up some chatter about people often referred to as survivalists. Frank mentioned them earlier."

"I've heard of them," said Dorothy. Aren't they some disenchanted soldiers from recent wars who have withdrawn from society and run around the woods playing war games?"

"That's the ones," said Amanda. "Only the buzz our veterans are hearing is some of these survivalists are getting excited about doing more than running around in the mountains. They have been angry at the government for some time and feel their leaders are totally corrupt. Some even talked about overthrowing the government, but until now it seemed like more talk than a possibility. Now they seem to be dreaming bigger dreams."

"Who's coordinating this diabolical plot?" asked the President. "Any clues on that?"

"I'm afraid we have only one possible clue," said Frank. "I've been struggling to make sense of this, but somehow the focus comes back to me."

"You?" said Dorothy.

"As you know, my church was the first victim, and the young shooter called my name a couple of times during his rampage and something about it all being a big lie."

"He could have seen your name on the sign out in front of the church," said Greg.

"I know," said Frank. "But he needn't have said it at all, and he acted like someone had drummed it into him so I would get the message."

"So you're saying this may have started as a personal vendetta," asked the President, "and that is why they shot at Rachel as well."

"It's at least a possibility" responded Frank, "and might be a clue we can trace back to those who are behind it."

"Whether you are right or not," said Jacob, "it has expanded beyond that now. Whatever triggered it, the Leader got seduced by his own craziness and developed visions of grandeur. I would not be surprised if there is another attack somewhere soon."

There came a knock on the door, and a woman came in with a piece of paper for the President. He looked at it, grimaced, and said, "Damn that idiot."

They all looked at him. "The great governor of Texas has just held a news conference. He took it upon himself to declare that Christianity is under attack, and true Christians everywhere should bring their guns to church on Easter Sunday to protect the faith. "Easter is the day of resurrection," the governor declares, "Let those who dare to challenge the resurrection test out their theory and learn hell is the destination for those who blaspheme the faith."

As he read more, his face grew red, and the veins on his neck began to pulsate. "The governor is my problem, but he also has a couple of prominent preachers in two of the biggest churches in Dallas who agree with him and are urging all their members to 'have a great Easter Sunday event where we show that we are prepared to stand up for our faith with force.'"

"Oh, Lord, with all those trigger happy nut cases crowding into the churches, it will be a wonder if a war doesn't break out," said Greg.

"Mr. President, regardless of what happens this weekend, I think you should address the nation on Monday evening," said Frank. "If we are lucky, and there is no massacre this Sunday, you will be laying the groundwork for how to respond down the line, and if there is a tragedy, you will help channel the anger and fear in a constructive fashion."

"I would like you to work with my speech writers to shape what I should say."

"Mr. President," Dorothy said, "I think you might consider having Frank follow your speech with some recommendations about what churches should be doing. He had some pretty good ideas for the churches in Wisconsin."

"You got that Frank?" the President asked.

"I'll do my best. I'd also recommend you find a nationally prominent rabbi, imam, Christian pastor, and perhaps an outspoken agnostic to stand with you as you speak, so it is clear this is not a doctrinal issue but an emphasis on the sacredness of sanctuary or divine space in this country.

"Let's hope that idiot governor's proclamation doesn't spread and our churches all become armed camps," said the President.

A CALL TO A NATION

CHAPTER 33

Even though it was going to be Easter Sunday, knowing it was going to be a tense weekend and he was needed in Washington to work with the speech writers to prepare for the President's address Monday evening, Frank called on a retired pastor friend to cover for him at John Knox's Church. Rachel wanted to return to Lincoln to check on how Brian was doing, and Jacob had students to attend to, so they both agreed to Amanda's offer for a flight home.

As they were entering the van that would deliver them to Andrews for their flight home, Frank gave them each a hug, and then added, "Don't get used to this private plane and personal delivery service, guys. It won't last long."

"It all feels so surreal, like I'm in a bizarre movie," said Rachel. "Who knew growing up being a preacher's kid would involve me in such a weird life."

"Because of the shooting incident, I'm sending an agent along with you," said Amanda. "This will probably add to the unreal quality of life, but please allow him to advise you on how to be safe. This was probably a one-time incident, but we don't want to take any chances."

"We'll be careful," said Jacob. "I've arranged for us to stay on the seminary campus rather than at Dad's home."

After they had driven away, Amanda turned to Frank. "Why is it you get involved in all these things? You must have some really weird karma in a previous life."

"I'm a Christian and not into the Hindu doctrine of karma, Mandy, but I don't understand it either. All I've wanted to do is be a good pastor and help people make sense out of their lives. I feel like one of the disciples who found Jesus asleep on the boat during the storm and wondered if Jesus was paying attention to what was happening to them."

"I remember the story. Didn't Jesus get up and tell the storm to calm down and stop misbehaving? I'd be glad for him to do it again at any time now. This is getting to be crazy."

Frank looked at Amanda in silence for several seconds and then said, "Mandy, I'm sorry for my behavior over the last year. I'm a whole lot better dealing with major issues than I am with my personal relationships."

With a slightly quizzical smile, Amanda shook her head. "That is not exactly breaking news, but I'll offer you conditional forgiveness, at least until we get beyond this."

"Would you like to have dinner with me tonight, and for a couple of hours see if we can step back and enjoy a good meal?"

"That would be nice, Frank. Though it can't be a long meal. I have to check in with my agents around the country and see if Brian's friends picked up any more gossip that will be helpful. The President wants you close by, so he arranged for you to stay at the White House. It's not exactly the Lincoln's Bedroom setting, but it should be comfortable."

─────── ♦•♦♦♦•♦ ───────

Most of Good Friday, Frank worked with the President's speech writers to play out different scenarios and how the President should respond in each case.

About noon Jacob called. Frank heard excitement in his voice. "All the way home, Rachel and I wrestled with the original message and how to break the code. We tried thinking like children. When we are together, we can get pretty good at that. It broke the tension of the trip.

Then, after I went to bed, my subconscious kept thinking about it. About four this morning, I woke up recalling in addition to a child's code, there were also some serious faith issues involved in this case."

"I agree. Someone is really angry at the church and religion," said Frank.

"They keep wanting to use religion against religion," said Jacob "and the phrase 'It's a lie' kept running through my head. What if this was a child-like code but was about the Bible? Play with those first three numbers, 1, 2, and 7 as locations in the Scripture."

"You mean like one Bible but the second part," he paused "wait a moment—it's a lie."

"Keep going Dad, you're almost there."

"Books of the New Testament, or the second part of the Bible, and the seventh book is first Corinthians."

"You're getting close, now look at the O, M, N part only substitute numbers—fifteen, thirteen, and fourteen."

"Fifteenth chapter, verses thirteen and fourteen," there was a moment of silence, "of course, that's where Paul debates those who don't believe in the resurrection, and he says something about if the resurrection isn't true, then the rest of what we are saying is a lie."

"That was my conclusion too."

"OK, but how does it help us?"

"I called Rachel early this morning to tell her about my discovery. You know Rachel, she wasn't too happy about being awakened at 6, but she quickly got caught up in the idea.

"By the way, we went by and saw Brian when we got back. He's doing quite well and is raring to go on his trip out West."

"He has the airline code so he can go whenever he is strong enough," said Frank. "So what did you and Rachel come up with?"

"As we talked this morning, Rachel came up with an interesting thought. If you were the terrorist leader and you knew the President was going to speak to the nation, what would you want to do?"

"Well, as I've worked with the President and his speech writers, part of our agenda is to calm the country by asserting some strong leadership and a rational plan for how this is going to be handled."

"Right, and he's doing it through the media. Given their past history and their rather childlike game playing, what might they try to do?"

"They'd want to do something to undermine the President's authority before the American people."

"Remember they have some media savvy people. Rachel suggests they will probably want to insert another banner during the President's speech to show they, not the President, are calling the shots."

"I can alert the President's media people. Surely they can figure out some way to block the banner if it starts displaying across the screen."

"That might be a small victory, but only the terrorists would know they had been frustrated. Rachel's idea is to allow the banner to play, but have the President acknowledge it as it's playing, and then announce he has a response banner to remind us we are not a country of despair and violence but a nation of hope and peace. When the first banner is through, the media plays his banner cast in red, white, and blue in a way that ridicules the first banner and plants questions in people's minds about the sanity of the Leader. If we are clever enough, we can plant some doubt in the minds of the recruited youth, and some might break ranks."

"That might work. Let me run it by the President and his writers."

"If the President is open to it, how about skyping us into part of the conversation. Rachel is working with one of her IT people on a way to insert some humor into a cartoon that might help undermine the Leader's authority. For example, if they again use a version of the code and we can break it, we could have a cartoon figure translate it on screen."

"Ha, remember that quote I love from the humorist, Judy Carter. When you want to overcome stress and anxiety, turn your problems into punch lines. We're certainly an anxious country, and we could use some good punch lines to reduce the tension. If we are quick enough, we can translate the message and turn it into a punch line."

"I'm sure the President has some skilled humorists he could have available. We have to be careful though. If we are right, this whole scenario builds on a number of youth in this country who already feel ridiculed. Whatever we do, it needs to be done in a way that doesn't make the young people feel demeaned but only sows doubt about the leadership," said Jacob.

"That's insightful. You're getting pretty good with that psychology stuff, Jacob."

"Thanks, but there is a spoiler in all this, Dad."

"What's that?"

"We have no idea what might happen on Easter, and how it will affect everything. It could be so horrible that any humor would seem inappropriate. We can't have it appear the President isn't feeling the pain in people's hearts."

"The problem is, we won't know until the last moment. We almost need two approaches, each of them very flexible, and then, be prepared to polish them up Sunday evening and Monday before the newscast."

"That's the way I see it, Dad."

"Listen, Jacob, see if you and Rachel can clear your schedules for Sunday and Monday. I'd like Amanda to fly you both back up here and have you available to help us as we make the final edits."

"Since most of the students are gone during Holy Week, I can come up in the afternoon. I'll check with Rachel. How big a bill are we running up for the government with all these private jets and everything?"

"Not nearly as much as they will pay if we fail to extract the poison from this insanity."

One of the President's men entered Frank's room and pointed to his watch. "Jacob, I have a meeting with the President about to start. Keep working on this, and I'll have Amanda let you know about the flights."

"OK, Dad. Be nice to Amanda. Rachel and I decided she's a keeper."

"Physician heal thyself," Frank said, laughed, and terminated the call.

As he headed down the hall towards the room where the President would be, he was joined by Amanda, who looked like she had not had a good night's sleep. "Hi, I was just talking to Jacob. If you can arrange it, I think it would be a good idea to fly them back up Saturday afternoon. I'll explain why when we are through with this meeting."

"Don't need an explanation," she said as she pulled out her cell phone. "I trust your gut on this." As they walked, she proceeded to make arrangements for the jet plane to pick them up Saturday afternoon in Lincoln. "Done."

Without giving it much thought, Frank reached out and gave Amanda a hug. "You are something."

"Thanks," Amanda said as a small smile interrupted the stern look on her face. "Maybe we should start this meeting by everyone having a group hug. This insanity is beginning to rub all our nerves raw."

When they were all gathered around the table, the President came into the room. He looked at each of them and then turned to Amanda. "You are coordinating this. What do you have for us?"

"I hear some rumors but nothing very solid. We are running on fumes and instinct. I haven't had a chance to catch up with Frank this morning, but I think he has some options he wants to lay out for consideration. His instincts and those of his adult children have been pretty good so far, so I'd suggest we begin there."

They all turned to Frank, and he shared with them the ideas he and Jacob had formulated.

"That's crazy," said Greg. "We have t the whole country on edge, and we want to talk about telling jokes! This is serious business, Mr. President. It's not some kid's game."

"Sadly, Greg, that is exactly what we are playing with—a violent game with children who are big enough to cause immense harm but without the emotional maturity to distinguish between right and wrong," said Dorothy. "I think we have to be ready for an explosion of violence but also have some intelligent words to say to the nation in case we find ourselves still in a holding pattern."

For about forty-five minutes, they continued to exchange ideas about what should be said on Monday evening. Then, the President said, "Everything is going to happen fast, and we need to prepare for a variety of outcomes. Amanda, we have to get a line on who is behind this. If we can identify this Leader, we will know what our options are. Let Frank work with my writers on the news conference angle, and you focus your resources on identifying the Leader. Anything you need, you tell them you are speaking for me."

"Frank, I'm not sure about this humor business, but I'd like to see what your kids come up with. We can bring in some quick-witted comedy writers for Monday night, but it will have to happen almost instantaneously and will be very tricky."

"It may be all for nothing," said Frank. "We don't know they will try the banner again or even if they do, they will include a coded message, but if they do, we need to be ready."

"We'll convene Sunday evening for a rehearsal depending on what happens," said the President. "In the meantime, I've got an international crisis in the Middle East and negotiations with some congressmen on healthcare to deal with. I also need to call some governors and hopefully convince them they don't need to arm their citizens against our youth.

"The problem is we have no idea where they will attack. If I were them, with all eyes focused on Texas, I'd choose another state."

"Or maybe they'll just skip Easter and let us stew in our own anxiety," said the President.

"I pray that you are right. I'm afraid, however, that Easter Sunday will be too great a temptation to resist."

IT HAPPENED ON EASTER

CHAPTER 34

Although Saturday night had been an intense effort to prepare for whatever might happen, Frank rose early Easter Sunday morning. He was tempted to attend worship at the Episcopal church near the White House, but instead he decided to go for a walk and worship at New York Avenue Presbyterian Church. In addition to having a rather famous history, the church had developed a reputation for being in the forefront of the justice issues and other challenges facing society. They had an informal worship service at 8:45 a.m., and he thought the walk from the White House would be good for him. His adult children, having arrived Saturday evening, decided maybe a later service might better meet their needs.

He walked up New York Avenue towards the large brick structure of the famous church. As he climbed the steps, he thought of the historic significance of this church. Though he never joined, even Lincoln had a special pew in which to sit. As advertised, the congregation reflected a polyglot of people in age, dress, and ethnicity. Frank walked into the sanctuary and felt uplifted. Not only did New

York Avenue Presbyterian show the rich history of our nation, but the very mix of those gathered spoke to him of what the church should represent. He did note several uniformed security guards on high alert as he entered.

As he observed their eyes move from one worshiper to the next, another thought struck him. Within the last few years, there had been some periodic shootings in faith communities around the country, but almost all of them involved a deranged response to the divisions of race or religion. This latest round of shootings had nothing to do with racism or our inability to relate to the Muslim world. These were Caucasian youth alienated from the very society that birthed them. Even their appearance fit in with what would make people comfortable.

He walked down the long center aisle towards a pew. He deliberately chose to sit where some young people sat. They seemed eager to welcome him as if to say we are not the problem. In fact, as he looked around, he was pleased with how many young people were present—young people refusing to be defined by the actions of a few. Ironically a few alienated young people had given a sense of purpose to others. Maybe we need to build this into the President's speech.

The liturgy was rich, giving voice to both the fears and faith of the nation. The pastor was at the top of his game and artfully interpreted the Ecclesiastes 3 passage on everything having its time. He spoke to the adults about this being a time to embrace our youth and to make sure they knew they are valued. He turned his attention to the youth, praising those present and challenging them to show their colleagues the future was full of promise. He led his listeners down the path of passion taken by Christ, reminding them if Jesus felt despair in the garden and the violence of the cross, then it was legitimate for members of the Body of Christ to share those feelings as well. However, he reminded them in a ringing conclusion, though Jesus experienced a time of darkness, he trusted God would, in God's own time, surprise us with a new birth of possibilities. "We call it resurrection, and, though some call it a lie, we know it is God's truth. Believe it, trust it, and in time we will experience it." He paused for a couple of seconds and then said, "let the people of God say . . ." There was a resounding, almost defiant "Amen" ringing from the congregation.

Frank thanked the pastor and felt renewed energy as he almost danced down the steps and onto the street. He wished churches across the country could hear that sermon. As he walked, he passed by a Dunkin' Donuts store and decided it was appropriate for a celebratory donut and strong cup of coffee.

He savored the rich aroma of the coffee and the sweetness of the donut, rationalizing he deserved this one detour from his attempt to eat more healthily. It was about 10:45 a.m. when he resumed his leisurely walk down the street towards the White House. He loved walking in Washington, especially on a Sunday morning when, though there was traffic, it seemed like more people took their time. He detoured over to the Mall where he could gaze on the monuments and historic structures that gave the city its distinctive aura. At 11:20 a.m., his phone buzzed. He noticed some erratic activity among some of the tourists as he punched his talk button and lifted it to his ear.

He didn't even have time to say his name before he heard Amanda shouting at him. "Frank, get back to the White House now. It's happened again. Hurry, I'll fill you in when you get here." She clicked off.

He broke into a jog, pulling out the lanyard that held his photo ID and hanging it around his neck. He headed towards the side street that would lead to the underground entry at the White House. If the shooters had hit several churches, it would certainly alter what the President needed to say tomorrow evening. How could a Presidential address possibly calm a nation that felt under siege? As he slowed to speak to the guard at the gate, he also received a text from Amanda. "When you arrive, tell them you are to go directly to the Presidential living quarters. They will take you."

He entered the building. A man waited for him, holding the elevator door. "I guess you know where you are to take me," said Frank.

"Yes, sir, right this way. This is a black day for our country. It wasn't right, but it was easier when we could blame it on the Muslims, the immigrants, or someone different from us. Now everyone is suspicious of those who used to be seen as the normal people."

Frank nodded and took a deep breath. "We'll get through this, but it is going to be rough going for a while."

The elevator arrived, and the door opened to the Presidential living quarters. He was ushered into the President's den. Four televisions were on different channels. The President had his head bowed as he listened. Amanda, Dorothy, and Greg sat on the edge of their chairs as they watched the news broadcasts.

"We only know of one site so far," said Amanda. "It was at the 10 a.m. service in a megachurch in Dallas."

Scott Pelley was speaking on the set nearest to where Frank entered. "Many churches traditionally have 11:00 a.m. services, and we are approaching that hour in Texas. No one knows whether there will be other incidents in Texas churches or even churches in other states. Reporter Barry Peterson has arrived at the scene of the Fresh Beginnings Baptist Church. "Barry, we've been getting all sorts of reports of a massive gun fight. What can you tell us?"

"It's pretty gruesome, Scott. Several people were killed and lots more wounded, including the senior pastor of this large metropolitan church. I have Deacon Wilkers here. Deacon Wilkers, I understand you were in the sanctuary when the shooting began. What can you tell us?"

"Our governor told us we should come prepared to protect our church. Most of us came packing. We thought that would scare any troublemaker off."

"The shooters got in anyway?"

"Not only did they get in, but since everyone came with their gun openly displayed, we couldn't tell who the good guys were and who the bad were. We're a large Bible-believing church, and not everyone knows everyone else. While these shootings had scared some away, we must have had almost a thousand people in there praying and singing."

"Can you tell us how it started?"

"We'd sung some songs, had some prayers, and the preacher was telling us to be seated so he could read some Bible to us. Since we were all standing, there was some commotion when we all turned to find our seats. Don't think anyone realized at first a young'un had pulled his pistol and hadn't sat down."

"Did he say anything?"

"Yeah, he started shouting that Texans were weenies, and he was going to teach them a lesson. Then it really began to get weird. Another youngster about ten rows back and over in the other section jumped up with his gun drawn and told the first to drop his weapon."

"So the second young person was trying to protect the others?" asked Peterson.

"That's what it looked like at first, but when the first guy shot a man a couple of rows in front of him, the second guy shot two or three times in his direction but hit people around him."

"Then what happened?"

"Well, several men jumped up with their guns drawn and started shouting. Then all hell broke loose. At first they all seemed to be shooting at the first guy, sometimes hitting him and sometimes hitting people around him. But as soon as he was down, people realized the second guy was laughing and continuing to shoot."

"So there were two shooters?"

There were a whole bunch of shooters. Problem was you couldn't tell who was shooting for the good guys and who was shooting for the bad guys. A couple of people were even firing from the balcony. When one person in the balcony tried to stop one of the shooters, he threw her off the balcony."

"How'd it stop?"

"That was rather amazing. It was all going to Hell in a hand basket when Sally, who played the electric piano, turned the volume up and struck a chord."

"It was like the music broke the choir out of their shock, and they all started singing "The Day of Resurrection." Pretty soon others began to pick it up, and all the shooting stopped." The deacon looked back at the church. "Got to go. They are going to need me.

Tell your people to keep trusting God to get us through this." He walked back towards the church.

"I'll keep trying to find more information, Scott. What we do know now is multiple people were shot, some by other members of the church who thought they were defending the faith. As reported, the pastor was shot in the melee, but we don't know how badly." There was almost a look of wonder in Barry's eyes when he said, "and it all stopped with 'The Day of Resurrection.'"

Scott Pelley, after summarizing what had been reported, added, "It is now 12:10 a.m. here on the East Coast, and we haven't heard of any other incidents. However, it is near 11:00 a.m. CST and ten states like Wyoming, Colorado, Montana, and the Pacific are approaching 9:00 a.m. so we have a long morning with many churches still to conduct their worship services. Everyone is on high alert. There is no way of knowing at this moment whether this is an isolated incident or part of a chain of events."

Frank looked around. The First Lady was standing in the back of the room with her hand over her mouth and a look of terror in her eyes. Most of the others sat in stunned silence.

The President stood. "I'm sure the switchboard is jammed with callers. I'll have to make a brief statement today and make a fuller statement on Monday. Amanda, let's get somebody on the ground to get solid information, and let's pray this is the only situation for today." He turned to Frank. "I think it's clear this will continue in some form or another until we identify who the Leader is, and I agree, in some mysterious way, you are a link to that. So stick around and draw on any help you need. We have to break this."

The President walked over and took his wife in his arms. He held her for what seemed to be at least a full minute. Then he turned back towards Frank. "How in the hell do you tell people to remain calm and everything is going to be all right when our own teenagers are shooting us in the very sanctuary where people should be safe?"

"We'll work on Monday night's speech." Frank looked around at the others. "Right now make a brief announcement expressing your grief and anger and assuring people you will use the full resources of the government to discover who is behind this."

The President nodded. "I have to call the governor of Texas and assure him of the same thing. He may be an idiot, but he doesn't deserve this. No one does."

MOM IS ACTING STRANGE

CHAPTER 35

By the time Bob Godwin completed the third and final worship service for Sunday, he was as drained as any time in his memory. Holy Week and Easter had been a marathon, but the Sunday following Easter everyone approached the 11:00 a.m. worship with high anxiety. The story of what happened in Dallas was all over the news. People were glued to their iPads and iPhones for the latest reports as they entered the church. He knew a number stayed at home to be safe, and he didn't blame them.

Bob was fairly certain whoever was behind this had moved beyond Lincoln, but when people heard about the attempt to shoot Frank's daughter, they still saw a connection with their city. Strange how our two families keep getting intertwined.

Not only did his church have security guards at the services, but he made sure some healthy young men were on the alert at various points in the sanctuary. Still, he entered each service with some trepidation, and he was pleased when they concluded without incident.

Now that part of his life was completed for the day, and he came home to rest. He tuned into the news to get the latest from the shootings in Dallas. Barbie, or Barbara, he swore he was going to stop even thinking the name Barbie because he knew it irritated her. Barbara told him she was going to run some errands after church and not to expect her until evening. He decided he would catch up on the news and rest a while before eating the salad she prepared for him and put in the refrigerator. She had been a little stressed lately and spent a lot of time in her private office, but, he had to admit, she was attentive to his personal needs—food always available, the house kept neat, and frequently she even initiated intimate interchanges. Given the sins I've committed, I guess I am a lucky guy.

About 2:30 p.m. he was dozing in front of the television when the phone rang. The caller ID indicated the call was from the prison where his son David was living. He punched the talk button. "David, how are you doing?"

"I'm fine, Dad, but I wonder if I could ask you to do me a favor?"

Still feeling guilty about his parenting skills contributing to David's being in prison, Bob was quick to respond, "Sure David, what can I do for you?"

"Well, I know you're tired after all the work you've done this morning, but I wondered if you could drive over to the prison and see me this afternoon. I've cleared it with the warden, and he gave me permission to see you about 4:30 if you can come."

"Uh . . . Sure David. Your mother is out right now . . ."

"Actually, Dad, I'd like it if just you came."

"I'll be there. Can you tell me what this is about, or do you just feel a need for a visit?"

"I've been doing some thinking, and I want to share it with you. I'll explain more when you get here. And Dad, for now let's keep this visit between you and me. Don't tell Mom until later, OK?"

"Sure David. You're all right, aren't you? I mean you haven't gotten into any more trouble, have you?"

"No, Dad, I just want to talk. I'll see you at 4:30. And thanks."

If I'm going to make it by four-thirty, I'd better get on the way.

I'll save the salad for later and grab a sandwich at the drive through at Steak'n Shake on the way.

As he drove, Bob thought about his role in what led to David being in prison. *I married a beautiful and supportive wife and had a fine son, but I messed up. I got so caught up in building my little religious empire I didn't give enough attention to either of them and what they needed. I was selfish; that's what I was.* He took a bite from the steakburger he had purchased. Then he held the sandwich out in front of him. *This is a good example of how I failed. It's quick, easy, and tastes good but is lousy for my health.*

A rest stop was coming up. He pulled off and paused near a trashcan. He got out and hurled the sandwich and the extra thick chocolate shake with whipped cream on it into the trash can. He reentered the highway. *Damn, I preach a good game, but I don't live it. I go for what is easy and feels good.*

He thought about his ministry. *He learned all the tricks about how to please people. He told them what they wanted to hear with enough religious wrapping to make them feel good about themselves. It wasn't total hypocrisy. In this stressful and guilt-ridden world, people do need to be lifted up. I'm pretty good at listening to people and helping them with their problems. People live sinful lives full of greed, hate, and pridefulness. They need to hear about forgiveness, and isn't that what grace is all about?*

The thoughts kept spinning around in his head. *I have gifts, but sometimes I don't have the discipline to avoid their temptations. O Lord, I know I've misused my talents at times. I knew and took pleasure in the fact I was attractive to women, and I played on that. And twice, once with Sally Flint and more than once with widow Marshall, I got involved. When I was exposed, I played that tearful sorrow act of Jimmy Swaggart to get out of it. I used religion to build my little empire, and the same religious game helped me get out of the messes I created.*

Look where it's got me. I know I hurt Barbara terribly. I'm amazed she is sticking around. I know David is responsible for his acts, but I also know if I'd been a better father, it might not have happened.

He's in prison as a serial rapist, but who showed him women were merely objects to be used? Who taught him religious hypocrisy was a way to appear pious while manipulating people to serve your own needs? Even as he drove, he banged his hands on the steering wheel. Oh, David, I am so sorry—I may preach forgiveness, but I don't know whether I can ever receive it for myself.

He was so lost in thought he almost sideswiped a car as he changed lanes. The other driver laid on his horn and flipped him the bird. He laughed out loud. You don't know how right you are, buddy. I've totally fucked myself.

He began to think about David's request that he come alone to visit him. Over the last couple of months, Bob noticed a subtle change in David. During their family visits, he seemed calmer and more introspective. It wouldn't get him out of prison, but he hoped David was coming to terms with what he had done.

He thought about how it all ended. Barbara blames it all on Frank Sessions, and in a sense it was—or at least a combination of him and his daughter. What was his daughter's name, Rachel? Now there is an attractive young gal. Damn, there I go again, focusing on a woman's body rather than the person. Anyway, the police and Rachel set a trap for David, using her as the bait. David had lost all mental balance and taken her to a cave for some weird religious ritual.

Bob ran his hand over his face and took a deep breath. If there is a God in heaven, I'm grateful they stopped him before he harmed her. My only hope is like his namesake in the Bible, if he truly confesses, God can offer him some healing, even if in prison.

As he pulled into the private road leading to the prison, his thoughts returned to the church shootings. Isn't it ironic Frank Sessions is part of this too? What is it about the man that he keeps getting involved in all these events? Well, at least he seems to have some authentic faith that will help him get through. We're in the Easter season, and the early shooters kept talking about the resurrection being a lie. I hope they are wrong. I could use a little resurrection in my life.

He drove up to the prison. After parking his car in the visitor's lot, he approached the large glass doors of the reception area.

As he entered, an officer approached. "Sir, visiting hours finished at four this afternoon."

"I know, officer. My name is Bob Godwin. My son David is here, and I think Warden Kramer has arranged special permission for me to visit him. Would you check?"

"Wait right there." The officer picked up the phone. After a brief conversation, he turned towards Bob. "Yes sir, you are cleared to proceed. Must be really important. I've never seen this happen before."

Bob thanked him and proceeded through the security check. He was pleased to discover not only were they prepared for his visit, but, after he had been checked through the procedures, he was taken to a private room without the usual Plexiglas partition. He knew he would not be allowed to give David a strong embrace, but, at least, he wouldn't have to look at him through that scratched up Plexiglass. Sometimes, he thought, it is little events that help restore a measure of faith.

The guard opened the door and brought David into the room. He had his usual hesitant look on his face, but there was genuine warmth in his smile. Bob took the smile as a good omen and extended his hand across the table, knowing that only a strong handshake would be allowed.

"Thanks, Dad. I haven't forgotten what marathon Sundays are like for you, especially in the Easter season, and I appreciate your coming on such short notice."

Bob felt his throat constrict a little. "I've let my work interfere with being a good father to you, David, but if you will let me, I'd like to do my best to change that." He looked around the small room void of any decorations that would give it warmth. "I'm so sorry it has taken this to wake me up."

David looked around too. "It's strange how being in a place like this can cause you to see things more clearly." He turned back to his father. "Do you believe in the resurrection, Dad? I don't mean whether it once happened to Jesus. I mean does God give us whole new beginnings after we've killed all our opportunities?"

Bob bowed his head and hesitated. "Funny you should ask. I was asking myself the same question on the way over here." Then he looked up and straight into David's eyes. "To be honest, and that's what I want to be with you from now on, to be honest, I don't know what I believe. I sure hope so, David. I sure hope so."

David spread his hands on the table and moved them around for a short while. "Dad, have you noticed anything unusual about Mom lately?"

Bob drew his head back and narrowed his eyes. "What do you mean, unusual?"

"Well, I'm not sure. It seems like she is less like the sort of fluffy blond and more steely or something. And there is a strange faraway look in her eyes like she is only partly here."

"Your mom's been through a lot, David. Mostly it was my fault, as you know. I hurt her deeply. We need to give her time, and I need to treat her better. I'm working on it."

"That's good, Dad, but there are times when she also acts a little weird—strange—even off the wall if you know what I mean."

"Tell me more."

"Well, lately she starts talking to me about what we are going to do when I get out of here. I try to explain, "Mom, that will not be for many years, if ever."

She doesn't seem to accept that. She said something really crazy last time. I'd tried to assure her I was prepared to take my punishment and be here for a long time. She reached over and placed her hand on the plexiglass. "Trust your mom," she said. "I just might tell the President of the United States to not only let you go but to buy us a place in Costa Rica near the beach. Wouldn't you like that, David? No one would know your past, and you could begin all over again. You could meet a nice Costa Rican girl and get a fresh start."

She had that faraway look in her eyes again. I said, "Mom, that's not going to happen—that's crazy."

"Just wait and see, dear," she said. "Few people understand how clever your mom is. It took me a long time to realize how this world operates. Greed and fear, dear, greed and fear."

Then she smiled, gave me a kiss through the Plexiglass, and hung up the phone.

"I'm a little worried about her, Dad. It's like she's gone off the deep end too. I wonder if this runs in the family."

Bob ran the conversation through his mind over and over again as he drove home. David seemed to be getting grounded in reality, for which he was grateful, but his comments about his mom disturbed Bob. Maybe it was time he and Barbara had a heart-to-heart talk.

As he came to his driveway, he was disappointed not to see Barbara's car in its usual place. It's possible she already put it in the garage or is just a little bit late getting home, he thought.

As he entered the house, he called out, "Barbara, Barbara, are you home?"

There was total silence in the house, almost as if his voice echoed in its emptiness.

He approached the door to her office and knocked softly. "Barbara, are you in there. I've been to see David."

When he helped her set up her office after the battle over Felicity Marshall, she made it clear that it was her territory, and he was only to enter at her invitation. He was so disturbed by what David said that he turned the door handle as he called out her name again.

She wasn't there, but the door was unlocked. He peered inside. Papers were scattered everywhere. He stepped inside. The TV was on Fox News and blaring away about the Texas disaster. Her computer screen had a map of the US and several circles around different cities across the country. A big yellow highlight made Dallas stand out.

He wasn't sure what it all meant. He stepped towards her desk and saw her notepad open. He knew he was risking all hell breaking loose, but he felt drawn forward and noticed some notes on her desk.

"That will teach those fuckers," a note said.

Bob was stunned and confused. He heard a car door slam and decided to exit the office quickly leaving no sign he had been there.

He was in the kitchen fixing himself a drink when Barbara came in with an energetic smile on her face. "Hi, Bob. Sorry to be late. I'm afraid that tragedy in Dallas has affected the traffic patterns around here as well. Though that doesn't make much sense." She came to him and gave him a strong hug and kiss. How was your afternoon?

He decided not to tell Barbara about visiting David. He was still trying to process what he had noticed in her office but knew now was not the time to bring that up. "Fine. Can I fix you a drink?"

"Sure, I would like one of those delicious chocolate martinis like you fixed on my birthday. Do we have the ingredients?"

"Uh, sure . . . At least I think so. Let me look."

"While you are preparing it, I'll go and change into something more comfortable." She winked at him and walked out of the kitchen.

I must be wrong. What was I thinking? He opened the cabinet door where they kept the liquors and found the ingredients. He began to make the drink. He smiled at remembering how much Barbara enjoyed the drink when they were celebrating her birthday. As he was mixing the martinis, his hand shook a little bit, and he spilled some of the vodka. He cursed silently under his breath. Get hold of yourself, my man. You're letting your imagination go wild.

Still, even as he carried the drink into the sitting room to meet his wife, some lingering thoughts kept nagging at his mind.

THE PRESIDENT'S ADDRESS

CHAPTER 36

As Frank, Jacob, and Rachel were ushered into the Oval Office, now set up for the broadcast, Frank prayed their work preparing for this speech would pay off. He noticed his thumbs rubbing his fingers, which he knew was a sign of how nervous he was. Why had he agreed to the President's suggestion he address the religious community following the President's address? He was grateful for Jacob's help in preparing what he would say, but soon it would be up to him.

He learned early in his ministry being nervous was both a natural and valuable part of making a presentation. This was more than a touch of nerves, however. He felt his stomach tighten as he assumed his seat off to the right of where the President would sit. Speaking to large crowds didn't bother him, but he had never before sensed so much was riding on what he would say.

He practiced the relaxation technique a friend taught him early in his ministry. He slowly took in a deep breath through his nostrils, held it for about five seconds, and let it out through his lips as he did a quick body scan in his mind and watched the parts of his body relax. He repeated the process about three times, almost oblivious to what was happening around him. When he again focused, he noticed Rachel and Amanda standing near the back of the room. She was whispering into Amanda's ear, no doubt explaining to her the ritual he was putting himself through. She saw him glance at her and gave him a smile and a small thumbs up gesture.

Several other White House officials were milling about in the room, and some technicians were adjusting the speakers. They also installed a special piece of equipment that would feed their special banner across the screen should their monitors indicate the Leader's group was trying to hack into their broadcast. While they still liked the idea of using humor to deflate the tension of the moment, they had agreed that with the Texas shootings, they had to be careful not to suggest they were making light of this tragic incident. It was a delicate balancing act. Jacob had worked with the White House tech officials to create three different types of responses. The President would choose which one to use depending on what the hacker banner said. Jacob had earned the respect of the President's advisers, and he was in charge of responding to the President's signal.

Frank was musing about how much trust the President was placing in the hands of his family. They barely knew each other. Jacob had a degree in psychology but wasn't licensed to practice. Rachel was a rookie cop, and he was a small town preacher. The nation was feeling under siege, and the President was counting on them to provide leadership in this critical moment. He was lost in thought when he felt a hand on his shoulder. He looked up into the eyes of the President. He could see the lines of worry on his face.

"Frank, you will do fine. Just go with your instincts. They have served you well up to this moment. We would be totally at sea without your help. Regardless of what happens in the next few days, already I am grateful to you. If you feel up to it after the broadcast, Karen and I would like you and your family to come by for a drink." He smiled. "If my instincts are right, you might invite Amanda to come with you, but that is up to you." Then he winked as he squeezed

Frank's shoulder and moved across the room to shake hands with the others who were present, including representatives from the Christian, Muslim, and Jewish traditions.

Frank noticed he particularly paused to speak and give a reassuring handshake to both Jacob and Rachel.

"Mr. President, it is time to take your place. We set up so a camera is focused on The Reverend Sessions when the moment arrives."

The President moved to his chair behind his desk, looked around the room, gave a calming smile, straightened his tie, and said, "Ready at your signal."

The camera operator counted out the last five seconds and then pointed at the President as the light blinked on.

Looking directly into the camera, the President began. "My fellow Americans, I speak to you at a very sad and tragic moment in our nation's life. As you are fully aware, yesterday, on Easter Sunday, during the worship service at Fresh Beginnings Baptist Church in Dallas, a gun battle erupted in their sanctuary. At least two, perhaps three, young people began shooting at those who were worshiping there. When they began shooting, some members of the church tried to protect the others with their guns. They had every right to protect their neighbors, but, in the ensuing confusion, it appears some of the shots went wide of their intended target and wounded several innocent worshipers. Authorities are still trying to clarify what happened."

Amanda smiled at Jacob. The President had been livid at the Texas governor's encouragement of members to carry their guns to church and the chaotic results of amateur shooters getting into a gun battle. He knew not even the security officers could distinguish between the terrorists and those who were seeking to protect the church. Jacob had persuaded the President to affirm the members' intentions and avoid the perennial arguments about who can carry guns. The facts will speak for themselves when this is sorted out, Jacob advised, and you want to speak to the larger tragedy.

"We know," continued the President, "this is part of an attempt to cast fear over our nation. All evidence leads to the opinion this is a completely homegrown effort and not part of any international conspiracy. Even as the FBI, in cooperation with law enforcement across our land, is pursuing every lead, it is important we, as citizens, do what we can to protect the right of this country to worship as we choose without fear of violence. It is equally important we do not allow our fears to exacerbate the problem and cause other innocent people to be injured.

"The shooters have all been Caucasian young people, between the ages of 15 and 25. We believe these young people have been seduced into taking this action by some angry adults. Some of these adults may have previously served in our armed forces. While we don't justify what they are doing, we need to recognize the soldiers who served this country deserve to be treated with respect and offered opportunities to advance themselves in our society. Our best connection with those who are alienated is other veterans who have shared the experience of war. Therefore, as your Commander-in-Chief, I ask all who served our nation in the military to be alert for individuals, and especially groups of soldiers, who indicate they feel left out of our society. Help us make the connection with them that can benefit the whole country. If you hear of active training camps, let us know. You've risked your lives and made a great sacrifice for the sake of those in other countries; now take a step to help us curb the violence that threatens our country.

"An additional characteristic of those who are involved in this tragic effort, whether they are from the military or not, are people who have been hurt by their religious experience. I am personally a Christian," the President smiled, "although as I admitted to the pastor I'm about to introduce you to, my Christian path has been somewhat ragged. While I have never been wounded by the church, I have been disappointed from time to time and had my share of doubts. I've also had friends who felt betrayed by religion and even years later speak with anger about their experience. Again, this does not justify the violent response some individuals are making, but we must recognize while all religions should give us hope and meaning for our lives, religion touches people so deeply that when it goes wrong, some people feel wounded at the deepest reaches of their soul.

"While the shootings took place in Christian communities, I have talked to some leaders in the Jewish, Islamic, and Buddhist traditions in the last several days, and they agree they are vulnerable to the same misunderstandings in their traditions. In recent years, we've seen examples of radical, violent actions among some members of the Islamic community, and like our current experience, it seems to be most attractive to young people who are disillusioned with their faith and the world around them. I have invited representatives of several traditions to be present tonight to express our solidarity in confronting this national tragedy." The camera panned over several people whose dress indicated their tradition.

"So we come to these young people who are committing these acts of violence. The first thing you have to recognize is these young people, as near as we can tell, are not what some of their peers would call nerds, but they are made to feel like they are losers."

Frank and Jacob had helped the President carefully craft his speech. Their intent was to convey to listeners that the President was aware of what was happening and to invite the whole nation into helping him put a stop to the violence. They wanted him to show enough empathy for those who were part of this action that people with similar feelings might be convinced someone else understood. At the same time, they wanted the President to convey he had a plan to bring this terrible chapter in the nation's life to a peaceful resolution.

"I believe the young people who committed these acts of violence were seduced by some sadly disillusioned adults—adults who are ready to sacrifice our youth without remorse to achieve their own revenge. The leaders of these events are willing to rob the nation of the talent of you young people rather than help you reach your potential. Here is the message I want to send out to all the young people in our country, 'Each of you has a value in yourself and are worth being listened to. You needn't die to achieve notoriety. You can live to make a difference. Like the soldiers I've asked to connect with other soldiers, so I'm asking you to recognize when one of your peers is feeling left out and work to include him or her in.'

"Further, I'm offering a reward for the young person who has the courage to give us tips to help us stop this so called Leader and the violence now being perpetrated on the churches in our country. I have established a Hot Line (225-843-7737, Call the Pres) to receive any information you can provide. If your call proves valid and helps us capture those who organized this, you will be put in touch with a counselor and provided up to $30,000 to develop your future career."

The President leaned forward and raised his open palm towards the camera. "I want to stop this violence, but I also want to hear the voices of you young people who feel alienated and not listened to by others. I'm your President, too, and I care about you. I have organized a task force that will operate this Hot Line for the next month. Even if you don't have any information about those who are behind this, I want to hear what you think needs to be done for other young people in this country. I will have your opinions compiled into a report that will be shared with the Congress and the public. Not every opinion is valid, but your voice deserves to be heard. The number for the next month will be 225-843-7737, Call the Pres.

"I don't condone what this so called Leader has done, but I owe him a begrudging word of thanks. Because of these tragic events, I, along with many other people, realize we have not been listening. I appeal to you to stop the violence, and let us begin to listen to each other as a country."

Everybody in the room was listening intently to the President and wondering whether the right people were hearing. Frank saw Jacob move towards his monitor, even as the President paused and looked at his monitor. A banner was starting to feed itself across the screen. They thought this might happen and had counseled him on how to respond, but Frank knew the President had to develop his response on the fly, and how he did it could have significant consequences.

The President glanced briefly at Jacob, nodded slightly while showing two fingers not visible by the camera. He continued, "My fellow Americans, you will see at the bottom of your screen a banner that conveys a message from the terrorist who is behind these events. In a sense, this is our opportunity to communicate with each other.

"If you are listening on your radio, the terrorist's message reads:

> Texans are weenies who can't shoot straight. Can even the President protect the next state?
> 'Abandon your churches and admit your lies, Listen to what the voice of youth advise.
> 'The President lost control; Humpty-Dumpty had a great fall.
> 'Maybe it's time for our leaders to take some Phenobarbital.

"Assuming the person or persons who cleverly had this message hacked into my news conference are also listening, let me respond directly to you. Neither Texans nor your President are afraid to take a truth serum, because, unlike you, we don't sacrifice our children while we go into hiding. You sent a message by banner. Let me return the favor. And if you are hiding in some dark cave and are only listening by radio, I hope you have someone who can show you a video of this message."

> Two little stick figures danced across the bottom of the screen talking to each other.
> "I just got a message from the Leader who said I should shoot a lot of other people and then shoot myself, and that would show the world."
> "Who's the Leader?"
> "I don't know; somebody on the Internet who is sending messages to teenagers who feel left out."
> "Is the Leader shooting other people too?"
> "No dummy. If the Leader shot other people, the Leader might get shot, and then nobody would listen."
> "But if you die, then you can't listen, so what good will it do?"

"I'd be like a soldier who died for his country. The Leader says people should be willing to die for the truth."

"How do you know the Leader is telling the truth?"

"I don't, but it was on the Internet. Who will listen if we don't scare them a little?"

"I hear the President of the United States will listen if you call him on the hotline. That might be better than dying."

"Maybe I'll try that. What was the number again? Do you suppose he would read a text?"

"The number is 225-843-7737 Call the Pres."

The stick figures disappeared and the screen filled with the President's face. "I'm telling you honestly. The Hot Line will not be perfect, but my task force will listen and tell me what you say. I want you to help me stop this craziness because your life has value.

"As the first banner from the terrorists threatened, there is likely to be more church shootings, so we must be prepared. As President, I am authorizing the use of the National Guard, in coordination with the local and state police authorities, to be on alert. However, since the only distinguishing characteristic of the previous shooters is they were well-dressed young people who would normally fit right into our society, we must choose an additional way to prevent these tragedies.

"Thanks to some advanced information, we were able to make some preparation in Texas, Wisconsin. We were fortunate to have the wise strategy of The Reverend Frank Sessions of the John Knox Presbyterian Church in Lincoln, North Carolina. You will recall his church was where the first shooting took place. I've asked him to share his approach and ask the religious leaders of our country to consider implementing his suggestions."

The camera light blinked on as the technician pointed to Frank.

"Thank you, Mr. President. While all of us are shaken by this terrorist activity, it seems to focus particularly on the churches—in this case the Christian churches, but we have no assurance it won't spread to other religious communities. As you heard, this began in my church in Lincoln. During that incident, the young person involved was known by some of my members. We are not necessarily dealing with absolute strangers. It was also obvious he was someone who felt left out of society. From what I've learned later, he was intelligent but pretty much a loner."

Frank glanced at the others in the room. All of them were listening as he continued to speak.

"Building on that description, when we learned in advance the next shooting was going to be in Texas, Wisconsin, we asked all the religious leaders of that community to help us implement a plan we called, "No Youth Goes UnFriended."

The idea is simple and something we should have been doing all along. Each religious leader organized a group of adults to stand at the church doors on Sunday morning. Whenever a young person arrived, one of the adults would usher him or her to a pew and the adult would sit on the outside of the pew. The adults would do their best to engage the young people in a conversation about what was important to them and what their hopes were for the future. If appropriate, they would also inquire about their faith and how the church could be of support for them. In short, no young person entered a sanctuary without someone taking a genuine interest in him or her."

Frank smiled into the camera as he warmed towards his subject. "What we discovered was while it did place an adult near the potential shooters, which lessened the injuries, it also had benefits for the churches that were blessedly free from any incident of shooting. Many adults learned from these young people and discovered several rich possibilities for ministry.

"What we are asking is the leadership, lay or ordained, in each of your congregations, implement a similar strategy in your communities. This is more than just preventing immediate violence. We want to sensitize this nation to the needs of our youth and to convince the young people they have value and potential in their lives. We want to prevent any person from believing there is more value in dying than in living.

"I am aware this plan seems idealistic, but, from our recent experiences, we believe this nonviolent approach to violence allows us to respond in a manner consistent with our faith and holds the potential of improving the quality of life in our nation.

"As I return you to the President, I would invite you also to draw on the resources of prayer for your church, for all congregations, and for this nation."

The camera switched back to the President. "My fellow Americans, this is a difficult time for our nation, but the history of this nation suggests we do our best when our back is against the wall, and we usually come out stronger for it. I join with The Reverend Sessions in inviting your prayers, and I will do my best to keep you informed as events develop. In conclusion, I urge you not to give in to fear. This is a time for us to stand up for faith and peace and not let the forces of fear and violence triumph.

"Good night and may God Bless America."

The camera lights went out. You could hear a visible exhale from everyone in the room. A buzz of conversation erupted. Frank took a deep breath and let it out slowly. He was aware his shirt was totally soaked. He was so focused that it took a moment to realize several people had crowded around him with big smiles on their faces and hands outstretched.

Ralph took his hand and pulled him to his feet. "I'm a skeptic, pastor, but I have to admit, this is a brilliant strategy. The organizers should be on edge wondering who among them might spring a leak, and the teens should have second thoughts about thinking no one cares about them."

The President finished shaking hands and moved towards Jacob, who was still talking to the other media consultants. "They say you have a degree in both psychology and spirituality."

"Yes, sir, and I fear I have just the subject matter for a post doctoral dissertation."

"This was a brilliant strategy, son. I was pleased you got my signal and played tape two. I think it was the right response to their banner. As I mentioned to your father, who hit just the right tone, by the way; I would like your family to come up to our family quarters so that we could debrief a little about what has just taken place and what our next steps should be."

The room began emptying as the President indicated it was time to leave.

The First Lady had organized some light refreshments and was waiting for them when they arrived. She briefly hugged her husband and turned to the rest. "I watched it from here, actually with our teenage son, and he agreed with me you all did great."

An attendant entered the room, and the President said, "Please tell Andrew what you would like to drink. In my case, I would like a double Scotch, neat." Then he turned to Frank. "We have the full range from soft to hard. Please ask for whatever would please you."

"I'll have some red wine, thank you."

The others placed their orders and then sat in a small circle around the refreshments."

"Each member of this family, along with you, Amanda, played a significant role in giving us some hope in the face of this violent onslaught," said the President. "Believe me, this country is deeply in your debt. I'd like to hear from all of you both how you evaluate this evening and what you think we should expect from here."

The President looked around the room and focused on Rachel. "I haven't heard much from you, yet, and I understand you were one of the first to help us recognize what we are facing. What are your thoughts now?"

Rachel had just popped a cracker with some cheese on it in her mouth. She held up her hand choking slightly as she swallowed her bite. "Well, sir, I think there are two key elements to our next steps. We sent some veteran friends out to several locations to see if they can pick up some chatter about these survivalist groups. Our theory is it will be easier for former soldiers to talk to former soldiers, and we want to find out if there are some likely training sites that might give us a clue on where the next strikes will take place."

"That makes sense. Have you heard any reports back?"

Jacob smiled as he saw Rachel blush slightly. "No, sir, but I expect to get a call tonight from the soldier who is coordinating the reports."

"You said there were two key elements. What is the other element?"

"We have to pin down this Leader thing. We don't know whether there is more than one or whether it is a man or a woman."

"A woman?" said the President. "I just assumed we were looking for a man."

Jacob spoke up. "When I interviewed the two youth in Texas, Wisconsin, there was something said hinting at the possibility a woman might be involved."

A WOMAN'S LEADERSHIP

CHAPTER 37

Without being obvious, Bob watched his wife as they sat together to watch the President's news conference. He wasn't surprised at some of the cynical comments she made as the President spoke. She was never very fond of the man.

"I wonder what our knight in shining armor will come up with in light of the Texas shooting?" Barbara said.

"He's sort of between the proverbial rock and a hard place," Bob commented. "He'd probably like to blast the Texas governor for his *everybody should take a weapon to church* speech, but he doesn't want to take on the divisive gun control issue right now when everyone is so unnerved."

"I heard he invited Frankie to the White House to tell him how to save the churches in our land."

"Barbara, you have to let go of your anger at Frank Sessions. I talked to David recently, and even he seems to have gotten beyond that. In fact I think he is making real progress."

Barbara took a strong sip of her drink. "All right, Bob, let's just agree to disagree about that idiot. How do you think the President will approach this? Is he going to call out the National Guard to frisk all young people who dare to go to church?"

"I think we are about to see." They turned to the TV where the President had just been introduced. Against his better judgment, but trying to be nice, he asked, "Can I freshen your drink?"

Barbara held the glass towards Bob. "Thanks, you make a good martini, Bob. You should try one."

When he returned, the President was in the midst of his speech, and Barbara was listening intently.

"How's he doing so far?"

"A lot of platitudes, but he's for free speech and the right to worship as we please. I don't think he is going to close down your church, Bob."

He watched her eyes narrow as he began to invite veterans to report on anything suspicious about other veterans. When he got to people being deeply injured by their religious experience, he noticed Barbara take a strong swallow, and there seemed to be just the hint of a tear in her eye. They hadn't talked about it much, but Bob knew her father's death left a deep wound in her soul.

Then the President introduced his "Call the Pres" hotline. "That's an interesting idea," Bob said. "I wonder whether it will generate real leads or just a lot of calls from youth who think it would be neat to call the President."

"Scratch below the surface of a young person, and they just hunger to be heard. I'll bet he gets lots of calls to whine until they realize he is not interested in hearing from them. What about the scholarship idea? Notice how he carefully framed it, so he never has to pay it? All he's doing is trying to create a society of snitches."

"He has to stop this madness, Barbara. Maybe he will convince some wavering youth they can do something worthwhile."

Then came the banner interrupting the President's speech. At first he thought he heard a slight giggle when the banner began with the line, "Texans are weenies who can't shoot straight," and a barely disguised smile as the President read the rest of the message.

But he saw her body tense when the President not only didn't seem thrown off by the appearance of the banner but acted almost like he expected it.

"I don't know how they did that," said Bob, "but I give the President credit. He's handling it pretty well."

They both watched as the little stick figures came dancing across the screen.

"What's he doing?" Barbara said. "This isn't time for cartoons. He's not taking this seriously."

"No, wait, Barbara. Think about it. He's trying to communicate with young people who are into cartoons these days. There is just enough mockery in the message to appeal to young people. I think it's brilliant."

"I think it's offensive," said Barbara, getting up to grab a piece of paper. "I expect more . . ." And then she paused as the President introduced Frank Sessions, and he began to speak. "Oh Gawd, just because he had a little luck in that Wisconsin town, now everyone thinks he's the Messiah."

"I know you don't like him, Barbara, but he has come up with a plan people can act on."

"This makes me sick," said Barbara. "I'm going to my office." As she walked into her office, she closed the door with a little more firmness than usual.

Bob went to the bar to clean up from fixing the drinks. *Oh God, what if it is true that my dear Barbara does have some connection with all of this? What am I going to do?* He knew he shouldn't, and it was entirely out of character for him, but as he put the bottles away, he opened a bottle of Scotch on the shelf and poured himself a drink. As soon as it hit his throat, he started coughing, and part of it came right back up in the small sink in the bar. *I don't know how people do that,* he thought. When he had the bar cleaned up, he slumped in his lounger and tried to think of his next steps.

He decided tomorrow he would call and set up a meeting with Frank Sessions. He didn't know when Frank would be back in town, but he figured he could reach him on his cell phone. *Strange,* he thought, how our lives have become so intertwined over the last couple of years.

At first he grabbed a book but couldn't concentrate. Then he flipped on the TV to listen to commentators react to the President's speech.

Barbara was beside herself. Such a perfect plan and it was going so well—until that bastard Frank Sessions messed everything up. I'm glad one of Jeb's deranged buddies took a shot at his daughter. Too bad he missed. Then the SOB would know what it feels like to have someone mess with your child.

She poured herself a small shot of Scotch from her secret stash and sat back in her chair. Now where should we go from here? I think the four-state attack is pretty well set, so unless one of Jeb's buddies suddenly gets a fit of patriotism, it should go off without a hitch. That will throw everyone into a panic. Jeb and I have been careful not to leave any tracks back to either of us, so we should be good for now. One of those snotty-nosed recruits could chicken out at the last moment, but the worst that would mean is there were three hits rather than four. We should probably send a message to them in the next couple of days and remind them of their historic significance. No youth unfriended. Ha, that's a laugh. Thanks to our brilliant planning, we've even got a way to make an end run around that defense.

I should be grateful to both the President and Frank. After their "we have everything under control," speech, when this comes off, they will look like fools. No one will guess Barbie Doll can pull this off. Actually, Barbara, you are a pretty brilliant girl.

She picked up her iPhone and texted Jeb. "Wednesday afternoon, same place. Got 2 talk re protect our backside."

She just had pushed send when she heard Bob through the door.

"Barbara, are you all right in there? Can I get you a snack or something?"

I guess that is one piece of unfinished business. I didn't cover up very well during the President's speech. Don't want Bobbie to get suspicious. She stashed her glass in a drawer, straightened her outfit, and opened the door. She greeted Bob with a hug and said, "Thank you for being concerned about me. I guess all this violence has gotten to me. I was a little cynical about the President, and you are right, dear, I need to get past my feelings about Frank Sessions. After all, he almost lost one of his children, too, in that drive-by shooting. You know what, sweetheart, if you keep being so nice to me, you might make me a more forgiving Christian yet."

She could see the look of relief come over Bob's face. He leaned in to give her another kiss. "I love you so much, Barbara. I know I've given you a rough time over the last several years, but I don't know how I would survive if something happened to you."

"Well, forgiving you for your little indiscretions taught me how important forgiveness is, and as you once said in one of your great sermons, virtues grow strong when you exercise them regularly."

She put one hand on his shoulder and one hand on the side of his face. "You know what, dearest, I think you should go relax in your chair while I go into the kitchen and prepare a little snack for both of us. It's been a long and draining day."

Tuesday afternoon, as Frank prepared to leave for the airport, his cell rang. Glancing at the screen, he recognized the area code was from Lincoln but didn't recognize the number. "This is Frank Sessions. Can I help you?"

"Frank, this is Bob Godwin. First let me tell you I thought you and the President did a great job last night."

"Thanks, Bob. Now we have to see what effect it has."

"Frank, I need to talk with you and soon. When are you getting back from Washington?"

"We will be back in a few hours. I'm not entirely comfortable with it, but the President arranged for us to fly back in a private jet.

We should be back in Lincoln at least by five, maybe earlier. What's up, Bob?"

"I can't talk about it over the phone, and it may be only my paranoia kicking up, but I need to talk to you in absolute privacy."

Frank could hear the strain in Bob's voice. "Sure Bob, how about we meet in the office at John Knox about five this afternoon?"

"That's great, Frank. No one will be there, right? This needs to be in private."

"Come in by the back door. If anyone is there, I'll meet you at the door, and we will go someplace else."

He had just returned the phone to his pocket when Jacob walked up. Jacob glanced at where he had placed the phone and at his father's face. He nodded to his father but didn't ask any questions.

As they boarded the plane, Frank said, "I know we are emotionally drained, but I think it might be helpful if we brainstormed some of our next steps during the flight home.

They all agreed and took seats so they could face each other.

Frank turned towards his daughter. "Rachel, while I know we have enjoyed kidding you about your interest in Brian, that is your business, but we do need to know any reports that he might have gathered."

"Thanks, Dad. We had one sort of casual date—pizza after I got off one evening, and then he met with us and . . .well, he probably saved my life. That's sort of hard to forget."

"I know. It still causes me to shiver when I think about it. I'm glad he wasn't hurt too badly. Has he picked up anything that may be useful in our deciding what might happen next?"

"He's been working the phones while he was recovering, and a couple of his buddies made use of Amanda's help in traveling to some spots to nose around. Nothing solid yet, but he did pick up some noise in California and Iowa."

"I'm not surprised by California," said Jacob. "There must be plenty of crazies out there, but Iowa, that's supposed to be the center of evangelicalism. Are there any locations we can guess are safe areas?"

"I'm afraid we've about run out of prejudices," said Frank. "All our stereotypes of places and people who should be avoided if you want to be safe are being shattered. It doesn't begin in New York City but Lincoln, North Carolina, and it's not Jews, Muslims, or atheists, but Christians. They're not Black, Hispanic, Asian, or Middle Eastern. They're dressed and behave like we hope all our children will. What's left?"

"One thing," said Rachel, "they have this thing about religion—so far the Christian religion. What makes a person so angry at churches they are ready to die to take them out?"

"I think," said Jacob, "it's the ultimate betrayal. To use that old cliché, 'Someone's mad as hell, and they are not going to take it anymore.'"

"What do you mean the ultimate betrayal?" asked Rachel.

"When I talk to the students I work with, even the most stable of them are very disillusioned with the society in which they live. Try to think of an institution in our society that hasn't betrayed their trust in recent years. The church, or at least the God of the church, should be the one source of hope we can count on. But they've begun to question whether even God can be trusted."

Rachel took a sip on her Coke. "I was pretty angry when Mom was killed—some of it at God, I guess—but I never thought about wiping out a church to get even."

"That wouldn't be in your mental construct," said Jacob. "You still felt you had a measure of control and could do something to make a difference. Didn't you say that was one of the reasons you joined the police force?"

"Yeah, so?"

"Try to get in the head of a person who was disillusioned by everything. Maybe in addition to God, you felt dissed by everyone around you and grew angrier and angrier every day, but you were totally helpless to do anything about it."

Frank had been listening closely to the exchange. "And along came someone who suggested a way that you could force the world to sit up and take notice. Even if it cost you your life; for once in your life, you felt empowered."

"But that's crazy," said Rachel.

"We are not talking about mentally stable here. There are lots of people who border on some form of mental imbalance," said Jacob. "All of us have crazy thoughts from time to time, but most of us have the restraint to evaluate and dismiss them."

"I think you are on to something, Jacob. But these youth are just toys being manipulated. The real question is who is doing the manipulation, and why?" said Frank.

"Brian said that there are a lot of disillusioned veterans out there who are angrier than hell at the country who sent them to risk their lives while everyone else sat in comfort and got rich," said Rachel. "Their moral compass was shattered when they were forced to violate all the standards they were taught, and now they can't find a new direction or purpose in their lives."

"They knew fear at its deepest level when they were in combat," said Jacob, "but they kept going because their buddies counted on them. When they returned, they couldn't fit back in. When they looked around, no one had their back, and most people walked around like zombies, protecting themselves but sucking the blood out of everyone else."

"Then someone showed them how to make society feel deep fear and be helpless to do anything about it," added Frank. "But who came up with that strategy, and how do we find them?" Something pricked in Frank's mind, but he couldn't bring it to the surface. "We had better tell Mandy about the rumors of California and Iowa. She can at least let the governors know and call out the Guard. If Brian hears more, make sure we tell Mandy."

They continued to talk, and Frank tried to access the back of his mind but with little success.

THE FIRST CLUE

CHAPTER 38

When they landed, it was late afternoon. Rachel wanted to check in at the police station, and Jacob had graduate students seeking his attention. Frank said he would call them tomorrow, and they all parted. Frank had left his car in the parking lot. Which row was it? Oh yeah, now I remember. Row J. I thought of Jacob when I parked. Now, how far down the row do I need to walk? He was grateful to whoever invented wheels for suitcases.

Once he found his car and started driving to the exit booth, he recalled what had been nagging at him. He was wondering what Bob Godwin could want to talk about. As he drove to his church to meet him, he recalled how insistent Bob had been the meeting be in secret.

Frank's actions led to discovering Bob's son, David, had been the "religious rapist" who terrorized Lincoln a few years back. David was now in prison. Frank didn't feel guilty, but he did feel an added measure of responsibility for helping Bob and Barbara cope with the reality of a son in prison. It would be hard enough for any parent, but Bob being the pastor of a large, growing church in Lincoln, made it both very public and extra difficult. Barbara, Bob's wife, seemed to withdraw after David was convicted and sentenced to prison. He hoped nothing had happened to her or their marriage.

He pulled into the church lot and drove to the rear of the church. He saw Bob's red Lexus RC near the back. He wondered if Bob realized how his car made him stand out wherever he went. So much for a secret meeting, he thought. As he drove up, Bob got out and approached Frank's window.

"Frank, thanks for coming. You must be exhausted from all you have been through." He glanced behind him at his car. "Not very discreet, is it? Do you mind if I ride with you to some little out-of-the-way restaurant?"

"Hop in."

Except for small talk, Bob was mostly silent as Frank drove. He shifted and squirmed in his seat but said little. As they approached the restaurant, Frank said, "I'm sure this will allow us complete privacy for our conversation."

They found a rear booth. A waitress came, and they both ordered a small sandwich. Bob ordered a Coke and Frank some unsweetened ice tea. The small talk continued until the food arrived. The sandwich smelled good. Frank took a bite and looked at Bob, who was fingering his Coke, his eyes focused on the table, his sandwich untouched.

"I'm not sure where to begin," Bob said, "but you were the only one I knew who might help me sort this out."

"Is this about David?"

Bob closed his eyes and ran his hand over his face. "No, in some ways I wish it was. Well, I guess he was the start of what I want to talk to you about."

"Begin anywhere, Bob. Eventually, it will all fit together."

Bob took a large gulp of his drink. He set the glass down, placed both of his hands on the table, smiled at Frank, took a big breath, let it out, and said, "OK, here goes."

"I have been working on my relationship with David, and, I'm pleased to say, we have the best relationship now we've ever had. I visit him regularly in prison and call even more often."

"That's good, Bob."

"It's a tough way to grow closer to your son, but it is what it is." He turned away briefly and returned his gaze towards Frank. "OK, here goes. Last Sunday, after the services, I was drained. Not only was it several services, but I think every preacher in the land wondered whether his church might be the next target."

"It was a tense Sunday. The Dallas tragedy raised the anxiety level for everyone."

"Since I'm using you as my confessor, I feel guilty as the devil about it, but when I heard about Dallas, I felt a little relieved. At least it moved out of Lincoln. Isn't that terrible?"

"Human, I'd say. I was in Washington on Sunday, but in the back of my mind I kept wondering if someone would come back to my church for a second round."

Bob nodded. "When all the events were finished at the church, I went home. Barbara was out, so I was sitting down having a Coke and resting a little. I planned to eat a salad Barbara had left for me in the refrigerator. I must have dozed off, and about 2:30 the phone rang. It was David."

Frank felt himself tense as David's name was mentioned.

"He told me he wanted to meet with me and had arranged with the warden to receive me even if I arrived after visiting hours. I told him his mother was out for the afternoon. He said that was good because he wanted to meet with me in private."

"So you drove over to the prison to visit him?"

"Yes, I arrived about 4:15, and, as David said, I was expected and ushered right in. After the usual greetings, David asked me if I thought his mom had been acting strange lately." Again Bob checked the room out to make sure no one was overhearing what was being said.

"I asked him what he meant, and he began to tell me a weird story about her last visit. He said she told him she was going to get him out of prison, and he should think about starting a new life in Costa Rica or someplace."

Frank's eyes narrowed. "You mean like she was going to help him escape from prison or something?"

"It's crazier than that," Bob said. "Apparently she told David she might talk to the President of the United States and demand he let David out."

Frank's head drew back and his eyes widened. "The President?"

"That's what David said, and normally I'd think Barbara had just gone around the bend, but with everything happening in churches lately, I began to think darker thoughts."

Frank felt his mouth go dry. He reached out and took a swig of his ice tea. "Bob, we'll think this through together. Tell me what darker thoughts you began thinking."

"Well, after my indiscretion" he paused and said, "Hell, I've got to learn to be more honest at least with myself. After I betrayed Barbara by having another affair, she laid down the law to me. First she took a break and went off to a spa in Arizona. I tell you, Frank, I wondered if I had totally blown it, and she would never come back. I was a horrible husband."

"But you are trying to face it now."

"I hope so. I sent her notes every day and some flowers, hoping she'd return. And she did."

Frank saw a brief flash of joy on Bob's face.

"I was so happy I'd have done anything. Actually what she asked for was reasonable. She said she wanted one of our extra rooms renovated into her private office and her private Internet service installed."

"Which you did," Frank said, more to encourage Bob to keep talking than anything else.

"I did. I made sure she had an office with all the frills. Her only condition was that it was her private office, and I only would enter it with her permission. I knew she was trying to reconstruct her personal identity, and I agreed. It seemed to work. She'd spend a lot of time there, but she became more loving and continued to do even little extra things for me."

"Sounds like there was some healing."

"I thought so. There were some little spats, but then we'd make up and move on. Strangely, I think Barb has become even more affectionate than before." He smiled. "She does know how to work me to get what she wants, but I decided after what I put her through, she deserved whatever I could offer."

"And then David mentioned this weird conversation."

"Yeah." He paused as if remembering the next thing he was going to say. "All the way home from the prison I kept turning David's thoughts over in my mind. I arrived home about six-thirty. Barbara wasn't home yet. She told me she had several errands to run, so that didn't worry me too much."

"So what happened next?"

Bob hesitated, lowered his head, then raised it up again as if he had made a decision. "I did something I promised Barbara I'd never do. I entered her office without an invitation. I wanted to look around—sort of ease my mind. I thought David was probably misinterpreting what his mother had said, but I wanted to make sure."

"I think what you did was understandable, Bob. So what happened?

"Well, the TV was on. She often leaves it on in the background. And the computer was on. I moved the mouse to awaken it, and I saw it." Bob paused.

"Saw what?"

"The screen had a map on it with circles around several cities and Dallas was highlighted in bright yellow. I went closer to look at the screen. I happened to glance down at her desk. Now understand, all the stories about what was happening in Dallas were all over the TV and Internet."

"No one could fail to see it," said Frank.

"But right there on her notepad, in big letters, it read 'That will teach those fuckers!!!' with three exclamation points after it."

"It sounds like she was pretty angry."

Bob's face brightened a little. "Yeah, that must be it. She has been angry—at you, at losing David, at my betrayal, at the church, at being put down as a Barbie doll. I mean that is a terrible response to the disaster, but she must have been listening to the broadcast and overreacted."

Frank was quiet for a moment and then said, "But you thought it was more?"

"Well, for a moment the crazy thought went through my mind that Barbara had something to do with all this." He paused and searched Frank's face. "That's insane isn't it? I mean how could Barbara have anything to do with all this horror? She may be angry, but she doesn't have the ability to do all this. I'm thinking crazy, aren't I?"

"Bob, I think this is probably a lot bigger than anything one woman could pull off. She's absorbed several blows lately, and maybe does need to see a counselor to help get her thinking straightened out."

Bob grimaced. "I wouldn't want to be standing in the same room when someone suggested that to her. She would make Mt. Vesuvius look like child play. Still, I'll think about whether there is a way to get her to consider it. Thanks, Frank. For a liberal, you are a stand-up guy."

Frank smiled at the gentle teasing. He knew, because he and Bob stood on opposite poles of the theological spectrum, they had both been cautious about extending friendship to each other. Still, they had faced some difficult moments together. "Bob, I think that is probably all there is to it, bad as it is, but we need to consider whether there is more to this. After all, her comment about demanding something from the President suggests she did think, however warped it was, she had some leverage."

Bob's color had improved in the last few minutes, and now it reversed itself and drained from his face. "What are you suggesting?"

"I don't know, but here are a couple of initial steps. You need to return home and try your best to be a supportive husband. If this is a slight mental aberration, Barbara certainly needs your support. Maybe the opportunity will occur for you to bring up the possibility of counseling. You might even begin by asking if she is ready for the two of you to take the next steps in some marital counseling."

"I could do that. I suggested counseling early on, but she said she wasn't ready. That's a great idea."

"While you are doing that, keep a careful watch on anything that might clue you into the possibility that more is going on. Keep note of when she goes out and where if she tells you, but don't ask. Make note of any comments that seem significant. Keep sort of a journal. Every once in a while we can get together and process the notes to see if there is some pattern we can spot."

"OK. But you suggested a couple of things. What are the others?"

"You mentioned there were several cities circled on the computer map. Do you remember what some of them were?"

"I didn't have much time because I heard her car come into the driveway, and I didn't want her to know I had violated our agreement."

"I understand, but do you remember any of them."

Bob fingered his now empty glass of Coke and played with the moisture ring on the table.

"Think about it while I order us another drink. Do you want anything different or another Coke?"

"I know this violates my image as a proper conservative pastor, but is there a beer you'd recommend?"

"Sure." Frank signaled the waitress. "I have just the thing for you." He turned to the waitress, "Bring us two Crabbies Ginger Beers."

While they waited, Bob pulled out a note card and began to doodle.

The beers came, and Bob took a careful sip. "Oooh, that's good. I'd better be careful."

Frank took his own sip. "So do any of the cities come to mind that were circled on your wife's computer map?"

"Bangor, Maine was one. We were going to take a vacation there but never did." He thought for a moment. "Oh," he held up his pen, "another one was Davenport, Iowa. We went through there once when we were visiting colleges with David."

"Good, Bob. Think of any more?"

"No, I only had a glance. Oh, wait, there was another one in California—Baker something."

"Bakersfield?" Frank asked.

"That sounds like it. What do you think it means?"

"Probably nothing. Though they are too spread out to be a trip she was planning. I'll keep them in mind just in case."

"There was some place south of us as well, in South Carolina or Georgia, but I don't remember the name of it."

They finished their ginger beers, and Frank drove Bob back to his car.

Bob got out of the car and turned to Frank. "It really is nothing, right? She was just angry, right?"

"I hope so, Bob. I hope so."

Frank headed home. He was both scared and energized about the possibility they had found a link that might lead them to the Leader of this terror event.

Entering the house, he dropped his briefcase and placed a call to Amanda. When the secretary said she was not available, Frank responded: "Listen, this is Frank Sessions. You find her, and tell her Frank Sessions called and wants her to get back to him immediately."

"I'll leave a message for her, sir, but I think she is in a meeting, and I don't know how long she will be."

"I don't care if she is meeting with the President of the United States; you interrupt the meeting and give her that message. I guarantee you if you don't, you will be criticized, and if you do, you will be thanked."

There was a pause on the phone line. Then a hesitant, "Does she have your number?"

Frank let out a chuckle. "Yes, in more ways than one. Thank you for your assistance."

Frank hung up and went to the refrigerator and grabbed a cold stout. I promise this will be the last one for today."

Within fifteen minutes, his Skype phone rang on his laptop. He punched the button to accept and saw Amanda's rather stern face on his screen. When she saw him, she didn't bother with pleasantries. "I assume this is important. You scared the pants off my assistant, and, believe me, she doesn't scare easily."

Frank smiled, lifted his beer towards her in a salute, and said, "I fear I may have discovered a possible link between the Leader of this whole mess and me."

"YOU WHAT! Wait right there. I need a colleague here, and I want to shut the door."

She disappeared from the screen, and Frank could see her desk chair and a flag and some pictures on the wall behind it. Soon she was back with a pad of paper and pen. "This is Mark," she said. "He is my top person on this task force."

Frank felt a flash of jealousy but greeted Mark with a wave as he appeared on the screen.

"OK, I may be off base, but my gut tells me this begins to fit together. You remember the mother of that serial rapist of a few years ago?"

"Yeah, Babs or Barbie, or something like that. Sort of a ditsy blond."

"That's the one. Barbara Godwin, wife of the pastor of a megachurch here in Lincoln."

"She was pretty devastated when her son was sent off to prison, if I remember. I think she had some choice words for you after the trial, didn't she?"

"Yes, and I tried not to take it too personally but to understand she was reacting to the pain of the virtual loss of her son. Now, I think I dismissed it too quickly."

"That ties in with what is happening now, how?" Amanda asked.

Frank described his interchange with Bob Godwin and the angry note on Barbara's desk."

"I can see she may never have gotten over her anger, and with her philandering husband, I can see how she is furious with the church," Mandy said, "but how could she play a role in the shootings?"

"I don't know, but that would explain why it started in my church, and the shooter knew my name."

"So you think she may be a link to this Leader somehow? Maybe they both have vengeance on their minds, and he had some way of organizing the youth who started with your church. What is he, some type of deranged youth leader?"

"I don't know, and it is pure speculation at this point. However, it is the only hint we have to next possible targets. What if we tried to organize special attention to California, Maine, Iowa, and Georgia?"

"It's the best we have. We have a couple of days before the weekend. We can try to get the clergy in those states to be on alert and beef up the National Guard in all towns possible. If we are lucky again, we may at least be able to reduce the damage." She turned away from the screen. "Mark, I'll finish up here, while you get on the horn and start alerting those we can reach."

Frank saw a hand on Mandy's shoulder as Mark's face appeared on the camera. "Frank, Amanda told me a lot about you. I just want to thank you myself. Without you, this would have been a worse nightmare than it is. Thanks ."

Amanda turned back to the screen and smiled.

Frank could see the worry lines etched on her face. He resisted the temptation to comment about Mark. "You look tired, Mandy. I think we both need to get some sleep and start fresh in the morning."

"Sounds good. And Frank, thank you. You have good instincts, and I hope this might be a significant break in this mess."

A WEEKEND FROM HELL

CHAPTER 39

May 14

Frank returned to his church on Wednesday. His secretary, Marcie, gave him a wan smile. "Not to be unkind, but you look like the final runner in a marathon. I hesitate to tell you how many notes and messages I piled on your desk. There might be real wisdom in turning around and heading back out. If it were me, I'd go for one of those full body massages, but you compassionate types would think it was a sinful indulgence. Isn't there something you could do that would feel good and relaxing?"

Frank raised his hands, leaned both left and right, and stretched his body. "Got to get ready for the next race. We marathon runners can't let a little stress or lack of sleep interfere with reaching for the runner's high."

"It's been three weeks since the last shooting. Do you think it's over? Are they making any headway in figuring this out in Washington?"

"I'm not sure, Marcie. I fear it is going to get worse before it gets better." He pointed towards his office. "I suppose you've done your usual excellent job of prioritizing the mountain of messages in there?"

"The mail was a challenge, but the phone calls were easy. They all want you to call them immediately. As long as each one is number one on your list, all will be satisfied. I did sort them into three piles. Pile one has those who think if you jumped off a bridge, all this would be over. Pile two are from those who think you are such an angel if you did jump off the bridge, it would be to swoop down and rescue all those in trouble. Finally, in pile three are messages calling to offer their support and to see if they can be of help."

Frank grinned for what he thought might have been the first time in days. "OK, pile three it is." As he started towards his office, he turned, "if you ever lost your slightly sardonic and cynical sense of humor, I don't think I could survive."

Over the next couple of days, Frank worked through his mail and returned phone calls. All the time he kept wondering what the next several weekends would hold. The Dallas shooting had removed any doubt this was a national issue, and the whole country was nearly paralyzed with the fear the next shooting might be in their town or city. Then three weekends passed without a shooting breaking the pattern. People began to hope the nightmare was over. Frank didn't think so.

He thought back to the sermon he was preaching when this all began. He had watched as people grew less and less trustful of the institutions in our society. It seemed as if every week there was a new story of corruption or blatant mismanagement from government to corporations, from churches to educational institutions, and from the courts to the major charities. People were beginning to resonate with the words of W. B. Yeats, "Things fall apart; the centre cannot hold; Mere anarchy is loosed upon the world, . . . "

He had wanted to acknowledge the challenges but fortify their courage with a vision of promise and possibility. He had begun with the image of God bringing order out of chaos and was developing the theme of God continuing to create and invite them to share in this courageous adventure. Then the boy had stood up and the shooting began.

Now there had been several more, and he knew the next shooting might be the worst yet. What could he possibly say to prepare his people for what might be happening even as he was preaching. In this day of instant communication, he knew even if it took place in another state, someone would be sneaking a peek at his or her phone during the service and would hear about it. People were so on edge if they heard it, they would likely shout it out. He prepared a second sermon to be used at the point of crisis. One to give them hope in the midst of chaos. The second sermon would be used if disaster struck. It was designed to quell instant panic if it erupted. He could only pray other pastors were preparing their responses as well.

The last three Sundays had passed without incident. After the expected two Sunday interval, Frank approached each Sunday with dread. He knew it was coming but didn't know when.

Each Friday Mandy called and updated him on the preparations being made for the weekend. "We know it can happen anywhere," Mandy said, "but we are trying to be especially alert in California, Iowa, Maine, and Georgia. Bakersfield, Davenport, and Bangor at least were specific enough to raise extra alerts, but what can we possibly do for all the towns and cities in Georgia or "South Carolina?"

"How is the National Guard being deployed?" Frank asked.

"We've placed them on high alert everywhere, but there aren't enough of them to be in every church, so they are stationed at key points around cities. We've done our best to communicate with as many pastors as possible. Do you realize how many churches there are in this country?" Amanda said. "It would make this a whole lot easier if they all got together."

"Jesus had that idea, too," Frank said, "but somehow between doctrinal arguments and egos, we've not been able to pull it off yet."

"We have tried to provide as many emergency buttons to as many of the large churches as possible," said Mandy.

"The problem is," said Frank, "if they just want to kill people and spread panic, they might find it easier to pick on the smaller churches. Small churches won't be able to afford extra security."

"Thanks, I feel a whole lot better hearing about that possibility."

"Sorry. I know you are doing the best you can."

"Have you heard anything more from Reverend Godwin?"

"No, I was going to check in with him later, but I'm sure if he had spotted anything, he would call me."

"They are trying to wear us down by waiting, aren't they?" said Amanda. "It could happen anytime. Oh God, Frank, how are we going to stop this? It's diabolical. At least schools, businesses, and movie theaters were one at a time. We can't even get a focus on whom to protect."

"My gut tells me that this may be the Sunday. Let's talk Saturday night."

They hadn't come up with any better ideas by Saturday night, and Frank rose early Sunday morning with knots in his stomach. He didn't know where, but he fully expected this nightmare was going to continue, and likely more than one church in more than one state would become targets.

When he arrived at the church, he found Harold Duggins and pulled him aside. "Harold, do you have your iPhone on you?"

Harold was a large, bespectacled man in his late fifties. As a stockbroker, he had become quite proficient with the latest technology. He looked at Frank with a puzzled expression. "Sure. You want to make a call, or are you just reminding me to place it on vibrate?"

Frank smiled, but placed his hand on Harold's arm and ushered him to a quieter corner. "Harold, I'm concerned that there will be more violence today, probably in another state. Can you get CNN on your phone?"

Harold took the phone out of its holster, tapped in a few buttons, and held it up for Frank to see.

"Good. What I want you to do is keep tuned in and position

yourself off to the side but down near the front of the sanctuary. Pay more attention to your screen than what is going on during worship."

"Whoa, I never thought I'd hear that from a preacher."

"Don't make it a habit, but this time you have special dispensation. If anything happens, I want you to signal me right away. Even if I'm praying, say something like 'Amen preacher.' I'll know what it's about."

"You think this may be the Sunday, Frank? This has been really evil, making us wait and never knowing when it is coming."

"To mangle an old cliché, this is where faith's rubber hits the road. I've primed Ariel, who is running the AV for the service. She has some special slides I've prepared. She is ready to flash them on the screen."

Harold's brow creased. "I know you always try to think ahead, Frank, but if people start shooting up churches, I don't know what good some words on a screen will do."

"They won't do any good for those poor churches that are getting shot up," said Frank, "but I'm hopeful they may help the people here not to panic. When people begin to freak out, it helps to have some familiar routines and liturgies to remind them of the faith they can cling to."

"Hope you're right, Frank. I'll be ready to do whatever you say."

Frank looked out over the congregation during the prelude. He could tell they were worried and anxious. He led them in a Call to Worship that reminded them of the sovereignty of God. Then he stepped to the front of the chancel steps. "I wish I could tell you the nightmare that started in this sanctuary a couple of months ago is over, but I don't think that is true."

There was a rustle among the people. He even saw some couples reach over and take the hand of their partner.

"I think," he continued, "we are safe in this sanctuary, and probably in this city, for now, but I don't believe it is true everywhere. I think somewhere in this country, there are those who are preparing to execute some more hellish acts even as we sit here."

There was a low murmur, but they were also looking at him intensely.

"I've asked Harold . . ." He pointed to where Harold was standing, "to keep an eye on his phone and tell us immediately if anything breaks while we worship. If it happens, there is nothing we can do by rushing out of here, and we are in no personal danger. I've asked Ariel to flash a litany on the screen that you can share with me. We will proceed with some prayer time for the victims and singing some familiar hymns to remind us of the faith that will get us through this. Are you with me?"

There was a lot of nodding of heads and several "We're with you preacher."

"Let's begin by reminding ourselves of who is on our side in this frightening time. Let us sing "A Mighty Fortress is Our God."

Frank heard the energy come from their singing. They were gaining courage as they sang with gusto "Did we in our own strength confide, our striving would be losing . . ."

He knew their faith would was being tested even in the waiting, but he was glad they could be reminded of it now. If chaos broke out, he wanted to provide his people with a liturgy that would cut through the fear and assure them of a light that the darkness of these days could not overcome.

"For our Scripture today, I will read to you Psalm 22. This was the Psalm Jesus shouted from the cross. It acknowledges his fears in the famous passage, 'My God, my God why have you forsaken me? Why are you so far from helping me, from the words of my groaning?'"

He finished reading the Psalm and lifted his eyes to see the congregation. "I know you are nervous, scared even, about what is happening in our land. Like Jesus in the Psalm, you want to know where God is now when all hell seems to be breaking loose." He continued to recognize the legitimacy of their fears but then pointed to the end of the Psalm where, having poured out his heart, Jesus was able to affirm once again the faith that sustained him.

He was about to recite those verses where, in the midst of terror, the psalmist was able to praise God, when Harold raised his hand.

"There has been a shooting in Maine and another one in South Carolina. Not clear how many are hurt yet."

There were groans and even a few screams from the congregation. "O Lord, make this stop," one lady screamed.

Frank signaled Ariel, who flashed an adapted version of Psalm 13 on the screen. "Pray with me as the screen indicates," Frank shouted into the mike. "It is important." Frank's commanding voice cut through the commotion as he began, "How long, O Lord? Will you forget us forever? How long will you hide your face from us?"

At first with hesitation some began to pray from the words on the screen. "How long must we bear pain in our souls and have fear in our hearts all day long? Lord, don't let these terrorists mock our faith."

Frank's booming voice rang out. "Consider and answer us, O Lord our God. Help us see light in this darkness. Don't let the mockery of these terrorists prevail. Don't let those who call resurrection a lie see us paralyzed in fear."

The congregation seemed to gain courage as they continued. Almost defiantly they shouted, "We trust in your steadfast love; our hearts shall rejoice and shatter our fear. We will sing praises to you and go forth in hope."

The very structure of the liturgy not only allowed them to own their fears but also claim their faith. Frank signaled the organist who struck a resounding chord, and he began to sing. "Amazing grace how sweet the sound . . ." As he continued, the congregation joined in. When they came to the third verse and the words, "Through many dangers, toils, and snares, I have already come . . , Frank could see them stand taller.

When they finished singing, he spoke again. "I've asked Harold to come and give us a report on this horrible event. The terror is not over, but our faith is in a God who is trustworthy. As Harold comes forward, I want you to pray the 23rd Psalm with me to affirm our faith that reaches back thousands of years and has triumphed over darkness and violence again and again.

Harold climbed the chancel steps even as the people began to say "The Lord is my shepherd, I shall not want." They almost shouted

"Even though we walk through the valley of the shadow of death, we will fear no evil." Frank positioned Harold close to the mike.

Harold helped lead the people praying the words, "Surely goodness and mercy shall follow me all the days of my life, and I shall dwell in the house of the Lord forever."

"Please sit," he said. "This is not going to be easy to hear, but we hear it in the sanctuary of our God who will give us strength."

They sat in deep silence as Harold began to speak.

"The first shooting was in Bangor, Maine, in a midsized Baptist church. The National Guard was patrolling the streets, and two youth dressed in guard uniforms entered the church announcing they were there to protect the people."

"People began to relax, comforted by the fact they were armed and stood along the side aisles. Then, just as the pastor was leading the congregation in prayer, there was a loud maniacal laugh, and when people looked up, both young men had their guns drawn and were pointing them at the people in the pews. They began shooting people in the pews.

"A young man, who is reported to be a linebacker on the high school football team, came barreling down the aisle and plowed into the first shooter. This distracted the second shooter and a couple of other men leaped up and subdued him. One of them was wounded in the process."

Harold raised his eyes from his notes. "I'm sure there will be much more, but that is what CNN is reporting as of 11:30.

"Wait, there is another report just coming in. Harold read off his phone screen. They tried to pull off the same tactic in Clinton, South Carolina. A couple of youth in uniform entered a Lutheran church."

Harold continued reading. "This time an alert young man, who himself had been in the guard, noticed the uniforms were not standard issue. Suspicious, he called the guard headquarters and 911. Then he followed the youth into the church. His father was on usher duty, so he told him what he had seen. As they approached one youth, he panicked and pulled his gun and began shooting. He killed two people and wounded two before he was subdued. His partner was distracted by these events and didn't see the men on the opposite side of the sanctuary coming towards him. There were some large festive banners hanging on the wall near where he stood. One of the men pulled a banner off the wall and covered him while he was trying to get his gun out of its holster. He was able to get one shot off, wounding a teenager sitting near him, but then they took him down."

Harold looked up from his notes. Normally a strong, steady man, his face had lost all color. The congregation sat in stunned silence.

Frank stepped forward and placed a hand on Harold's shoulder.

"I know you will all want to tune into the news to hear more. The tragedy is many worship services will be commencing further west from us in earlier time zones. Let us pray nothing more happens.

"I would urge you, if you are single, to gather with friends. We need to support each other. Let me conclude with words from another hymn. Frank read the words, 'If thou but trust in God to guide thee, with hopeful heart through all thy ways, God will give strength what-e're betide thee, to bear thee through the evil days.'"

Many people just stood around, hugging each other and weeping. Slowly they began to make it to their cars to return to their homes or the home of a friend.

Frank left Harold in charge. Harold was still watching his iPhone. Everyone gathered around him and watched his screen. It distracted them from seeing Frank step out of the sanctuary. He ran to his office and grabbed his phone. He speed dialed Amanda.

"Frank, all hell is breaking loose here. What have you got?"

"If Bob's memory was right, the next target will be in Iowa, in a city called Davenport. I know you have The Guard there and have done your best to forewarn the pastors. I'm sure they must have a citywide fire alarm or something that alerts the community in times of disaster. Tell them to set it off. At least it will put everyone on alert. You probably have about ten minutes."

Frank could hear Amanda shouting orders in the background.

Then she returned to the phone. "OK, I hope that works. I guess

Georgia was the wrong pick, but we got lucky in Clinton. The body count was minimal if you can say that in this type of mess."

"There is more. If we are lucky, and they stick to 11 a.m. services, you have three hours to alert Bakersfield, California—maybe only two if they have a service at ten. Do everything you can to shut the town down. If we create enough chaos, it's possible the shooters will panic and run."

"With a larger population, 350,000 I think, it is a little harder to shut down, but we will set off all the alarms and police sirens possible. Let me call you back in the next half-hour. We need to consider our next move with the source of your information."

"In the meantime, I'll contact Rachel and see if they can't find an excuse to visit the Godwin home. It's almost certain that Barbara is connected with this somehow. It's important Rachel get a warrant to look at her computer and papers."

"I'll have the justice department contact a judge there in Lincoln and clear the way."

Frank could hear the shouts in the background. "They've hit Davenport."

"Got to go, Frank. I'll call you."

BARBARA DISAPPEARS

CHAPTER 40

Like Frank and most other pastors, Bob tried to prepare his congregation for additional shootings. He did his best to remain calm and reassuring. He also had alerted some church officers to monitor the media during the service. When a deacon came running up to the chancel area with word of the shooting in Bangor, Maine, Bob almost fainted.

He now knew somehow his wife was connected with the shootings. Later he would marvel at the fact his first thoughts were not about how this would affect his reputation. The shock of David's alert and his discovery in Barbara's office had galvanized an inner strength in Bob.

He was ashamed that a lot of his energy when David was arrested centered on how to protect his image as the esteemed pastor of a major church in the city. Over the next couple of years, his frequent visits to see David shook him to the core but also began to transform him. While some members left, and he received a number of nasty and accusatory letters, to his great surprise, a large part of his congregation rallied around him. Some even said they thought his sermons were better and had more depth. As one member shared, "I can feel the pain in your sermons, and it helps me to realize I can wrestle with my pain and my faith too."

That was all before he knew Barbara was at the heart of what was ripping this nation and its churches apart. How could he possibly survive that? Did he even want to?

He did his best to calm his congregation when the news came in. He turned the closing of the service over to an associate pastor and left the sanctuary. His feelings cascaded in large waves, alternating from fury to abject terror. How could he have been so stupid not to read the signs? How could his beautiful wife have become such a monster? What had he done to create this satanic presence? What can be done to end this evil before it consumes the church?

It's time to be a man and stop acting as if I'm walking on eggs around Barbara. He entered his office and called home. There was no answer. He knew Barbara would see it was him on call identification, and if she was in a foul mood, she may have chosen not to answer. When the message machine came on, he said, "Barbara, this is Bob. I'm coming right home. Do not, I repeat, do not leave the house until we talk."

He didn't worry about the speed limit as he drove home. Barbara's part in this nightmare had to stop right now, and he was going to make sure it did. He pulled into the driveway and saw her green Subaru was missing from the usual spot. He prayed that didn't mean she was gone. He slammed on his brakes near the front door. He heard the sirens of several police cars entering his driveway and screech to a stop. He noticed the front door was open a crack.

A commanding voice over their loud speaker said, "Will the driver of the red Lexus please exit the car with hands raised?"

I guess they came to the same conclusion I have, thought Bob. He slowly opened his car door, raised his hands, and stepped out.

"Bob, it's Rachel Sessions. Please walk towards the lead police car. I'll meet you."

He was relieved to see Rachel and responded immediately.

"Rachel, I just got home from church. I assume you are looking for Barbara. I haven't been inside yet, but I suspect she has left."

"We need to look. We have a warrant to search the house and confiscate her computer and files."

"You also have my permission. You won't even need a key. For some strange reason, Barbara must have forgotten to lock the door."

Because Rachel was a member of this special task force, the other officers listened to her direction. She called four of the officers to proceed to enter and clear the house. They headed towards the front door.

"I don't understand," said Bob, "I might leave the door open when I was in a hurry, but not Barbara. She never acts without a plan in mind."

Sometimes in police work you have to trust your instincts. Rachel could not explain why, but before the officers reached the door to the house, she shouted out to them. "Stop. Don't touch the door."

She triggered her radio and called into headquarters.

When they responded, she didn't waste any time. "This is Officer Rachel Sessions. I am outside the door to the house of Bob and Barbara Godwin. I want you to dispatch the bomb squad with the new Remotec ANDROS F6A to this site. Time is of the essence."

Bob and the other officers stared at her.

"It may be unnecessary, but we are going to make sure the door is not rigged before we go in."

"Rachel, that's not necessary. I assure you Barbara would never do something like that."

"Bob, I can't believe the Barbara I met would be involved in any of this, but the evidence is mounting she may be. I'm not going to take any chances with the lives of my officers."

Within ten minutes, a van arrived and took a small robot-like machine down from the back. The man who controlled the Robot affectionately gave it the nickname Robbie after one of his favorite Sci-Fi movies. Rachel directed them to send the robot with its special bomb sniffer into the house. As it neared the door, it was instructed to examine the area with its camera and use its sensor to determine if any explosive materials were in the area.

The officers were tense as the robot approached the door. The controller adjusted the camera and the arm with the special sensor to inspect the door.

"The door appears clear," the officer reported, "but there is a faint odor of bomb material."

"Move everyone back behind our cars, and then we will tell it to enter," said Rachel.

When everyone was safely behind barriers, the controller was instructed to direct the robot to enter. "OK, Robbie, do your thing." When he opened the door and entered without incident, there was a visible sigh of relief.

"OK, maybe I was overreacting," said Rachel. "Be careful as we go in, however. We have to find out why it sensed the odor. Check the basic house out, but don't open any doors that are closed until Robbie has checked them."

Within about ten minutes, the "all clear" shout was heard.

Rachel, accompanied by Bob, entered the house.

"Show us where Rachel's office is, Bob."

"Oh, it's right this direction." He walked to a door near the rear of the house. "I'll have to provide you with the key. Barbara always keeps the door locked. Funny thing, last night she said she thought I should have a key in case of emergency. I have it right here."

As Bob moved towards the door of Barbara's office, Rachel once again called out, "Wait. Don't touch that door until it's been checked."

The controller brought Robbie, the robot, into position, and Bob provided the mechanical arm with the key. As it approached the door, the alarm went off.

"Out! Everyone out of the house now," Rachel commanded. She grabbed Bob by one arm as another officer took his other arm, and they hustled him out the door.

Once all were in the clear, the controller again instructed the robot to proceed with caution to the door.

As the camera watched, the robot inserted the key and began

to open the door. As the door swung open, the camera showed a chair to which two shotguns were strapped. A large sign was visible. "You bastard!"

Some fish line had been affixed to the triggers, and both guns erupted at the same time, damaging the robot's camera.

An auxiliary camera was activated, and the robot proceeded to survey the room.

Bob was allowed to look over the shoulder of the operator. The desk where Barbara had set her computer and screens was bare. As the camera swung around, he saw file drawers open and empty.

Rachel keyed in her radio. "Put an all points bulletin out for a green Subaru, license number," she looked at Bob, who gave her the license number, and she repeated it over her radio.

Then her father arrived.

"She's not here, is she?" Frank said. "I just got a text from her."

"You got what?"

"A text. She's on the run, but still has some more bullets to shoot."

Bob and Rachel moved towards Frank. "What did she say?"

"It was rather cryptic." He showed his iPhone to them.

Printed on the screen was, "Partial victory. Watch the news, U SOB. Fire next time. B.T.L."

"Better call Mandy," Rachel said. "We'll finish up here, but I doubt if we will find much. If we are lucky, watching the news may suggest whatever is going to happen is in the future. Maybe we still have some time."

Rachel looked at Bob and her father. "Dad, I think it would be good if you took Bob with you." Bob walked, half in a daze, out the door. Rachel stepped towards her father. "Maybe it would be a good idea to call Jacob and have him meet you." Nodding her head at the door that Bob had exited. "He doesn't look so good."

"Wise advice from a wise daughter." He nodded at her. "Let me know when you are free to join us."

* * * * *

Frank helped Bob into his car. "Sit there. I'll be with you in a few minutes. I have to call Mandy and give her an update.

He walked away from the car and hit the speed dial for Amanda. When she answered, his first words were, "How bad is it?"

"We were late getting the alarm on in Davenport, but when it went off, the target church was just being interrupted. The shooter heard the alarm and panicked. He shot at a few people, wounding several, and ran screaming up the chancel steps crying out 'I'll be remembered. It's a lie.' He tried to climb on to the altar.

"The minister shouted at him that it was a sacred table and leaped at him. He shot the minister in the shoulder as the minister grabbed his legs. As he was falling off the table, he shot himself. You have some pretty tough preachers in these churches, Frank."

Right now we are counting two dead and eight wounded including one very brave preacher. The rest of Davenport is in a panic, but they are all right."

"What about Bakersfield?" Frank asked.

"The alarms went off all over the city, and people exited their churches in droves. With all the extra guards and police cars patrolling, the shooter, as you predicted, abandoned ship."

"They aren't professionals." Frank said, "Just some teenagers that have had a few hours training on how to pull the trigger."

"Did you find Barbara?" Amanda asked.

"She packed up her computer and files and fled while Bob was at the church. Rachel tells me she rigged a pair of shotguns to go off if Bob tried to enter her office."

"Is he all right?"

"Yes, thanks to Rachel. For some reason, she became suspicious and brought in the bomb-sniffing robot. It opened the door to Barbara's door and took the full blast."

"She has really gone over the edge."

"I'm afraid so. Bob is a basket case. I'm taking him home with me."

"So where does that leave us? I hope they have an all points bulletin out on her."

"Rachel put that out, but I doubt if we will catch her right away. She seems to have been well prepared in case she had to flee. She did send me a text, though."

"She what!! You sure waited long enough to tell me."

Frank heard the irritation in her voice but also knew it was exacerbated by the stress she was under.

"Her words were 'Partial victory. Watch the news, U SOB. Fire next time.' signed BTL. I gather by the tone of your voice, you may agree with her characterization of me?"

"Sorry, that's for another time. What do you make of the message?"

"First, she has some further plans for violence, and second, in some bizarre way, she is the person we are looking for."

"What's the B.T.L. bit?

"My guess is it is very simple. Her codes have never been elaborate. It probably is her signature—Barbara the Leader."

"So what's supposed to come on the news?"

"We'll have to wait and see. My guess is it will be an attempt to raise the level of fear and not let our partial victory, as she put it, calm people down."

"And all this started because she was angry with you?"

"Seems like it."

"Frank Sessions, you do have a powerful effect on women."

He grunted into the phone but didn't know any words to say.

"Let's hope we can catch her before she can execute this next part of her plan. I'll talk to you later."

I WILL BE HEARD

CHAPTER 41

Barbara had sensed that Bob knew more than he was letting on. He may have been a lying, cheating, SOB, but he was not very good at disguising his feelings. In the last couple of days, she knew that something was different about how he responded to her. One moment he was solicitous and caring and the next he was looking at her with a strange look in his eye. It was as if he was trying to see what was behind the curtain.

She had been sure that he was too frightened to enter her office uninvited, but now she began to wonder. She had been careless to leave that nasty note about her response to the Dallas shooting where it could be seen on her desk. she had awakened her screen and seen her map of the states to be hit. It was stupid of her. Now she began to question whether he had seen that as well.

She decided she could not take the risk that he had become suspicious and even mentioned his thoughts to someone else. She knew that this weekend, with the four states being hit, the heat would be on. If there was any chance that Bob had become suspicious, and especially if it had been mentioned to anyone else, the FBI, or whoever the hell was in charge of such things, would be coming for her. She thought she had covered her trail well, but she didn't want to take a chance.

Over the past few weeks, she had been talking to Jeb about one big, spectacular finish. She talked to him about the terrorists who wore vest bombs and blew up whole buildings. She researched it on the Internet and had a rough understanding of how that worked.

"You don't want to do that, babe," Jeb said. "There is no coming back from an operation like that."

"You don't understand," Barbara said. "I don't intend to come back. I just want to go out with such a big bang that everyone in this country will be sorry they didn't listen."

As she argued with him and he became convinced there was no turning back, he grinned. "Wow, if I'd of known there were tough bitches like you, maybe I wouldn't be gay. You got balls, lady."

"You show an appalling lack of knowledge of both a woman's anatomy and the indelible nature of your sexual orientation." Then she smiled. "I've never met a man like you, Jeb. If there were more like you, we'd be a better country."

Jeb grimaced and nodded his head. "OK, if you are going to do this, I have enough guts to make sure you do it right. I have a buddy who has lifted some C-4 from a military depot. We can mold enough of it into a belt that will make the whole sky light up, even if you start in a large building."

"I'm starting in one very big building," she said. "Make sure there is enough of it that all the kings' men can't put Humpty Dumpty together again."

She met with Jeb a couple of times to learn how the vest bomb worked. Those terrorists were geniuses, or at least their leaders were. Who would have ever thought that you could take a basic light bulb, coat the wires with a flammable material, attach it to your C-4, and all you had to do was turn the bulb on. She had joked with Jeb, "You throw the switch, or, in this case, push the button to turn the light bulb on, and lights out."

When she concluded that Bob had both discovered what she was doing and betrayed her, she also decided she wanted to take her final revenge on his hypocritical soul. So early Sunday morning, after good old Bob had left for the church, Jeb came, helped her move out of her office, and set up the shotgun trap.

She smiled at remembering how touched Bob was last night when she said now that she could trust him, she was giving him a key to her office just in case there was ever an emergency. All he has to do is stick to his promise not to come into my office, she thought, and he will be OK. But if that lying bastard has been sneaking into my office, I will have a little surprise waiting for him this time.

Then another thought struck her. What if Bob had been talking to Frank Sessions? Maybe he will come over and be with Bob when they open the door. Or maybe, oh it would be so delicious, if that self-righteous daughter of Frank's, the policewoman, would come by and she would get blasted all to hell. Then maybe Frank would understand what it is like to lose a child.

She knew that once the alarm was set off by the multiple church shootings, they would put out an all points bulletin to take her down. She couldn't be driving her beloved Subaru. Again, Jeb had come through for her. Love that man. Too bad he's gay and is not interested in her showing her gratitude.

She pulled into their prearranged spot in the woods where she could hide her Subaru and switch cars. It took her a few minutes to switch her computer and files into the trunk of the Ford Escort. She also hid the vest bomb where no one would spot it. She was ready to go. No one was around, so it was no problem to strip down to her underwear and redress with the outfit she had purchased at Goodwill. Then she adjusted the wig she had purchased, added some makeup that enhanced the lines on her face rather than disguised them, and looked into the mirror at a frumpy, sixty-five-year-old woman that could pass any police roadblock without question.

She flipped on her radio as she drove and found the public radio station. She was looking forward to being a hundred miles from Lincoln when the first news broke about Maine and South

Carolina. When the reports first came in about Maine, she knew that something had gone wrong. While people were killed in the church in Bangor, Maine, it was clear by the reports that the officials had been put on the alert. Then, when the South Carolina report came, with a young man becoming suspicious of the National Guard uniforms, she felt for sure that somehow officials were prepared. There should have been at least 20-30 deaths and twice that many wounded. Still, it had been a partial victory, and there was still Iowa and California to come. The West Coast would be most delicious, she thought. Then they will know this is a nationwide phenomenon.

A hundred miles later, Barbara knew that the shootings were far less successful than she had hoped. With Bakersfield a flop, and some very quick actions on the parts of several people, the death toll would be under 30. It was enough to create panic as long as they didn't know who was behind it, but not enough to paralyze the country totally. If she was going to make a statement, it had to be a big one.

She had decided to hide out in a small motel in West Virginia and had just entered the state when she experienced her first roadblock. The traffic slowed to a crawl. She had an opportunity to exit but didn't want someone getting suspicious, so she moved slowly towards the officers who were checking the cars. *Might as well test this disguise out.* She tried to think about how a frumpy, older woman would respond to being stopped by the police.

When an officer came to her car, she rolled down her window. "Good afternoon, officer. What is this all about?"

"Nothing to be concerned about, mam. May I see your driver's license, please?"

"Certainly, officer. My billfold is in my purse, on the floor. Just a second." She leaned over, pulled her large purse up on the passenger's seat, and began to rummage through it. "Oh, here it is, officer. Now let me see, where is my license?"

It amused her to notice that the officer was growing impatient with the line building up behind but trying to be nice to this elderly lady in the car. One of her Internet connections had shown her how to create a fake driver's license and to place a cloudy picture on it.

When she finally handed it to him, he barely glanced at it before urging her to move along.

By early evening, she had arrived at a Red Roof Inn where she had made reservations under her new identity. Fortunately the clerk had no objections to her paying with cash. She was able to move into her room without incident. She immediately flipped on the TV as she unpacked, prepared to stay a couple of days.

Her plan was to stay in several motels over the next few weeks, each time moving closer to DC so that she would be able to arrive at the National Cathedral in ample time on Pentecost Sunday. She had a couple of different old lady disguises just in case someone had spotted her along the way. She wished she could go out and get some sun at the motel pools, but she could hardly strip down to a bikini and then go back in her old lady disguise. *Oh well, soon it won't matter what color my skin is.*

CODE BROKEN

CHAPTER 42

"Hi, guys," Amanda said. She was greeting the Session family over a special Skype Account projected onto a larger screen she had arranged for through the Justice Department. "I'm sorry I can't be with you. As this gets worse, the President is more and more insistent I stay close to my office. I think he would prefer I sleep here, but he hasn't had a cot delivered here yet."

"I talked to his speech writers before he went on tonight," Jacob said. "I think he hit a good balance between acknowledging the tragedy and congratulating the police and Guard for keeping deaths to a minimum."

"I also liked recognizing those civilians who acted so bravely," Rachel said. "Since we are dealing with rising fear of young people, it was a nice touch to highlight both the football player in Maine and the alert youth in South Carolina. If we are in a battle for the souls of the young, it's good to celebrate how youth are standing up for the good."

"I think you had a voice in that decision, Jacob," Amanda said.

Jacob acknowledged the compliment. "We are playing a game of chess, and I wanted us to show the difference between pawns sent out to sacrifice themselves and pawns that make critical contributions to our future," said Jacob.

Amanda sat back and looked past Jacob over his shoulder. "What, pray tell, is the sullen one over in the corner thinking about?" asked Amanda.

Frank raised his head. "Does the President know all of this might not be happening if it wasn't for me?" He had not slept well since the shootings on the previous Sunday. He knew Barbara was behind much of this violence, and her anger at him was one of the motivating forces. He couldn't get it out of his mind that he was responsible for so many people dying.

"He knows," said Amanda, "if it weren't for your brilliant family and your uncanny intuition, we would be running blind in the worst domestic terrorism ever to hit this country."

Frank shrugged as he stood and approached the computer. "OK, I'm feeling sorry for myself. I guess there isn't time for that. Are there any clues to what happened to Barbara? She seems to have disappeared from the face of the earth."

"She may be crazy, but she is an absolute genius in the way she set this up. She's never part of any of the shooting incidents, and the youth involved don't even know who she is. So even those we catch alive can't help us track her down. I'd like to hire some of those Internet nerds she recruited. Their operations are brilliant. The messages bounce off so many points before people see them they are impossible to trace."

"We were trying to break her last coded message when you called," said Jacob.

"Have you made any progress?" asked Amanda.

"It's so frustrating. They sound so juvenile, like kids taunting each other on the playground," said Frank. "Read it to us out loud, so we can hear it coming from the screen."

Amanda reached across her desk, picked up a piece of paper, and began to speak in a singsong voice like a child.

"Never fear, your leader is here. The church is lying up, the church is lying down, the church is about to hit the ground. Superman stops bullets. Superwoman breathes fire." This is followed by a string of numbers—16191432343.

"If they used a number code like last time, it comes out a,f,a,i,a,d,c,b,c,d,c which doesn't make any sense," said Rachel.

"Wait a minute," said Frank. "Jacob, what was one of the biggest challenges when you first started trying to translate Hebrew texts?"

"I'm not sure what you are talking ab . . . oh, yeah, the problem was they tried to save space on those scrolls, so they didn't leave any spaces between the letters or sentences."

"The first part of this string keeps repeating the number 1," said Frank, examining the paper. "Look for letters combining more than one digit. One six could be sixteen."

Everyone grabbed some paper and started playing with the new possibility.

"P, S, N but what does 32, 34, and 3 mean?"

"C, B, C, D, & C."

"Or," said Jacob, "twenty-three might be the letter W."

"So," said Frank, "the last three letters could be W, D, C. What does that suggest?"

"The last two, DC sound common, but W, . .oh, wait, . .what if it were Washington, D.C.?"

Frank continued to probe. "Break them up into the smaller letters. What are the letters for 3, 2, 3, 4, and 3?"

Everyone continued to scribble on their paper.

"NC could stand for North Carolina" said Rachel.

Frank began pacing. "Remember, this is an act of vengeance on the churches. If the city is DC, what is the most prominent church in DC?"

"The National Cathedral," shouted Jacob. "Do you suppose they think they can hit the National Cathedral?"

"And when?" Amanda asked.

"Remember this has all centered around the church. What is the next prominent Sunday on the liturgical calendar?" asked Frank.

"Pentecost Sunday," Jacob and Rachel both said together.

"So all those years of Sunday school paid off," said Frank. "Pentecost Sunday, National Cathedral, Washington, D.C."

"It sure fits the code," said Amanda. "I'll make sure the D.C. police are all over any youth who comes near there."

"You should do that," said Frank, "but I don't think that is the way it is going to go down."

"What do you mean?" asked Jacob.

"Read the part of the message with words," said Frank.

Amanda glanced back at her paper, "Never fear, your leader is here. The church is lying up, the church is lying down, the church is about to hit the ground. Superman stops bullets. Superwoman breathes fire."

"Sounds like to me the Leader is giving up being in the background," said Frank. "Remember, as badly as we feel about what has happened, the several past incidents weren't as successful as the terrorists might have hoped."

"And this time, it will be more than a few flying bullets," said Rachel.

"You guys are great," said Amanda. "I'll alert everyone that I can to protect the Cathedral. Since they practically dared us to discover what they are up to, they must have figured out a way we won't easily spot. We don't have many days to crack this. You keep working, and I will be back in touch."

"Mandy, will you be around for the next hour?"

"It's beginning to look like I'll be here permanently. What do you have in mind?"

"I need to check on a couple of things first, but I may need your help." Frank smiled and lifted his right eyebrow. "How are you at breaking people out of prison?"

Amanda opened her mouth, exhaled a big breath, closed her eyes, shook her head, and said, "Sure, Frank. I know your penchant for prison reform. How many prisoners do you want me to set free? Maybe I can save the state some money by clearing out the residents on death row."

Jacob and Rachel laughed, but Frank was deep in thought. "We can work on that later. I have something different in mind. I'll call you within the hour."

"I can hardly wait." She smiled a thin smile, shook her head, and reached forward to disconnect.

As she faded from the screen, Jacob and Rachel turned to Frank. "So are you going to let us in on your big secret?" Rachel asked.

"In just a moment, but I need to make a call first. Excuse me for a second, I'll be right back." Frank grabbed his phone and walked into another room.

Frank dialed and waited for an answer. "Bob, how are you holding up?"

"Not too well. To think my wife may be behind these shootings is overwhelming. It goes against my faith, but I've seriously considered killing myself. At least then I wouldn't have to face the shame."

"I have a better idea. I need your cooperation to end this nightmare. You are key to what I have in mind."

After a moment of silence, Frank heard a couple of sobs. He waited, knowing it was important to let Bob work through his emotions on his own.

Finally, Bob spoke.

"I don't know what you're thinking, but I'll do anything you want. Maybe I can set myself on fire like that monk did several years ago. I'm going to burn in Hell, anyway. Might as well get started."

Frank took a deep breath and let it out slowly. He waited for Bob to continue.

"I'm sorry, Frank. Things are so confusing. I guess I'm just grasping for one dramatic act to end this all."

"We can talk about the details later, but right now I need your permission to set some plans in motion."

"Just tell me."

"We're pretty certain Barbara is planning a dramatic act of her own. We think she wants to make one final statement, and we think we know where."

"She's gone completely crazy, hasn't she, Frank?"

"I'm afraid so, Bob, but we are hoping there may be one thread connecting her back to reality."

"Not me, Frank. I betrayed, wounded, and deserted her in her time of need. I doubt she feels any real connection with me. Don't forget the shotgun surprise she left for me."

"You don't arrange such a devious event for people you don't care about, Bob. She may be deeply wounded and furious with you, but you are still significant in her life."

"I'm not so sure, but what do you have in mind?"

"It does involve you but also David. That connection might even be stronger."

Frank proceeded to explain his plan, and Bob agreed to participate.

RELATIONSHIPS ARE IMPORTANT

CHAPTER 43

Barbara rose early on Pentecost Sunday morning. The last several weeks were a drag. Living in cheap motel rooms was not Barbara's idea of fun. Yet, every time she was tempted to go out, she turned on the news and was reminded of why she needed to stay in deep hiding.

On the second day after the President spoke, the FBI held a conference in which they posted her picture. They said they saw her as a key participant in the recent events. They placed a million dollar reward on information leading to her arrest for questioning. She had never heard of anyone placing a million dollar reward before. In one sense, it thrilled her to be seen as that important. It also reminded her of why it was so critical not to take any chances. She did not make all these sacrifices only to have it fail because she became careless.

She texted Jeb a couple of times with questions about the explosives, but she never let him know where she was. She trusted Jeb as much as she had trusted anyone since her father died, but a million dollars could turn anyone's head. Besides, after a couple of days, some wealthy business leaders announced they would add their own million dollars on top of the government reward. Two million dollars—WOW she might even squeal on herself for that much.

The media went wild trying to develop stories behind the FBI's announcement. There were big headlines about the pastor's wife of a major church in Lincoln. They rehashed the story of David's arrest a few years ago. Column after column speculated on what would motivate an educated, attractive woman to take such a dark turn in her life.

Another group of articles philosophized on what it suggests about our society to discover alienated youth who were willing to sacrifice their lives to make a statement. Still others asked what were the churches failing to do that had generated the anger and violence against them? How had churches become the enemy?

It was as if, one columnist mused, the whole theological structure holding society together had imploded. Many prominent faith leaders reduced faith to complex hair-splitting arguments instead of offering people hope, resulting in division and despair. Other church leaders disdained reason and offered emotional responses and dramatic rituals as alternatives. Like drug highs, the columnist mused, they eventually crashed and left people hopeless and helpless. At ground level, noted another columnist, the greed, corruption, and division of society seemed to triumph over the ideals and promises of faith.

Now the day had arrived when she would pull the trigger and expose the hypocrisy. Both Bob and that limp-dicked Frank Sessions will soon be out of a job. It made her giggle just to think about it.

She carefully assembled her vest bomb, threading the wires that would trigger the bomb through her sleeve. Jeb had shown her how to attach it to the adapted light bulb and from there to the small battery and button that would detonate it. Being satisfied all was connected except for the battery charge, she donned her outfit. Quite a comedown from those stylish clothes she used to wear. Some stylish clothes were available at the Goodwill, but she didn't want anything that would call attention to herself. She deliberately dressed in layers, like she had seen poor people do, but, in her case, it was both to hide her figure and to cover up the vest bomb.

Then she sat at the mirror and carefully applied the makeup that gave the appearance of an elderly woman. When she placed the wig on her head, she marveled at how different she looked. I wouldn't even recognize myself, she thought. None of those security people and their multiple cameras will come close to spotting me.

Satisfied with her disguise, she turned on the television to get any final news bulletins before she left. This morning, she chose NBC. As she flicked it on, the Special Report banner was moving across the bottom of the screen. It reminded her of the banners her hacker friends had projected across the screen interrupting the President's speech. She wished she had arranged one final banner exposing the hypocrisy of Christian leaders to the American people, but as the search for her grew more intense, she was afraid NSA would intercept her communications. She was afraid they could use her computer signal to locate her. The genius of her strategy was so few people had contact with her, so almost no one was in a position to betray her.

As the sound on the TV came on, the broadcaster was announcing, "We interrupt our normal programming to bring you breaking news related to the wave of terror shootings sweeping across this country. The FBI has confirmed a green Subaru, owned by a chief suspect in the case, has been located in a forest in North Carolina."

They flashed a picture of Barbara on the screen. Not a bad picture, she thought. Bob must have given it to them.

"We are only now learning authorities went to the home of Barbara Godwin, wife of the pastor of the True Vine Church in Lincoln, to talk with her after the last shooting. When they arrived, they discovered she had packed up and left. In leaving, she booby-trapped the house in a manner that would severely harm either her husband or any other visitors. The quick thinking of Officer Rachel Sessions, member of the local police task force investigating the Lincoln shootings, averted tragedy. They made use of a recently acquired bomb-sniffing robot, Remotec ANDROS F6A, affectionately known as Robbie the Robot, and triggered the trap without significant damage."

"Dammit," said Barbara, "how does that Session family get so lucky?"

The broadcast continued, "A two-million dollar reward has been issued for anyone who can help in apprehending this suspect. Authorities now think she may be the one referred to as "the Leader," who deviously manipulated psychologically confused teenagers into sacrificing themselves to advance her agenda against the Christian churches in this country."

You have it partially right, Barbara thought. Only I didn't deviously manipulate people. I brilliantly organized the young people you have ignored.

The newscaster continued. "They have asked people to be particularly alert this Sunday. They are speculating, based on a coded message left by "the Leader," she might try to engineer another attack on this Pentecost Sunday. While they have some ideas as to the general location, they are not releasing information because previously "the Leader" tried to mislead authorities by providing false information about an attack."

Barbara turned off the television, looked once more around the room, and took her suitcase out to her car. It was still early on Sunday morning, and there weren't a lot of people having breakfast at the motel. She checked out and decided to have a cup of coffee and a sweet roll before she left. She didn't want to eat too much but wanted the sugar to provide some energy for her final trip. After all, she thought, I no longer need to worry about weight or diabetes. I think I'll take an extra roll with me in the car.

She carefully pulled out of the parking lot and entered the highway. She decided to travel the interstate to enter Maryland but had plotted the use of local roads as she came closer to DC. She figured if they broke the code, as she guessed from the newscast, there would probably be extra roadblocks, and she preferred to be seen as a little old lady who was winding her way to her church on a Sunday morning.

She entered DC from Maryland and made her way down Wisconsin Avenue. When she came to Woodley Road, she decided to find a place to park and walk the rest of the way.

* * * * *

Bob went with Frank to the prison. The President had used all his political chips and the specter of a national emergency to convince the governor of North Carolina to release David into Frank's custody. When they drove up to the prison, the guard viewed their identification and directed them to the warden's office. It was Sunday morning, and there was little activity around.

When they entered the warden's office, David was already there, dressed in civilian clothes and waiting for them. Warden Gilbert greeted them, had Frank sign a release for David, and said, "I don't know what this is all about, but given the young man's relationship with the suspected Leader of this horror, I imagine it is about that."

Frank started to respond, and Warden Gilbert held up his hand. "No explanation necessary. The Justice Department and the governor made it very clear I was to cooperate and ask no questions. I will only say good luck for whatever you are doing. I hope to God we can do something to stop all this mess."

He turned to David and stuck out his hand. "You have been a good guest here. It must be rough thinking your mom is involved in this. May God bless you, and may this venture prove successful."

They were soon on the road to the airport where Amanda had arranged for a private jet to take them to DC.

Bob sat silently by his son while Frank explained what they had in mind.

"I can't believe Mom's doing this. I mean she always seemed so fragile and a little ditsy."

"I'm afraid that is the way we always treated her," said Bob. "We never gave her a chance to be the brilliant person she turns out to be. Plus, David, you need to know your father was a horrible husband to her and hurt her deeply."

"So what makes you think we will be able to stop her in this insane action she is bent on taking?"

"We don't know that we can," said Frank. "She has clearly slipped into some type of psychotic break with reality. We are hoping there are still some relational bonds with you and your father that might be able to reach her."

"Was this caused by my behavior and arrest?"

"I'm guessing that it goes way back, but I won't lie to you. What happened to you may have been one of the stressors that tipped her over."

"I'm probably primarily at fault," said Bob. "My behavior, not only regarding my unfaithfulness but also by my total focus on work and success, prevented me from being supportive when she needed it."

"A psychiatrist might figure it out," said Frank, "but we don't have time for that now. I've had Amanda set up cameras at all the main entrances, especially the front entrance to the National Cathedral. We will be able to see everyone who approaches."

"Do you really think she will come in with guns blazing?" asked David.

"We guess it will not be like that," said Frank. "When my daughter sent her robot to sniff out your house, the trap she set was a pair of shotguns. However, the robot also sniffed out some bomb-making material that wasn't found at the house. We think she might have brought a bomb with her."

"A bomb? How could she carry a bomb with her?" David asked.

"I think you've seen enough pictures in the paper of the terrorists in Iraq and elsewhere to understand the concept of a vest bomb."

"Yeah, but that would have to hide under a lot of clothing. Mom has always dressed in a way that left little to the imagination."

"So, if we are right, we need to expect your mom to be wearing a disguise that includes wearing some layered clothing," said Frank. "The cameras will try to view everyone who comes in, but we are hoping you and your father will be able to recognize clues the rest of us might miss. Maybe it will be the way she walks, a mannerism she has, something that will signal you even though it doesn't look like her, it is still her."

"I'll do the best I can," David said.

"You need to understand, son, this is dangerous. Your mom has lost touch with reality, and if she is wearing a vest bomb, we might well get blown up."

"Dad, whatever else might be true; we know you and I contributed to this dreadful situation. I may have been in prison, but I read the papers and watch the news. Lots of people have been killed or wounded because of this mess. The truth is, it feels kind of good there is something specific I can do that might help. It's penance for all the sins I've committed in the past."

Bob looked at his son. Tears began coming down his cheeks. "Not long ago, you asked me if I believed in the resurrection. Joining my son, risking our lives for others, being unselfish for once, feels like resurrection to me."

"I love you, Dad." David and his father rose out of their seats and they gave each other a good strong hug."

"OK," said Frank, "as that guy in the plane captured by terrorists a few years ago said, 'Let's roll.'"

When the jet landed at Andrew's Air Force base, they were met by Amanda and her associates with transportation ready to carry them to the Cathedral.

Mark brought out some Kevlar vests. "We are just guessing, but we think these will fit each of you. Just to be clear, however, they are better at stopping bullets than bombs. If you are within a 100 feet of one of those vest bombs, depending on what it is made of, nothing is likely to protect you."

"We understand," Bob said. "Let's get it on and hope for the best."

As they were getting dressed, Amanda turned to Frank. "You know that Bob and David are the keys to this. You don't have to get too close."

"I'm afraid I do. She has become almost obsessed with my family and me. While she might like to take me out, I'm also part of her slim connection to reality. Did you get that portable fire extinguisher and stun gun I asked for?"

"You know that the extinguisher is unlikely to work even if they chose the light bulb trigger."

"This all came about quickly, and that is one of the simplest triggers to set up, so maybe we'll be lucky."

"Even if they do use the light bulb, you will only have less than a couple of seconds to freeze it, probably less than a second. My people say they have never heard of it being done before."

Frank looked at Amanda and saw the fear in her eyes. Her arms hung limply at her sides. "Mandy, I know that you care and are frightened for me." He saw the tears start down her face. "Before we go, since we don't know what will happen, let me say this clearly. I have never fully recovered from Rosie's death, and because of that I've been fearful of making any real commitments."

"It's all right, Frank. I understand."

"No, it's not all right. I've treated you poorly, and I'm sorry. If we get through this, I want you in my life. Now let's hug and resume behaving like professionals."

Soon they were in nondescript cars that were supposed to blend in and headed for the National Cathedral. All were lost in their own thoughts, and there was little conversation.

EXPLOSIVE LOVE

CHAPTER 44

Frank had worked with the Bishop to create a special Pentecost display off to each side at the top of the cathedral steps. The displays had several red banners buffeted by the breeze. The bulky display disguised a small observatory room from which they could see the camera feeds and observe the worshipers as they arrived for worship. The people worked the cameras from another location. They were of the highest resolution so they could zoom in with precise clarity on any individual chosen. Amanda was in constant contact with them. She directed them to focus in on anyone wearing extra clothes or a coat under which a vest bomb might be concealed.

On the opposite side of the steps, was another large display. Inside it were three people. One was the best sharpshooter they could find. The other two were dressed in hazard suits. The design was carefully crafted, so the sniper had an excellent sight line and a rest for his gun barrel.

When they arrived, David, Bob, and Frank joined Amanda in one booth to see if they could spot Barbara among the sea of people who flowed into the Cathedral. People, even crazy people, tend to follow patterns, and they counted on the fact all the incidents happened during the eleven o'clock service. They calculated that in Barbara's mind, she could do the most damage at the late service. They held their breath during the early services, and when nothing occurred, they prepared for the people who arrived for the Holy Eucharist at eleven-fifteen.

On this bright, sunny Pentecost Sunday, people started arriving about ten-thirty. There was enough chill in the air that women had at least a light coat or shawl. For the most part, they figured people who arrived as families deserved less attention than the single people. Since they knew Barbara must have had some adult help, they examined closely the couples but paid particular attention to older single people.

About eleven, David indicated an older woman at the bottom of the steps. Before she began to climb, she looked up as if evaluating the climb. "Mom always did that when we had a long set of steps to climb."

Amanda quickly spoke into her radio. "Camera 1, focus closely on the gray-haired elderly woman at the base of the steps to the left."

As the camera zoomed in, both Bob and David bent into the screen and examined her.

"Dad, look at the bracelet on her right arm. Isn't that mom's? You gave it to her on her 35th birthday."

Frank watched the older woman begin to climb. He noticed even though she appeared to be about eighty, she showed none of the hesitancy in her steps as she climbed.

The three men began to exit the rear door of the display.

Amanda reached out and squeezed each of their arms as they passed. Then she spoke to the shooter and hazard-clad men in the other booth. Focus in on the elderly lady climbing the steps to the left. No action until my call."

Amanda realized she was exceeding her authority, but she unlocked the handcuffs from David's wrist and laid a hand on Frank's shoulder. "This had better work or it won't just be David who is going back to prison."

As they appeared around the corner of the display, as agreed, David took the lead.

"Mother, it's David. You were right. The President pardoned me this morning. I'm a free man."

The older woman froze four steps up and stared at him as he descended towards her. Frank knew they made the right choice. Now can they talk her down?

"Mom, it's me, David. Don't do this. There are children here. They don't deserve to die."

"Barbara, even if I betrayed you, listen to your son. He made mistakes, but he has become a good man," Bob said, as he too appeared at the top of the stairs.

"How'd you recognize me?" Barbara said.

While he knew that it was impossible, Frank thought he could almost see Barbara switch in and out of reality as she tried to process what was happening.

She reached up and tore off her wig and opened her coat revealing the vest bomb. "Don't come any closer. This is full of C-4, and I can set it off instantly."

"Mom, Dad and I both hurt you, but these people didn't do anything to you. Don't do this horrible thing."

Several ushers, really with the secret service, began to clear people who had reached the top of the steps out of the way. Others, at the bottom, prevented people from climbing the stairs. Instead, they directed them to move back away from the Cathedral. The men in the hazard suits quietly moved out of their shelter and into position to act if things went south.

"It's not these people; it is that lying faith and stupid God they think they are following. That God killed my daddy, and He's a liar. They think if they build a big enough building, it will protect them. Well, it won't. I have enough explosives on me to bring the front of that building down from right where I stand."

"Barbara, I put your son in prison, but I also got him out today.

People listened to you, and it happened. You are a brilliant woman, and we can figure out a better way than this. It doesn't need to be all violence and destruction."

"Well, well, if it isn't the self-righteous, super pastor Frank Sessions. This is great. I will finally get to destroy the two men who I most hate in the world."

Bob took a step down towards her.

"Stay back, Bob. See this little button in my hand. Do you know what it's attached to?—A light bulb. Isn't that a hoot? When I push this button, it turns on the bulb that detonates the bomb, and lights out." She howled at her own joke.

Frank stepped a step closer. "Barbara, why don't you let David and Bob go. You can blow me up and get your revenge, but at least your heritage will continue."

Amanda keyed her radio. "If I say go, I want one instantly right between her eyes. I want as little twitch in her hands as possible."

"Roger that."

"Mom, I'm not leaving. I was a narcissistic bastard, but you gave me your best, and I'm a better person for it."

"David, I'm sorry. It's gone too far. I would never be as strong as you. I couldn't survive prison, and they would never let me go."

"Barbara, you are right. After all these killings, they would never let you go. But you can go out the right way. I'll go with you. We'll walk over to the Bishop's garden, and you can push the button. We'll go together the way we should have been all along."

Barbara hesitated and looked at Bob. "You'd do that? You would deliberately sacrifice your life for me?"

"I remember our wedding day, Barbara. You were the most beautiful woman in the world. I thought, then, if I died and went to heaven, it couldn't be any better than this. I lost my way because I was too egotistical, but I know who I want to be with at the end of my life." Bob stepped closer to Barbara and reached out his hand slowly towards her.

Frank hesitated. This is not part of the plan. He saw Bob with his hand stretched out near Barbara.

"Bob, I don't think . . ."

"Shut up, Frank, This is the way it should be. There is no other path for either of us."

"We'd get to find out if the resurrection is real or not, wouldn't we?" Barbara said.

"Yes, Barbara, we will know for sure."

"I'm keeping my hand on the button, and if you try to betray me again, I'm pushing it."

"I know, Barbara. I will never betray you again. Frank, take David, and walk back up the steps. I love you David—we both do."

Frank moved slightly to the left, which blocked the direct sight of the sharp shooter.

"I've lost the line of fire."

"Damn that idealistic idiot. Stand down and wait."

Slowly Bob walked with Barbara down the steps, shielding her with his body but staying away from her hand with the button so she would not think he was betraying her. Once they reached the bottom of the steps, they made their way along the path to the Bishop's Garden. When they opened the gate, Bob said, "Wait just a moment, Barbara. I want to say goodbye to some very special people. She cautiously turned and watched him as he shouted up at the people at the top of the steps.

"Frank, blessings on your family. Don't be stupid, hold on to Amanda. She's good people. David, we love you. If there is an afterlife—a matter about which your mother and I disagree—we'll be watching you. In either case, make us proud."

Then he turned back, took Barbara's other hand and entered the garden.

As they passed through the gate, Frank heard Barbara say, "You can call me Barbie, if you want. I sort of like the way you say it."

Amanda came and stood by Frank and David as they looked out at the Bishop's Garden. In about five minutes, there came an eruption of sound, fire, and smoke that shook the area around it.

Fire came down.

RESURRECTION

CHAPTER 45

Three weeks later

Frank had received permission from both the President and the governor for David to stay with him for a few weeks, so they could talk about all that had happened. Now Jacob, Rachel, Amanda, and Brandy had joined them. They were all still reeling from the events that had taken place.

"David," Amanda said, "I talked to the President yesterday. It isn't definite yet, but both he and the governor have advocated for the state to have you transferred to the Forsyth County minimum-security facility in Winston-Salem. You will be assigned work detail with the Highway Patrol. It isn't freedom, but it is a good step in that direction. If your sessions with your therapist go well, you might be able to secure parole in a couple of years. It will take a few days to handle all the paperwork, and, in the meantime, you are in Frank's custody. When you are ready, Frank can drive you back up to the prison to gather your belongings, but hope is you will never have to live there again."

"I guess Mom was right. She told me she would get the President to release me. I just didn't realize the cost."

"None of us did, David," Frank said. "Your mom was in a psychotic state, but her love for you was right. You will honor the good in her and your father if you accept the conditions of the transfer, and we figure out how you can move on."

Jacob brought two bottles of wine into the room and began serving those present. He also brought a bottle of water and handed it to David. "At least for the moment, one of the conditions is you avoid alcohol and any form of drug use until you are cleared by your doctor."

"While drugs were available in the prison, I didn't use them, and I haven't had a drink in a long time. What are the other conditions for my transfer?"

"The main one is you have regular sessions with a professional counselor who will focus both on your past and how you adjust to your new freedom. Working with the highway patrol can't hurt either. "

"I think what Amanda has worked out is a good step," said Frank. "Your earlier behavior may reflect a psychosis of its own, and what you have just been through, witnessing the death of both your mother and your father, could result in all sorts of bizarre effects."

"This will provide some protected custody while you adjust," said Amanda.

Jacob moved over and sat by David. "Just a reminder, this family is always available to you as friends. We've been through enough trauma to understand how difficult it is, so don't hesitate to give any of us a call."

"I know what Mom did, but I don't understand how she was able to convince all those young people, and apparently even some veterans, to help her out. They weren't all psychotic were they?"

"I'm not sure the label you put on them, but with my work at the seminary, I talk to a lot of young people who feel a low level of desperation in their lives. Most of them will adjust and make an accommodation with the world and its failures that still allows them to feel worthwhile. Some, however, are so hungry for a clear answer to the complexity of life; they are very vulnerable to a charismatic leader who offers them a path that won't allow them to be ignored."

"I think Jacob is on to something," said Frank. "History is full of examples where people became so frustrated with the power games played around them and their sense of helplessness, that they didn't want to think anymore. They just wanted to demand they be noticed. It happens in political movements, in religious cults led by charismatic leaders, and in violent responses to the world around them."

"Are we likely to get more church shootings guided by some other leader?" Rachel asked.

"You heard the President's speech last week," Amanda said. "I think he is right. On the one hand, this series of actions is probably over. We haven't had any more incidents for the last couple of weeks. At the same time, as the President mentioned, we cannot wait for someone else to emerge to give voice to their hurt and confusion. The churches need to aggressively continue to reach out to their youth and neglected adults around them. The Veteran's Administration needs to insist on dialog with these survivalist groups, and most importantly, we cannot allow the ideological divisions in our country to go unattended. Violence usually occurs when people feel they can't be heard."

"Oh, I almost forgot to tell you," said Rachel. "Brian called earlier with some exciting news."

"Wait, don't tell me," said Jacob. "He found a girlfriend that no one is trying to shoot and he feels safer now."

"No, lame brain," Rachel said, sticking out her tongue in Jacob's direction. "The Veteran's Administration has offered to hire his group as consultants as they develop a strategy to reconnect with disaffected veterans."

"That's great," said Frank. "This might provide a real test case for how PTSD is affected by discovering how to integrate their traumatic experiences with a positive purpose."

David turned to Rachel. "Rachel, in my crazy season, I treated you in an unforgivable fashion. You have every reason not to trust me near you. The fact your father can treat me so kindly, in light of the way I treated you, is unbelievable to me. I don't expect you to trust me, but I want you to hear directly from me I am deeply and profoundly ashamed of my past behavior."

Rachel shifted her chair, so she could look at David. "My father has tried to teach me no one is beyond redemption. You did a brave thing by coming to stop your mother on the Cathedral steps. I respect that, and I'm working on the forgiveness piece one step at a time."

"Sometimes the hardest part is learning to forgive yourself," said Frank. "If you can't do that, you are bound to mistreat others from time to time."

"Is that what happened to Mom and Dad?" asked David.

"I'm not sure, David. I do know what has happened for me. When it was clear our lives were at risk a couple of Sundays ago, it helped me see how foolish I've been behaving—especially in relationship to Amanda."

"Hallelujah!" shouted Rachel. "It's a miracle. My preacher father has begun to see some light. Maybe there is hope for this world yet."

Amanda smiled but didn't say anything.

Jacob smirked a little and said, "As my therapist would say, 'Very interesting. Tell us more about how you are feeling.'"

"Good for you, Freud," Rachel said. "And what does the patient have to say?"

"David, you don't know, but my wife was killed in a robbery incident several years ago. Rosie was the center of my life and my strength for facing the worst of conditions." He looked at Jacob and Rachel. "These two were becoming young adults, but they still had to face losing their mother through violence."

"Dad held in there," said Rachel, "and showed us how to recover from the trauma, but it wasn't easy for him."

"Some of you know part of this, but in addition to losing my beloved wife, I also felt deeply responsible for her death."

"The cookies," Amanda said, with understanding dawning on her face.

"Yes, the cookies. You see, David, Rosie and I loved to have some tea and cookies, preferably chocolate chip, before we went to bed at night. It was our special time when we caught up with each other and tasted the sweetness of our life together. But that day I'd forgotten to pick up the cookies on my way home from work."

"So Mom went out to buy up some cookies from the convenience store," added Rachel, "and that is where she got killed."

"I was so fixated on some big deadlines I was facing, I forgot. It's odd how little incidents like that can tear apart your universe."

"And then Amanda, who you'd known in college, came back into your life, and I thought this great lady was going to be the final healing for you."

Frank looked at Amanda, who was gazing at him with a mixture of pain and love in her eyes. "She did bring healing, but I was afraid of committing myself again and making myself vulnerable to more pain, so I pushed her away."

Amanda smiled. "I knew part of that. I just didn't know how to break through the wall."

"Please forgive me, Amanda. I do love you, and as I told you on the Cathedral steps, I do want you to be part of my life."

They stared at each other while the others looked on.

In the uncomfortable silence, Jacob rose from the table and walked around to the other side where Brandy sat. He knelt by her side.

She shifted, so she faced him.

"What my father said to Amanda is part of what I want to say to you as well. I confess I have neglected our relationship. When we met, I hadn't had a serious relationship since Mom died. I was frightened by how much I was attracted to you. Then I ran and hid in my books. I ask you to forgive me and see if we can start over again."

Brandy stood up and reached down to the kneeling Jacob. "Get up you bookworm, and give me a hug."

"You know, I'm not a prude, but I feel like I'm listening to private conversations," said Rachel. "I think I am seeing both of the men in my family beginning to get their feet on the ground. You see, David, people can change."

"I surely hope so," said David. "With the support of people like all of you, I'm certainly going to try."

Amanda grinned and said, "Though I'm not the reigning psychologist here, I would suggest that the most psychologically healthy step we could all take at this moment is to order a couple of large pizzas and pig out."

Cheers went up around the table as Jacob hit the speed dial on his phone to place the order.

www.ingramcontent.com/pod-product-compliance
Lightning Source LLC
Chambersburg PA
CBHW020453030426
42337CB00011B/98